Governance and Internal Wars in Sub-Saharan Africa

Exploring the Relationship

Published by
Adonis & Abbey Publishers Ltd
P.O. Box 43418
London
SE11 4XZ
http://www.adonis-abbey.com
Email: editor@adonis-abbey.com

First Edition, April 2007

Copyright 2007 © Abdulahi A. Osman

British Library Cataloguing-in-Publication Data
A catalogue record for this book is available from the British Library

ISBN: 9781905068531 (PB)
The moral right of the author has been asserted

All rights reserved. No part of this book may be reproduced, stored in a retrieval system or transmitted at any time or by any means without the prior permission of the publisher

Printed and bound in Great Britain

Governance and Internal Wars in Sub-Saharan Africa

Exploring the Relationship

By

Abdulahi A. Osman

To my mother Binti Sharif Hussein and the loving memory of my father Sharif Ali Osman who lived under colonialism, witnessed the birth and collapse of the Somali state, and passed while still waiting its rebirth.

TABLE OF CONTENTS

List of Tables	vi
List of Figure	viii
Acronyms and Abbreviation	ix
Foreword by Dr. Frederic Pearson	x
Acknowledgements	xiii

Chapter One
Internal wars in Sub Saharan Africa — 15

Chapter Two
Conceptualizing the relationship between governance and internal wars — 27

Chapter Three
Peace-to War Countries: Rwanda, Sierra and Somalia — 63

Chapter Four
Peace-to-Peace countries: Ghana, Tanzania and Zambia — 110

Chapter Five
Findings, Conclusion and Implication — 142

Appendix 1
Note on methodology and Data Sources — 157

Appendix 2
African Presidents since independence — 164

Bibliography — 170

Index — 199

LIST OF TABLES

2.1	Factors and indicators of governance	34
2.2	The percentage of DFI and ODA in selected regions 1970-1989	40
2.3	Regime type and ICRG governance scores	45
2.4	Inequality and in the world measured in GINI selected regions	54
3.1	Contextual factors for war countries: Number of ethno-linguistic groups and ODA for war and no war countries between 1960 and 1989	100
3.2	Structural factors for all countries: Number of coups d'etat, government consumption, investment, Infant mortality, literacy rate, life expectancy, GDP per capita for war and no war countries 1960-1990	102
3.3	Policy factors for war countries: military, education and healthcare expenditure	103
3.4	ICRG governance scores for the war countries	104
4.1	Contextual factors for no war countries: ethno-linguistic groups, ODA, per capita in 1960 and 1989	135
4.2	Structural factors for no war countries: Number of coups d'etat, government consumption, investment, Infant mortality literacy rate, life expectancy, GDP per capita 1960-1990	137
4.3	Policy factors for war countries: military, education and healthcare expenditure	139
4.4	ICRG governance scores for the no-war countries	139

5.1 Number of ethnic groups in the no-war and
war Countries   144

5.2 Contextual factors for war and no war countries:
ethno-linguistic groups, ODA, per capita in
1960 and 1989   145

5.3 Structural factors for no- war and war countries:
number of coups d'etat, government consumption,
investment, Infant mortality literacy
rate, life expectancy, GDP per capita 1960-1990   148

5.4 Policy factors for no-war and war countries: military,
education and healthcare expenditure   149

5.5 The ICRG score for war and no-war countries   150

LIST OF FIGURES

1.1 Summary of the causal link of what caused internal wars in Sub Saharan Africa in the 1990s.   25

2.1 Summary of the theoretical framework   30

2.2 Average of governance score for war and no-war countries   35

2.3 Colonial powers and average governance scores   36

2.4 The GDP per capita for Sub Saharan Africa 1960 -1990   42

2.5 Number of attempted and succeeded coups in the war and no-war countries 1960-1990.   48

2.6 Military expenditure in Sub Saharan Africa 1960-1990   58

2.7 The per capita spent on military, education and healthcare of the war and no war countries 1960 and 1990   58

5.1 The ODA receipts between 1986 and 1989 for war and no war countries   151

ACRONYMS AND ABBREVIATIONS

AFRC	Armed Forces Revolutionary Council
ANC	African National Congress
ASP	Afro-Shirazi Party
CCM	Chama cha Mapinduzi
CND	Conseil National du Developpement
CPP	Convention People's Party
ECOWAS	Economic Community of West African States
FAI	Funda Aiuto Italiana
FDI	Foreign Direct Foreign Investment
GNR	Gendarme National Rwandaise
ICRG	International Country Risk Guide
IFI	International Financial Institutions
IMF	International Monetary Fund
MMD	Movement for Multiparty Democracy
MNRD	Mouvément Revolutionaire National pour le Dvelopment
MPLA	Movimento Popular de Libertaçao de Angola
NLC	National Liberation Council
NRC	National Reformation Council
ODA	Official Development Assistance
OECD	Organisation for Economic Co-operation and Development
PARMEHUTU	Parti du Mouvemento de l'Emancipation Hutu
PNDC	Provisional National Defense Council
PNP	People's National Party
PP	Progress Party
RPF	Rwanda Patriotic Front
RUF	Revolutionary United Front
SAP	Structural Adjustment Programs
SLPP	Sierra Leone Peoples Party
SMC	Supreme Military Council
SNM	Somali National Movement
SRC	Supreme Revolutionary Council
UDP	United Democratic Party
UNAR	Union Nationale Rwandaise
UNDP	United Nations Development Program
UNIP	United National Independence Party
ZANU	Zimbabwe African National Union

FOREWORD

"Many of Africa's people felt they were unjustly condemned to be exploited and oppressed, generation after generation, since colonial rule had been replaced by an inequitable economic order on the global level, and sometimes by corrupt rulers and warlords at the local level."
– Kofi Annan, General Assembly farewell speech, Sept. 19, 2006.

Africa's place in 21st century global politics is still being shaped. Will the vast and diverse continent continue as it has for more than three centuries to be a largely neglected net supplier of resources— human and material—and raw materials to the world, or will it develop a modern economy based on international communication links, investment and the skills and educational attainment of its people? Will the future Africa more resemble the desolate killing fields of Rwanda and Sudan or the vibrant streets and markets of Libreville and Cape Town? Will it fall victim to the whims of outside powers coveting its diamonds, gold, petroleum and mineral resources for gadgets, such as cellular phones, made elsewhere? Or can Africa score a technological and social break though, including the development of indigenous and international industry, somewhat akin to the remarkable, if still incomplete transformation of India, which just two generations ago also seemed hopelessly mired in poverty and periodic famine? Can the African continent overcome the tragic loss of human potential in its raging health crises and wars?

Indeed, after years of dislocation and violence, hopeful signs are emerging in African governance. The popular and reasonably free elections experienced in Liberia and the Republic of Congo in recent years, along with South Africa's challenged but proud governing institutions serve as examples that democracy, human rights, and popular sovereignty are attainable even in war weary environments. While Sudan's decades long north-south civil war has formally ended through inter-cultural and inter-regional bargaining and sanctions, the killing has spread among recalcitrant groups and government forces involved in the Darfur region. Thus despite hesitant progress, hanging over the scene is the threat of reversion to dictatorship and oppression, corruption and "kleptocracy," territorial and ethno-political victimization by which national treasures are stolen by unscrupulous leaders in league with their international patrons.

In fact Africa's future is not beyond redemption. If African international debt burdens are reduced to manageable proportions so that more money is not going out to international lenders than is coming in, if Western commitments to meet the HIV crisis through pharmaceutical supplies and public health measures are actually met, if corporations and financial institutions begin to pay the type of attention to African market and production potential that they have paid to Asia, if international governmental and non-governmental organizations provide the relatively affordable inoculations and hydration kits to prevent child and infant deaths, if the African Union's considerable peacekeeping efforts are supported and augmented by UN and global agencies, significant life improvement on the continent could be attained in a relatively short time.

The answers to the questions about Africa's future depend, as African politics always has, on the complex interplay of outside intervention and the quality of Africa's emerging indigenous leadership. Too often in the past this has been a lethal mixture, as seen in the years of shortsighted Western strategic support for leaders such as Zaire's Joseph Mobutu. As with colonialism the cold war played out in Africa with tragic consequences; the potential of the talented founding leadership generation, Nkrumah, Nyerere, Kaunda, and others, was squandered in ill-devised schemes for wealth and glory. Now with that era behind us, there is the possibility, still unrealized, for less manipulative more collaborative forms of international involvements and of leadership more attuned to building viable states.

Professor Abdulahi Osman is uniquely able to comment on these alternate possible paths for Africa's development. He has grasped the interplay of the local and the global in African history, putting proper emphases on both sources of de-stabilization and mismanagement. He understands and identifies with African aspirations for better government and the subtle nuances and manipulations of identity politics that often stand in the way, including issues of race, ethnicity, and kinship, in the region as a whole, and in its sub-regions. Thus he weighs the various factors that have led to the unraveling of Africa's social and political fabric, and he highlights the changes and reforms necessary to mend that cloth. His is a sophisticated understanding all too rare in social science analyses and in government circles.

Forword

Dr. Osman instructively contrasts cases of more and less successful conflict settlement in recent African history, cases of states that sank into civil war and those which managed to avoid the abyss. The focus on conflict resolution is especially pertinent since one detects a far worse overall fate in war-torn African societies than in those that have experienced relatively peaceful political transitions. The phenomena of child soldiers and victimization of women, of insurgent fiefdoms and confiscation of resources for illicit purposes, of destabilizing arms importation, of ethnic "cleansing" and terrorist havens, of raging epidemics and of tragically misplaced budgets are far more prevalent in warring societies, not just in Africa but throughout the world.

In developing his insights, Dr. Osman reflects both sound scholarship and high scientific standards, applying the stark outlines of quantitative indicators and the rich details of qualitative histories in comparable cases. He brings politics alive for the reader in a way that will make this book valuable both as a textual primer and as a guide for policy reform. Readers will be better off for both a deeper understanding of the political forces at work in Africa and for a clear specification of trends that must be overcome in order for Africa to become a more integral part of the "global order." In the words of the early 20th century geographer George Kimble, "The darkest thing about Africa has always been our ignorance of it." Dr. Osman has taken important steps to let the light shine in.

Dr. Frederic Pearson, Director
Center for Peace and Conflict
Wayne State University
Detroit, Michigan

ACKNOWLEDGEMENTS

At various stages of writing this book I have benefited greatly from critical judgments, support and advice of a number of people. At Wayne State University I have received a great support from the faculty and staff of the Department of Political Science and Center of Peace and Conflict Studies. Dr. Frederic Pearson, the Director of the Center of Peace and Conflict, my advisor and mentor, whose continuous support, encouragement and push towards excellence I gained great insights of this topic and the completion of this project. Additionally, I would like to thank other supporters including Drs. John Strate, Brad Roth, Anthony Perry and Eboe Hutchful. I also would to thank to the late Dr. Otto Feinstein for his support, inspiration and friendship. I want to also thank Dr. Eroll Henderson for his role in sharpening my theoretical argument. I want to thank to my colleagues and friends at Wayne especially Dr. Marie Olson Lounesberry and Michael Alandu for their friendship, criticism and unconditional support. Additionally, I have benefited greatly from my current position at University of Georgia. I would like to thank the entire faculty and staff of the Department of International Affairs and African Studies Institute at the University of Georgia who provided me friendship and encouragement in finishing this book. Especially, I would like to thank Drs. Howard Wiarda and Lioba Moshi. I also like to thank the Willson Center for Humanities and Arts, especially Dr. Betty Jean Craige. Finally, I have greatly benefited from support of Amasale Abegaz, Kathryn Johnson, Bill Zachamnn, Nada Moris and Murat Bayar.

I want to thank my fellow Somali academics, mentors and brothers Drs. Mohamed H. Mukhtar, Abdi M. Kusow, Ali Jimale Ahmed, Omar Enoo for their continuous encouragement, critique and support. I also want to thank to the hundreds of people who in one way or another supported me in the completion of the project. I also want to thank to my dear friends Omar Abukar Shekhey, Farhiya Mahdi and Mohamed Ahmed Nurow (Yare) for their support and encouragement. I want to express special thanks to Dr. Jideofor Adibe my publisher whose quick turnaround and professionalism made the completion of this book possible.

Acknowledgement

I cannot end without thanking my family, whose constant encouragement and love I have relied throughout my life. I want to thank my sisters Maryan, Zeynab, Khadija, Miski and Faisa and my brothers Abdulqadir, Hassan, Mohamoud and Mustaf, my nieces, nephews and my brother in-laws Mohamed, Wardi and Omar. I also want to thank my uncles Abdulakadir and Osman for their support and encouragement over the years. I want to thank to Cheryl Larry and my boys Ali and Abdihamid. I want to thank my wife Anisa Hussein whose patience and understanding made this project possible. Most importantly, I would like to sincerely thank to my pareants and all my extended family whose unflinching courage and conviction will always inspire me, and I hope to continue, in my own small way, the noble mission to which they so believed and pushed on us. It is their strong shoulders I stand upon and it is them that I dedicate this work.

CHAPTER 1

INTERNAL WARS IN SUB-SAHARAN AFRICA

Following the end of the Cold War and the collapse of the former Soviet Union the number of internal wars[1] defined by Regan (2000, p.21) as "...an armed combat between groups within state boundaries in which there are at least 200 fatalities" in Sub Saharan increased (Adedeji, 1999; Elbadawi and Sambanis, 2002). According to Wallenstein and Sollenberg (1999) there were 108 conflicts in the world between 1989 and 1998. Only seven of these were interstate wars and the rest were internal wars. A majority of these wars were concentrated on the African continent. For example, in 1998 there were a total of 13 conflicts in the world (an increase of 7 from the previous year); of these, nine were found in Africa. These wars caused thousands of casualties[2] and thousands of refugees and internally displaced persons.[3]

Adedeji (1999, p.5) divides the continent into three categories:

Category 1: Countries with severe armed conflicts and internal war
Category 2: Countries in prolonged political crises and turbulence
Category 3: Countries that enjoy a relatively stable political system

On the basis of these categories, Adedeji points to the increased number of conflicts in Sub Saharan Africa. For example, in 1996, of the 48 countries in the region, 12 (25%) belonged to category 1, 12 (25%) belonged to category 2 and 24 (50%) belonged to category 3. By 1998 this figure jumped to 18 (38%), 11 (23%) and 19 (39%) respectively.

The devastation of the 1990s presented conditions that dashed Africa's high hopes for stability and development that began with the independence period of the 1960s, a period that earned Africa the nickname "continent of the future." Most countries emerged out of decades of colonial rule only to be shattered because of lack of good governance, democracy, rule of law, economic growth and stability. The 1990s were supposed to bring a second wave of hope due to the end of the Cold War, which promised the emergence of a "New World Order" that would create opportunities for many countries in the region. On the contrary, in the 1990s many African countries witnessed unprecedented violence, economic decline and suffering (Sambanis, 2002; Adedeji, 1999). Gurr et al. (2000) argue that Africa has not been part of the post-Cold War dream of stability and prosperity. Instead the post-Cold War era is being associated with: a) relatively little international effort devoted to their conflicts, unlike conflicts in Europe, as in the Former Yugoslavia; b) failed democratic transitions, and c) heightened poverty (Gurr et al., 2000, p. 11). From West to East Africa and from Central to Southern Africa, most states began to face an ever-growing challenge to maintain peace, stability and growth. Additionally, the quality of life declined and today Africa shoulders the largest burden of AIDS.

It should be noted, however, that all is not lost in Sub Saharan Africa. In the post-1990s four different realities existed in the area. Some countries experienced internal wars and in some cases state collapse after years of relative stability, e.g. Somalia, Liberia, Rwanda, D.R. Congo and Sierra Leone. Other countries that had experienced war sustained their war experience during the 1990s, e.g. Sudan and Angola. Additionally, some countries showed signs of development, pacification, democracy and positive change in the 1990s. Lastly, democracy is consolidating in places like Botswana, Benin, Tanzania, Senegal and Mauritius; peaceful transitions of power took places in Ghana, Mali and Burkina Faso. The two giants of Sub Saharan Africa - South Africa and Nigeria - have also witnessed peaceful political transition despite the existence of acute racial, ethnic or religious differences and economic difficulties in their midst. Finally, the long tragic internal war in Mozambique actually came to an end in 1992. Therefore, the leading question for this book is: *How and why did some countries manage to avert internal wars, while others did not?* This chapter sets out the tone of the book and will be divided into three parts. First, the causes of Africa's internal wars will be examined. Second, the guiding theory of the book will be introduced. Finally, the organization of the book will be outlined.

II. The Causes of Internal Wars in Africa

The causes of Africa's violent conflicts are diverse and complex. Some sources are internal; some reflect the dynamics of a particular country or a sub-region; and some have important international dimensions. These varied causal factors are thought to include the lingering effects of colonialism (Rodney, 1982; Okigbo, 1993), imperialism and neo-colonialism (Parenti, 1989; Nkrumah, 1966); economic breakdown, foreign aid and debt crises (Adedeji, 1995; George, 1993); ethno-political differences (Gurr, 1994; Zimmerman 1993; Gurr and Harff, 1993, 1994; Horowitz, 1985); the Cold War and militarism (Gavshon, 1981; Odetola, 1982); bad governance and corruption (Schroeder, 2000; Herbst, 2000; Adedeji, 1999; La Billon, 2001; Braathen et al., 2000); and greed and the struggle for resources (Collier and Hoefler, 1999; 1998; Collier, 2000; de Soysa, 2000).

The literature on the causes of internal wars in Sub Saharan Africa has often given "ethnicity" and "contested identity" a priority. The majority of the scholars, for example, concentrate on ethnicity or ethnic-primordialism as the main cause (Zimmerman 1993; Gurr and Harff, 1993; Horowitz, 1985.) Obviously, ethnicity is an important factor in explaining these wars. This is so because most of the warring factions belong to different ethnic, tribal, religious or other identity groups. Additionally, the killing or the suffering of these groups is based on their group affiliations. Most of us, to some degree, are members of certain groups.

Other scholars argue that economic factors including economic hardship, unequal economic distribution, and failure of economic development and modernization (Samarasinghe and Coughlan, 1991; Rule, 1988). Still others have blamed the nature of the politics in the postcolonial states of Africa. These factors include bad leadership, unequal and discriminatory political institutions, exclusionary national ideologies and inter-group politics and issues of citizenship and nationality (Ekeh, 1975; Berman, 1997; Mamdani, 1996; Adedeji, 1999).

Africa's internal wars have resulted from the nature of political power in most of their states, making power central to understanding internal wars in their countries. The political system in postcolonial states in Africa, like the preceding colonial states, has been centralized with most of the governmental power being concentrated into the hands of, and benefiting, the states' leaders and their cronies (Chazan, 1999; Adedeji, 1985; Calaghy and Ravenhill, 1993; Herbst, 2000; Leonard and Straus, 2003). It is important to understand that the rewards or consequences (real or perceived) of capturing and maintaining state power have over the years become a key source of wealth and privilege. The African political system has been the main source conflict as state power has always been a zero-sum game, where the winner gains all. As a result of this reality African states have witnessed numerous violent military coups.[4] The control of the state in Africa brings wealth and resources, patronage, the status and prerogatives of office for the office holders and his cronies, often his tribesmen. Therefore, the conflicts that arise have been accompanied by a communal sense of advantage or disadvantage. Communal support has been a basis of power because most states in Africa tend to be highly personalized regimes that lack accountability, transparency, and adequate checks and balances.

In most of the states in Africa, there is lack of obedience to the rule of law, a lack of social and political cohesion, a lack of respect for human rights and most of all, frequently, an absence of any peaceful means of regime change. Thus, control of the state's coercive machinery becomes extremely important, simply because the stakes are comparatively very high. Moreover, postcolonial states in Africa have often lacked legitimacy and internal cohesion (Englebert, 2000). They possessed few of the normative characteristics associated with the welfare state, hence over the years they came to be known as: the lame leviathan (Callaghy, 1987); weak (Migdal, 1998); predatory (Fatton, 1992); vampire (Attiyey, 1999); criminal (Bayart et al., 1999), shadow governments (Reno, 1995).

After their independence, most of the African states maintained a structure of inequality, where the members of the ruling group benefited handsomely from that control (Ayittey, 1998; Braathen et al., 2000; Herbst, 2000). The rest of the society suffered from the strong arm of the state and gradually acquired a deep resentment against it. After independence, many regimes maintained their power through the financial support of the international donors in addition to the rents they receive from the exports, which made them less accountable to their own societies. In the 1980s, however, the amount of support they received was severely reduced owing to the imposition of programs such as Structural Adjustment Programs, which severely limited the states' capacities. Additionally, during this period the price of the commodities from African countries declined. These two factors, in turn, weakened the capacity of the state to reward or punish and created high inflation and in some cases the collapse of many economies in the region.[5] The net result was a severe decline in security both economically and physically. In many parts of the continent, food became a luxury item, and this, in turn, triggered a struggle for survival. Members of the society, including bureaucratic officials, began to trade in anything they could find, including weapons from the military that found their way into the hands of many resentful groups.

Postcolonial leaders in Sub Saharan Africa over the years have been described as: 1. criminalizing the state by preying on state properties (Bayart *et al.* 1999); 2. Using patronage as the only legitimacy for their states by using state property to reward or punish on the basis of clan, tribal or regional lineage (Chabal and Daloz, 1998). This makes the postcolonial states the creators and enforcers of social inequality, which in turn creates resentment among the numerous "losers" in society. Frederick Forsyth (1977. p.25) described African politics in this way,

In Africa as elsewhere political power means success and prosperity, not only for the man who holds it but for his family, his birthplace and even his whole region of origin. As a result there are many who will go any length to get and having got it will surpass themselves in order to keep it.

III. Governance and Africa's Internal Wars

The literature listed above briefly described the causes behind the increased number of conflicts in Africa. However, there is a gap concerning the reasons why the wars increased during this period and only in certain countries despite the presence of the political, social and economic factors that led some countries to the war path. The main hypothesis of this book is that the key to understanding the genesis of internal wars in Sub Saharan Africa is bad governance attributable to the postcolonial state and its failure (or success) in bolstering economic development (Braathen *et al.,* 2000; Herbst, 2000; Adedeji, 1999).

Sub Saharan Africa's internal wars in the 1990s occurred not specifically because of the primitive social settings, as some have argued, but rather because of the "power game and the arena of modernity." (Braathen *et al.* 2000, p.10). This arena of modernity is "...the state and the fight to gain control of state resources, power and possibilities." (Ibid) Specifically, the wealth that accompanies the capturing and maintaining of state power has been a key source of conflict and political violence across the continent. Therefore, this book argues that the internal wars in Sub Saharan Africa in the 1990s are largely the result of ruthless, exploitative and ineffective states. More specifically, states that were "captured" by ethnic or tribal groups that compound the anti-government resentment and lead to inter-group warfare.

At this juncture, explanations based on policy – on the issue of good governance – deserve further discussion since little doubt exists about the relationship between bad governance and internal wars (David, 1997; Herbst, 2000; Schroeder, 2000). The quality of governance is a good indicator of social cohesion or social unrest. Zartman (1997, p.1) argues that: "Governing a state is not only the prevention of violent conflict from destroying the country; it is the continual effort to handle the ordinary conflicts among groups and their demands which arise as society plays its role in the conduct of normal politics."

Many Sub Saharan African states have had openly corrupt governments that ran their economies into the ground and hence created an environment conducive for the power and resources struggle. Michael Brown (1996) argues that the prospect for conflict in a country to a large extent depends on the type and fairness of the political system in place. Over the years, many states, especially those in Africa, have generated considerable resentment, often because the interests of some groups are extravagantly served while others are completely neglected (Brown, 1996, p.160). Thus, the importance of understanding the role of governance for the onset of internal wars is imperative. Hyden (1991) suggests that "governance" is an approach that can provide a comparative-analytical framework of macro-politics. Since this study intends to compare countries that experienced internal war to those that did not in Sub Saharan Africa, governance becomes an appropriate framework.

The objective of this study is to investigate, describe and compare governance of African states from the contextual, structural, and policy perspectives that led (or did not lead) to war in a country during the 1990s. Thus, the goals of the book are description and explanation of governance. Specifically, the book examines how various factors within countries since independence, e.g. colonialism, environment, culture, economic dependency, ethnicity, etc. led to war or no war outcomes in the turbulent 1990s. The study will utilize descriptive-explanatory analysis and synthesis. It involves analysis and comparison of historical records of two sets: one group of countries that experienced relative peace in the 1980s and internal war in the 1990s and another group that maintained peace from the 1980s through 1990s.

Since the research question is an open-ended question that cannot be easily quantified, the book will use a qualitative design supplemented where possible by quantitative indicators. Qualitative research employs inductive analysis to identify critical variables (Patton, 1990), and is appropriate in situations where the numbers of variables with important effects are numerous and are contextually bound. Therefore, our role is to provide rich, contextual description that provides a basis of comparison to other situations. In this book the occurrence or non-occurrence of an internal war is already known. Strauss and Corbin (1990) claim that qualitative methods can be used to better understand any phenomenon for which much is already known, and also involves in-depth information on phenomena such as complex internal wars that are difficult to convey quantitatively.

The book will utilize pattern-matching as a technique for linking data to the hypotheses (George, 1979). A series of in-depth focused case studies will focus on the contextual, structural and policy variables that led to the onset of internal wars (Eckstein, 1979; Yin, 1989). The same questions will be applied to each case systematically and consistently, thus eliciting key comparisons. The underlying hypothesis is that similar patterns exist in the states where internal war occurred. Another series of in-depth case studies, with the same basic questions, will investigate states where internal war did not occur.

Despite sampling across geographical regions, the limited number of cases feasible for in-depth comparison has several disadvantages, including the possibility that the observed relationships are due to the uniqueness of both the cases and the time they were observed and thus may lead to incorrect conclusions. However, there also are advantages in using small number of cases, including the ability to do a thorough analysis (Lijphart, 1975). Moreover, the problem of excessive differences among the cases is limited because we will examine countries that are located in Sub Saharan Africa that have similar features, including colonial history and an indigenous postcolonial state apparatus with at least two or more ethnic groups. We will analyze the cases systematically for presence (and absence) of factors hypothesized to be the causes of internal war. The book employs replicated, multiple cases and increases confidence in results beyond what can be accomplished by a single case study. (Yin, 1989)

In order to address the research question, the book will compare two scenarios that existed in the Africa during the 1990s:

1. *Peace-to-war:* countries that previously had relative peace, defined as absence of an all out internal war in 1980s, but began to experience internal war in the 1990s, e.g. Somalia, Sierra Leone, Liberia, etc.

2. *Peace-to-peace*: countries that had peace in 1980s and continued relatively peacefully, e.g. Botswana, Tanzania, Senegal, etc.

The model will compare these two scenarios examining similarities/differences in contextual, structural and policy variables. The unit of analysis for this book is the country, and the temporal domain is the period between 1989 and 1999. The cases were selected based on two criteria: a) geographical location of the countries, which are located in East, Central, and West Africa, and b) a difference in the outcome variable: internal war/no internal war.[6] Two countries were selected from each region -- a total of six. Within each region, one country experienced internal war and one did not.

There are a large number of potentially relevant contextual, structural and policy variables. Based on the literature, several indicators are chosen for each variable. Measures for these variables come from existing global data sources and records, such as World Bank, SIPRI, UNESCO, etc. Overall, this book expects that governance - measured as contextual, structural and policy variables - will be found to have either triggered or buffered internal war. In this section, a summary and overview of the variables and the expected patterns is presented, and in the next chapter, the inter-relations between these variables and patterns will be examined more extensively.

Contextual Factors

The term context is generally defined as the overall idea, perspective or viewpoint from which a topic or matter is discussed and presented. This term also may be referred to as the big picture, rather than a single idiosyncratic factor. Context in this book will refer to those factors that states confronted initially and in their relevant environments, including traditional and socio- and geo-political conditions in their neighborhood. The most important historical factor for most African states is their colonial experience, along with the type and extent of anti-colonial struggle.

Colonialism left behind states that were largely extractive, dependent and more importantly socially divided. Also, colonialism provided the basis for the current political structure as well as the factional conflict that African societies have experienced since their independence. More specifically, social divisions were often enforced along ethnic lines, with the arbitrary drawing of borders and economies that were often dependent on a single crop, with the state and infrastructure set up only for extractive purposes. Since all the countries examined in this book experienced colonialism, these colonial legacies are accepted as given unless otherwise specified, though differences in colonial experiences – as between British, French, Portuguese or Belgians – will be considered. The model will include variables relevant to the functions of the postcolonial state, simply because African states, although they nearly all experienced colonialism, did not all descend to internal war and chaos.

Culture and Ethnicity. Most African states contain multiple ethnic groups. Contrary to the argument of the ethnic "primordial school" of thought that violence is endemic to multi-ethnic societies, many multi-ethnic states did not experience internal war. For example, Tanzania, which has over 130 ethnic groups, had no full fledged internal war in 1990s, while Somalia with fewer than 10 main groups did. The model will look at how ethnicity is related to state functions, and specifically how benefits are distributed among the ethnic groups. In other words, who rules and who gets what?

Economic dependency. Most African states, like their counterparts elsewhere in the developing world, have been economically dependent on the international economic system. An "exploitative" system that benefited the North and made the South poorer was created and enforced through trade imbalance, exploitation, conditional foreign aid, etc. Still, many African countries maintained some economic independence and stability (e.g. Tanzania, Botswana, Swaziland and Lesotho) and enjoyed special ties with their former colonial powers in the European Union.[7]

Structural Adjustment Programs. In the 1980s the International Financial Institutions (IFIs) began to impose Structural Adjustment Programs. These programs were designed to get the developing countries to pay back the loans that they owed. The program mandated shrinking the size of state functions as well as privatization of some of them. Many states found themselves bankrupt and incapable of providing even basic services (Englebert, 2000; Ndulu and Van de Walle, 1996; World Bank, 1998-99). During this period, poverty increased tremendously throughout the whole region. Still, some countries passed this harsh test relatively intact and even experienced relative economic growth.

Structural Factors

Structure refers to the institutions that make the system function. These institutions encompass political, social and economic domains. In other words, structure describes the overall governance system including political and economic institutions, their impact on the society and eventually on the outcome of either internal war or no war situations.

Regime Type: The type of the regime that rules a country – whether this is autocratic or democratic – determines levels of legitimacy and popular trust. These factors relate to political violence in the following ways: many states in the developing world are described as weak and ineffective. The inhabitants of these states do not identify themselves with the state. Other related structural factors include: leadership, stability, size of the state, quality of life and investment the country has attracted over the years. The model proposes that the war countries had military rulers, "bad" leaders, unstable regimes, and that the state consumed the largest portion of the economy. As a result, it attracted less investment and its people were poorer compared to the no-war countries.

Policy Factors

The institutions in all political systems, from a normative perspective, should produce policies designed to meet societal needs for defense, education, healthcare and social services. States opt for a variety of policies, some geared towards social programs, i.e.

healthcare and education, and others towards the military, but most opt for combination of policies. Because of potentially violent and expensive effects of militarization, a likely hypothesis is that the war countries invested more heavily in the military than social programs, as compared to the no-war countries. Of course, one must look at military spending before war breaks out, since wars tend to increase military spending in turn.

The model will compare these factors in the two groups of countries. It may lead to the identification of trends that are warning signals for future conflict. In theory, all of these factors in political systems, in combination, led to either internal war or no internal war outcomes. The model is summarized in the Figure 1.1.

Figure 1.1: Summary of the causal link of what caused internal wars in Sub Saharan Africa in the 1990s.

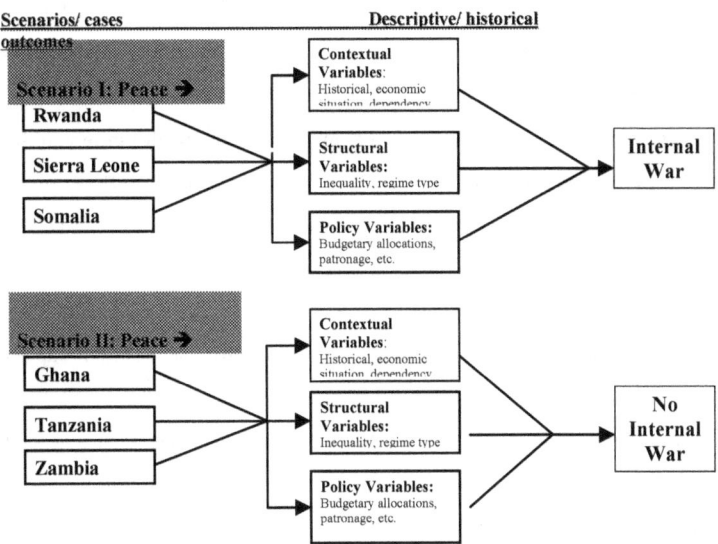

IV. Plan of the Book

Chapter 2 will provide details of the theoretical arguments and hypotheses that predict patterns of the war and no-war countries and detail the methodology to be used. Chapter 3 will analyze countries that went from peace-to-war, while chapter 4 will analyze countries that went from peace-to-peace. Chapter 5 will present a summary of the major findings and recommendations concerning potential mechanisms for the effective resolution of violence prone situations.

Notes

1 Throughout this book I will be using the internal war as opposed to civil war. Henderson (1999, p.279) defines civil war as, "...a sustained, violent conflict between the military forces of a state and insurgent forces of the state." He differentiates, however, civil wars from internal wars, mainly on the basis of who are the combatants. In a civil war one of the combatants is the government; whereas in an internal war the combatants can either be government forces or any other organized groups within the state. This distinction is important for the current study because in many of the selected cases the government had collapsed or was near collapse.

2 For example, an estimated 2.5 million or 5% of the Congolese (formerly Zaire) population since August 1998; see http://news.bbc.co.uk/hi/english/world/africa/newsid_1308000/1308963.stm Also, nearly one million people were slaughtered in the Rwandan hundred days' genocide. See Gourevitch (1998).

3 For example, the United States Committee for Refugees reports that there were 4.5 million internally displaced people in Sudan, Somalia, Ethiopia and Eritrea alone. In 1997 Sub Saharan Africa produced nearly 24% of all the world's refugees, which is the highest proportion in the world. See, United States Committee for Refugees at www.refugees.org

4 Between 1960 and 1985 there were 60 successful coups and 131 attempted coups. Only six out of 54 countries in the continent have not experienced an attempted or successful coup since their independence.

5 For example, according to the World Bank the average per capita income in Sub Saharan Africa (including South Africa and Nigeria) in 1965 was $499 and by 1995 this figure moved to $494 (in constant 1987 dollars). Source World Bank Africa Database 1998/1999.

6 For details on strategies for utilizing case studies see Lijphart (1975)

7 Although Lesotho's economy has been dependent on South Africa, still its economy showed great independence and steady growth. For example, the manufacturing sector, which accounted for 7% of GDP in 1980, had risen to 18% by 1995 and altogether industry accounts for 56% of GDP (World Bank, 1997). For more details, see Pierre Englebert (2000).

CHAPTER 2

CONCEPTUALIZING THE RELATIONSHIP BETWEEN GOVERNANCE AND INTERNAL WARS

In the course of the past two decades, governance has become an important issue in social science and development studies; however, the word has suffered from a lack of conceptual consensus. Many African states have experienced continued conflicts since the 1990s, while others have enjoyed continued relative stability and growth. Moreover, many African states also witnessed significant governance changes from the 1990s (Bratton and van de Walle, 1997; African Development Bank, 2001; van de Walle, 2002). In fact, there was a paradigm shift during this period from autocratic to democratic governance (Hyden, 1992). Despite the modest recovery in some countries during the 1990s, African countries continue to have the slowest growing economies in the world. The factors that led to this slow growth include a combination of high indebtedness, HIV-AIDS, unfavorable terms in international trade of African commodities and continued political instability.

This chapter provides a framework and analysis of the relationship between governance and internal war. The chapter will first present the theoretical framework derived from the existing literature. The objective of this chapter is to examine governance quality retrospectively in two types of countries: war and no-war. The chapter will begin by establishing a definition of the concept, measurement and methodology. Second, governance will be examined from three perspectives: context, structure and policy. By examining each of these perspectives, several general patterns that were present in the two categories of countries will appear. The chapter will conclude with specific hypotheses to be tested against the cases in chapters 3 and 4 of this volume.

I. What is governance?

The previous chapter established the central hypothesis for this research. This hypothesis proposes that "bad governance" is the primary cause of Africa's internal wars during the 1990s. Defining the concept of governance is a difficult task for it requires value judgments. The definition of the concept can be equated to the likes of twelve blind men asked to describe an elephant with each one describing a single part of its body. Before tackling the definition of the word governance, it is useful to look at three interrelated concepts: political system, government and governability.

According to Bealy (1999), a political system has four elements: (1) the branches of the state institutions: legislature, executive, and judiciary as established by laws or constitution and their interactions; (2) the wider society that encompasses political parties, electoral system, and the machinery that propels one into the political system; (3) the methods of decision-making and the underpinning values regarding the relationship between the state and society; and (4) a structural-functional model which explains the situations of survival, maintenance, decay, and collapse of the system.

The second concept, "government", refers to control. The legal and supreme controlling force within society is the government or state. Government is an abstract concept that includes style, scope, purpose, and degree of control. There are two schools of thought that explain the concept of government: mechanistic and organic. The mechanistic theory views government as a necessary instrument that maintains law and order and resolves conflicts within members of the society. The organic theory views government not only as the entity with the power to maintain law and order in the society, but also as a tool for the achievement and maintenance of higher moral order intended to bring humanity to higher forms of decency and civilization. The third concept is governability. This can be generically defined as the ability of a country's political system and institutions to direct its economy and society (Bogdanor, 1991). In other words, the nature and acceptance of the governed and the ability of the state to meet the welfare and security demands of the society are both important.

Using these three concepts, it is easier to define governance. The concept incorporates all of the elements that were introduced above: political system, government and governability. Macridis and Burg (1991) suggest a two level analysis of a political system: normative and functional. At the normative level the authors suggest values such as freedom, equality, and justice. At the functional level they suggest the ability of the state to have: 1) the decisional efficiency that creates an adoptive, responsive and inclusive system; 2) the legitimacy that comes from the consent of the population and their belief that the state has the authority to rule them; and 3) the ability to maintain civil order, which is highly influenced by the distribution of goods and values within the society.

In this book, good governance is understood as accountable and predictable regimes, which effectively exercise the power and authority of the state institutions in a manner that improves the quality of life of its citizens. This includes the use of state power to create a society in which it is possible for individuals to fully develop and exercise control over their lives. These states do not necessarily have to be democratic in the pluralistic Western sense as long as there are significant forms of accountability over the rulers and institutions (Englebert, 2000; Hyden and Bratton, 1992). Therefore this book is concerned with results of state functions, specifically whether it has succeeded to improve the lives of its citizens regardless of the ideological trait it adopted.

As the above narration indicates the word governance is concerned with and has indeed been borrowed from development literature. Recently, the term found its way into the social science fields including political science. More specifically, many political scientists accept that good governance leads to development (Hyden, 1990). Hence, well-governed states improve the lives of their citizens, deliver security, provide a strong rule of law, respect political freedoms and human rights, foster strong institutions, provide quality educational and health services, strengthen or regulate effective infrastructure, and bolster an economic framework conducive to growth and prosperity.

In contrast, instability and stagnation tend to be more prevalent in states where these traits lack (Rotberg, 2003; Englebert, 2000). Failed governments or states such as the Democratic Republic of Congo, Liberia, Somalia and Sierra Leone had predatory states that delivered few public goods for their citizens, as opposed to states such as Tanzania and Botswana that delivered relatively better social services. Governance quality appears to play a large role in explaining the war/no-war distribution among countries. This book posits the argument that where relative development occurred, internal war was avoided, as opposed to places where it did not (summarized in Figure 2.1). Before testing this argument, it is useful to look at two schools of thought that examine the effectiveness of governance and factors that contribute to its success or failure.

Figure 2.1: Summary of the theoretical framework

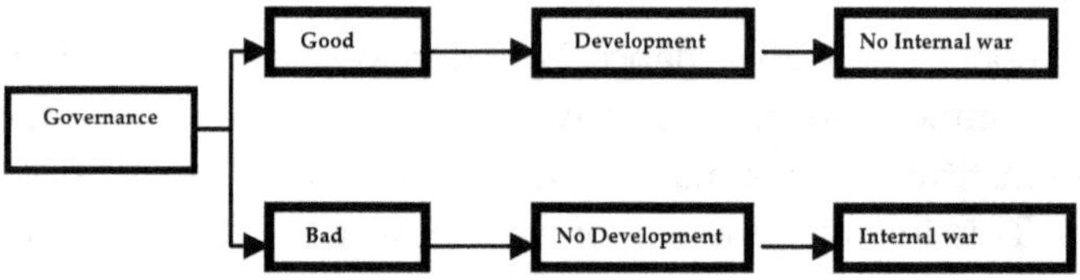

```
                    ┌─→ Good  ──→ Development  ──→ No Internal war
    Governance ─────┤
                    └─→ Bad   ──→ No Development ──→ Internal war
```

Structuralism v. Institutionalism

The literature that analyzes governance in general and governance in Africa in particular stems from two platforms: structural and institutional. Structuralists view governance in African states as a set of entities and political actors that rationally respond to their inherited settings (historical, social, and economic). These settings constrain their actions. The primary subscribers to this school are the dependency theorists who argue that the world is divided into core and periphery.

They argue that the core has the capability to exploit the periphery as a result of years of colonialism, imperialism, Cold War, and general geo-political settings created and enforced with mechanisms of exploitation. The current abundance of bad governance in many countries of the Third World has, therefore, been set up and maintained through economic mechanisms and military support regardless of the regime's behavior, so long as the regime meets with the interests of the core. In other words, the practices of colonialism, imperialism, and their constraints continued, even though these countries were independent for decades.

Institutionalists on the other hand, believe ineffective governance is a result of the failure of the respective states and their institutions. Proponents of this viewpoint include the World Bank and IMF. The basic assumption is that after independence these countries essentially had the freedom to choose their fate. As a case in point, although Botswana went through all the historical constraints, such as colonialism, neo-colonialism, and the Cold War, the country still managed to have the fastest growing economy in the world between 1960 and 1985 (World Bank, 1993). For the current book, both the structuralist and institutionalist viewpoints will be adopted in order to provide valuable insights in explaining the occurrence of internal wars in one country while another enjoys relative peace and prosperity.

Good governance and Africa

The postcolonial states in Africa, in most cases, have been characterized by the inability or unwillingness of the ruling elites to deliver the functions of good governance. This has resulted in many negative outcomes including civil disorder, corruption, and violence. These states became known by several scholars as neo-patrimonial states. In such states there is a blurring of the boundary between the public and private spheres through nepotism and favoritism.

Neo-patrimonialism is a hybrid of patrimonial and legal-rational state structures. On the one hand, strong familial ties between the ruler and the ruled characterize the patrimonial state (seen in other regions as well). The term, derived from Max Weber, refers to an authority and relationship in which the leader controls administrative staff selected for their personal loyalty to the leader, thus making the state essentially the private property of the leader. This is in contrast to the Weberian legal-rational state, which is characterized by impersonal or unbiased transactions and adherence to the rules of the state. The emphasis of this state is on formal procedure and regulations and the individual powers to obtain recourse for injustices.

A neo-patrimonial state has three main features: personalist rule, patron-client relations and "kleptocracy." Personal rule increasingly prevailed overtime in Africa's postcolonial states. There is debate concerned with whether this stemmed from colonialism itself and its tradition of appointed governors that were mainly interested in economic extraction or from postcolonial national leaders responding to the conditions of international economic structures (Mamdani, 1996; Davidson, 1992). In either case, the majority of the postcolonial states became one-party or military regimes unaccountable to their people; this allowed dishonesty and corruption to flourish.[1]

Many scholars described these states as weak, although many of these states have proven to be very capable of maintaining themselves in power for long periods of time using oppression as their most valuable tool (Jackson and Rosberg, 1982; Adedeji, 1999; Fatton, 1992). Between 1957 and 1990, there were more than 150 African presidents and only seven stepped down voluntarily: Nigeria's General Olusegun Obasanjo in 1979 (after one year); Somalia's Adan Abdulle Osman in 1967 (after 7 years); Senegal's Leopold Senghor in 1980 (after 20 years); Cameroon's Ahmadou Ahidjo in 1982 (after 22 years); Tanzania's Julius Nyerere in 1985 (after 23 years); Sierra Leone's Siaka Stevens in 1985 (after 14 years); and Abdul Rahman Swareddahab of Sudan in 1986 (after one year). The remaining leaders in Africa's were removed by military coup d'état or assassination or war, or else died in office.

Personalist states in postcolonial Africa, like their preceding colonial states, have been able to extract resources and redistribute rewards privately to their clients. Braathen et al. (2000, p.11) describe this process by stating that, : "...the independent states created a specific patrimonial path of redistribution which divided the indigenous majority along regional, religious, ethnic and at times familial lines." This process in the long run creates huge social inequalities, and it is the spoils of power inequality that leads to resentment and eventual violence (Gupta et al., 1998; Reno, 1995; McMullan, 1961). Neo-patrimonial states and their elites have occupied a central stage in which they controlled the largest portion of economic activities in Africa. Over the years they acquired large military forces and bureaucracies that provided protection and jobs for the elites and their supporters. Overall, both economic and physical security of the members of the society became closely related to the state.

Measuring Good Governance

The issue of good governance, even if one manages an acceptable sufficient definition, is still difficult to quantify and measure. This multi-faceted concept encompasses all aspects of the exercise of authority throughout state institutions in the management of the country's resources. The ultimate indicator of governance is thus determined by how states exercise their power, which in turn impacts the quality of life of their citizens.

In developing governance evaluation, already established and existing indicators will be used. The ability to create an index of governance quality has been enhanced by the existence of several quality of life indices such as previously published indices measuring health and education. The economic dependency of most developing countries can be measured by examining available data from a variety of institutions such as the Organization for Economic Co-operation and Development (OECD), World Bank, and International Monetary Fund (IMF). The index developed in this book takes advantage of the increased data availability as well as more traditional research of historical, political, and economic narration through the case studies.

As noted, there are two school of thoughts underpinning the issue of governance: structuralist, which views governance and its impact as part of its setting (historical, social, economic and environmental); and institutionalist, which views governance from the immediate postcolonial institutions and their chosen behavior. These schools will be used as a base for creating indicators of governance quality and ultimately the occurrence of internal war. More specifically, governance will be examined from three perspectives: context, structure, and policy. It is important at this juncture to note that for the purpose of this book structuralist arguments indicate context or setting, whereas institutionalist arguments indicate what is termed as governmental structure and adoption of various specific policies.

Traditionally, several indicators of governance frequent the literature. These include the availability of security, rule of law, infrastructure, economic development, physical quality of life, and more. Some of these indicators are relatively easy to measure, while others are more problematic. Indicators such as economic development are measurable in GDP per capita (even allowing for vagaries of estimates in less developed or dictatorial states); others such as rule of law are very difficult to measure the existence of courts may be apparent, but measuring the independence of the courts can be more challenging.

Using the schema of context, structure, and policy, several indicators and measurements of governance quality as related to internal war have been selected (see Table 2.1). Context refers largely to factors inherited by governments as "given." Structure refers to governments' institutional arrangements. Policy refers to decisions about how and for what or whom to expend resources. These three domains can affect one another in complex ways.

The rest of the chapter will focus on how these factors interact and explain the relationship between governance and internal war in Sub Saharan Africa. The factors will be used both in initial quantitative comparisons and later in the case studies. Other existing indices of governance quality will be employed as well.

Table 2.1: Factors and indicators of governance

Factor	Indicators
Context	Historical Ethnicity Economy
Structure	Regime type Leadership Stability Size
Policy	Expenditure Social Military

The contextual, structural, and policy factors in which African countries have found themselves or for which they have opted since their independence will be examined. Some preliminary propositions that point to differences between the war and no-war countries are also identified. The theoretical argument will be constructed that internal wars are the result of bad governance, or operationally "worse governance" than in comparable states, and suggest several general propositions. These propositions will be examined later in the case studies.

Several scholars have attempted to measure and quantify various aspects of good governance (Mauro, 1995; Keefer and Knack 1995; Saachs and Werner, 1997). Most of these empirical studies concentrated on how the state facilitates development in the country, which in turn makes the society more or less prone to conflict (Englebert, 2000). The Inter-Country Risk Guide (ICRG) compiles one of the most widely used datasets related to good governance. According to this dataset, the majority of the countries on the African continent scored lower than their counterparts in Europe and South East Asia; however, on the war or no war comparison, the trend of governance has been worse for African countries experiencing war with an average score of –2.96

compared to no-war with −1.43. Botswana, for example enjoyed political stability and economic growth and had the highest ICRG score of 1.30, whereas the Democratic Republic of Congo (formerly Zaire which since 1997 has continued to suffer from devastating internal violence, scored −4.10.[2] (see Figure 2.2)

Figure 2.2: Average of ICRG governance score for war countries (n=25) and no-war (n=6) African countries

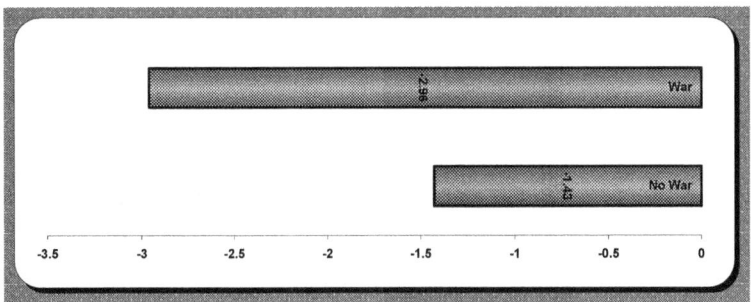

Data: Englebert, 2000

Indicators of good governance (e.g. low crime rates, economic growth and prosperity, high literacy and rich cultural life, etc.) were largely absent in many of Africa's postcolonial states. It should be noted, further, that few African states have shown sufficient growth and stability to pull their societies out of the poverty and violence cycle. Based on this preliminary analysis, one could conjecture that war countries generally have had lower governance scores compared to no-war countries.

Contextual Factors

The selected cases in this book vary in their social, political, and economic situations. The sources of these variations are both internal (e.g. ethnicity and culture) and external (e.g. economic pressure, international markets, neo-colonialism, Cold War and nearby or regional wars). They differ, more importantly, in the achievements of good governance and their avoidance of internal war.

Historical: The most pervasive governing context, as argued, is the colonial legacy that nearly all African states experienced even though each country was affected differently. The colonial state shaped Africa's present-day political systems and, in particular, left behind three interrelated problems. First, colonialism created the current borders of states that include and divide numerous ethnic groups (Herbst, 2000; Schroeder, 2000; Mazrui, 1967; Young, 1982; Clapham, 1994; Davidson, 1992; Ofiaja, 1979; Boahen, 1987). Second, it created or magnified divided and hierarchical societies, mainly using ethnic, linguistic, and cultural differences.[3] Third, the colonial state created economic problems that left enduring scars on many African economies: specifically, the impact of the single-crop economic model, which persists today and severely hinders the evolution of strong market economies in this region (Bates, 1981; Ake, 1981; Jackson, 1986; Young, 1982). Overall, despite educational opportunities for some and establishment of parliamentary traditions, colonial rule was poor preparation for stable governance and independent rule. Few people were educated beyond the primary levels.

As argued, different colonial states left behind diverse imprints. Using the ICRG scores, different in colonial powers, and vulnerability to war, it can be concluded that British colonized countries had the best ICRG score average of –1.12, and one (or 8%) out of these twelve countries went to internal war. France with 11 postcolonial countries had an average ICRG governance score of –1.85, but all of them were at relative peace at least by 1990. The worst records, however, were those of Belgium (Rwanda, Burundi and DR Congo), Italy (Somalia) and United States (Liberia) with –2.49, –2.88 and –4 respectively. All of these countries were at war in the 1990s (see Figure 2.3).

Figure 2.3: Colonial powers and average governance scores

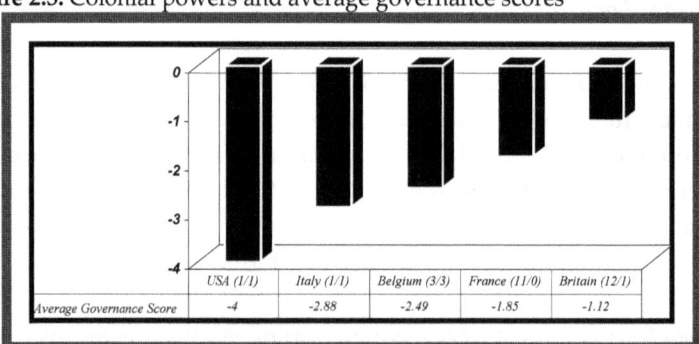

Data: Englebert, 2000

Ethnicity: In most African postcolonial states, another key contextual governance factor concerns ethnicity, tribalism, and culture.[4] High degrees of ethnic diversity offer the possibility for unscrupulous leaders to play on the fears and insecurities and use groups against each other much like their colonial predecessors.[5] This has been further facilitated by the existence of the over 2,000 ethno-linguistic groups in Africa.[6] Most independent African states, therefore, faced the dilemma of creating nations out of highly diverse and often resentful societies. The creation of European style modern states along with the artificial borders created a situation of security threat perception for all competing ethnic groups. The resulting states created and enforced social inequality based on tribalism. In other words, the members and friends of the tribe or clans that control the state tend to receive the most benefits from it.

In order to understand this disparity, one must examine the sociocultural setting in which the African leaders and bureaucrats function. Ekeh (1975) suggests the existence of two politically involved with social realms that have two different types of moral linkages to the private realm in postcolonial Africa. The first is the primordial public, which is identified with primordial groupings, sentiments, and activities such as ethnic groupings. The primordial public is usually understood as moral, at least by its members. The second realm is the civic public, which is historically associated with the colonial administration and became identified with popular politics. The civic public in Africa is seen as amoral and lacking in the generalized moral imperatives which operate in the private and in the primordial realm. This public is based on civil structures such as military, civil service, and police. Ekeh (p. 92) suggests that these two public realms create a different meaning of citizenship from that understood in the West.

In most African societies citizenship acquires different meanings depending on the realm (primordial or civic) in which it is conceived. In the primordial public realm, the individual is morally obligated to maintain solidarity with his/her group. The individual, in turn, gains benefits in the form of identity, sense of belonging, and psychological security (Fajnzyleber *et al.* 1998; Hsieh and Pugh, 1993). In the civic public realm, the individual seeks to gain materially and does not have moral obligations and duties based on identity groupings. Given the state breakdown and resource control issues raised in the prior section, there is considerable violence potential in Africa's civic public realm. Ekeh argues that the educated Africans belong to both of these realms, but that this puts them in a dilemma because of the dialectic tension between the two.

This tension manifests itself in African politics in the form of an unwritten law that "...it is legitimate to rob the civic public in order to strengthen the primordial public." (Ekeh, 1975, p.108) It is this individual identity whereby social inclusion/exclusion is created and enforced. The departing colonial powers gave advantages to some groups, while depriving others. The idea of government, therefore, is at the heart of the process of social exclusion in Africa (and elsewhere). This exclusion is never the result of a spontaneous process, rather it is the result of initial imbalances of power and practice of the more powerful group or groups in the society to maintain and augment power.

In Sub Saharan Africa, as in many other regions, there tends to be a close relationship between holding positions of power in the state and the acquisition of wealth. The ethnic groups of the office holders also benefit in this system through nepotism and favoritism. They, in turn, provide legitimacy and support to the office holders. Lonsdale (1986, pp.106-7) compares these groups and argues that "...states have some moral force in the modern world and some international standing; they are licensed to use violence against their citizens and to incur debts. Ethnic groups are allowed none of these strengths...and Ethnic politics is stigmatized as tribalism." Lonsdale further argues that the morality of new forms of social inequality was the "tribe" where the included persons took on "...the duties of patronage" and justified their actions by "...creating communities in which they had a moral standing and beyond which they acted as brokers of political alliance within the new arena of the state." (Lonsdale, 1986, p.143).

In most cases, the issue of ethnicity impacts on the creation of good governance. The issue of governmental legitimacy, which is an important ingredient in governance, is hindered by ethnic based nepotism and favoritism (Ayittey, 1998; Englebert, 2000). Many scholars suggest that ethnicity, as it exists, is the result of years of colonialism that shaped present-day tension (Ofiaja, 1979).

Economic conditions: Another contextual indicator includes the issues of economy, and economic development and available resources the governments use. For the purposes of this book all the economic and economic development related indicators will be grouped under the economy. Africa is a continent well endowed with vast natural resources; however, the 1980s came to be known as, "Africa's lost decade."[7] The continent faced unprecedented political instability, economic stagnation, migration of huge number of refugees, the scourge of diseases, and enormous foreign debt. Between 1980 and 1989, per capita income declined by an average of 2.8% (World Bank 1989; Ravenhill, 1986). The situation did not improve in the 1990s. In 1992 the Gross Domestic Product growth rate for the continent was 1.9%, compared to 1991's 2.6% (Adedji, 1993). Africa's debt mounted to US $ 225 billion by the end of 1992 with a debt payment service of 32.4% of export earnings (Adedeji 1993; George, 1993).

Foreign aid and dependency: Upon independence a majority of African countries began to depend on foreign aid. This dependency increased in the 1970s, a time when many African countries began to accumulate large amounts of Official Development Assistance (ODA) and Direct Foreign Investment (DFI) was declining. African countries for example received 8.3% in ODA in 1970. By 1989, this figure grew to 37.8%. During the same period the DFI figure declined from 15% to 8% of GDP. This trend was the opposite in Southeast Asia (See Table 3.2 below). The Asian ODA figure was 15.3% in 1970 and 13.7% in 1989, while the DFI figure was 11.7% and 33.3% of GDP during the same period (UNDP, 1992, p.37). Perhaps this explains why South-East Asia countries, in spite of eventual economic problems of their own, gained the title "Newly Industrializing Countries." The African continent, however, with lack of export revenue and foreign aid dependency, found itself facing further economic stagnation. In some circles the debt crisis is regarded as a: "...silent and undeclared economic war for the recolonization of Africa." (Onimode, 1989, p.1-7) In the process Africa's debt has kept growing larger over the years (Nafziger, 1993, pp.67-74).

Table 2.2: The percentage of DFI and ODA in selected regions 1970-1989

Region	DFI % 1970 / 1989	ODA% 1970 / 1989
Sub-Saharan Africa	24.8 / 33.3	8.3 / 13.7
Southeast Asia	15.0 / 40.4	37.8 / 7.7
Latin America	11.7 / 29.4	15.3 / 11.6

Source: Adopted from Adedeji, 1993, p.6.

Commodities: The debt crisis and deficit were further compounded by the decline in commodity prices and food production. From 1970 to 1992, for example, Sub Saharan Africa experienced a 52% decline (or 38% from 1980 to 1992) in commodity prices (Nafziger, 1993). During the 1960s food production matched population growth, but by the 1970s, food production per capita was in decline. Moreover, Africa's share of the world market for many agricultural commodities decreased during the 1970s; in the meantime, food imports grew at three times the rate of population growth.[8] By the early 1980s the average real income in Africa south of the Sahara was only 80% of the 1970 level. During this period, the number of people living below the absolute poverty line increased by more than 80 million. The purchasing power of the region's commodity exports over its manufactured imports declined by 37% (UNCTAD, 1998).

The vast foreign debts accumulated during the 1970s and 1980s paved the way for the Structural Adjustment Programs (SAPs) imposed by IMF and the World Bank in the 1980s. The general belief was that Africa's swollen and inefficient states were the main cause for economic decline. The proposed remedy allowed the market forces to operate freely and set economies on the right path. Over the years, the adjustment programs have received mixed reviews. The World Bank argues that these programs have produced positive results.[9] Others argue, however, argue that adjustment programs had a negative impact on many Third World countries.[10]

The adjustment programs mainly affected the poor in the developing countries. As a result, the 1980s became associated with decline in Physical Quality of Life Index in many parts of the continent. The adjustment programs were mainly trickle down economies that granted a few elites more economic power (Berg, 1995). Adebayo Adedeji (1993, p.7), a leading African scholar, described the effect of these programs as,

> "...a highly polarizing social and political concept was superimposed on existing structure and led to disappearance of the center, a small urban based but rurally connected middle class...A tiny group of actors in the unproductive and often illegal sector of the economy is setting the beat."

The result of the adjustment programs was the birth of huge informal economies controlled by the ruling elites. These elites began to shift their efforts toward political survival and wealth accumulation, all courtesy of the adjustment programs. The privatization sermon of the adjustment programs generally failed to materialize; however, the already existing severe poverty crisis was significantly heightened (Clapham 1997; Reno 1998).

The pressure of the adjustment programs created a situation where the ruling elites often abandoned good governance and instead concentrated on augmenting their wealth. In the meantime, they continued to pay lip service to the externally imposed financial regimes. The elites of these states were therefore able to branch out into informal networks and seize control over exploitable resources (Reno, 2000; Herbst, 1996). As the size, strength, sophistication, and most of all the profitability of these networks increased, the ruling elites increasingly relied on violent coercion. Violence became the tool of economic regulation; it was spread into most economic spheres and set the stage for the growth of armed conflict and anarchy, a pattern seen earlier in places like Katanga in the Congo during the 1960s. Now this pattern is seen repeatedly and more harshly across the continent. Some ideological and factional rebellions, such as those in Angola and Sierra Leone, utilized regional resources, such as diamonds, to fund their armed resistance. Some leaders, such as Charles Taylor of Liberia, also set themselves up as regional power brokers in these informal and corrupt economic networks.

The economic performance of most of the countries in this region has been declining since 1970; however, different patterns can be observed, whereby "war countries" experienced more economic decline compared to their counterparts. Adedeji (1999) argues that the African countries that experienced war in 1998 had also experienced prior economic decline. Similarly, Auvinen and Nafziger (1999) found that the countries that did not experience internal war had an average GNP per capita of US $1,300. This figure was US $550 for countries that experienced internal wars. Even though the causal relationship between economic decline and internal war can be equated to the "chicken and egg" question, still, according to Wallensteen and Sollenburg dataset (1999), war countries had been experiencing steeper economic decline than the no-war countries since the 1970s. The GDP per capita of war countries declined by an average of US $11 annually from 1970 to 1990, whereas the no-war countries' actually increased in GDP per capita by over US $66 annually during the same period (See Figure 2.4). Ominously, the no-war states also saw relative declines between 1980 and 1990, indicating that the potential for future violence is also rising among them.

Figure 2.4: GDP per capita for Sub Saharan Africa war and no-war countries between 1960 and 1990

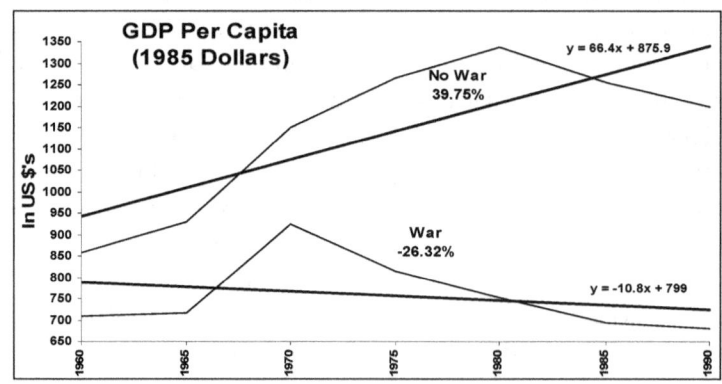

Data calculated from the University of Pennsylvania World Tables. War n=10 and no war n=26; N=36

Two major contextual factors resulted from Africa's colonial heritage. The first factor is the effects of economic dependency, which subsequently led to politicized foreign aid and later Structural Adjustment Programs. The second is the effects of incorporating an often hostile and suspicious, multi-ethnic population inside borders that were arbitrarily drawn and enforced, first by the former colonial powers and then by ethnically driven states. Although nearly all countries inherited these contextual factors, they have still shown differential economic growth, stability, and variations in violence patterns. Two distinct patterns can preliminarily be investigated in the case study analysis differentiating between the war/ no-war countries. One pattern suggests that: war countries had more ethno-cultural diversity, were more economically dependent experienced steeper economic decline, attracted less investment, had lower quality of life, and had lower governance scores than the no-war countries.

Structural Factors

A second set of explanatory factors is entailed in the structure of the state. The majority of African states have been, at least initially, highly influenced by their former colonial powers. These powers left behind European-type political institutions that lacked the underpinnings of democracy and rule of law and more importantly the educated cadres and citizenry equipped to run the political system. Thus, since their independence the overwhelming majority of African states can thus be described as models of ineffective governance. In this sub-section, the functions of the postcolonial state in Africa will be examined from different perspectives including regime, leadership, size, kleptocracy, and inequality.

Regime type: The majority of the postcolonial African states have been ineffective, totalitarian regimes. Those describing African states as weak (Jackson and Rosberg, 1982; Migdal 1988) note that very few such states have had a monopoly of legitimate force throughout their territories and across time. Goran Hyden (2000, p.7) describes the Sub Saharan Africa states by saying, "…it is not only the state that lacks capability to get things done. The same applies to society, or civil society." Hyden further argues that the state is not only weak and unable to successfully implement policies, it also lacks legitimacy.[11] Others argue that the states in Africa are not weak but strong and predatory (Fatton, 1992). They do, however, add that the African states also have strong linkages to rural ethnic elites, which provide some legitimacy to the ruling elite (Bayart, 1983; Leonard and Straus, 2003; Herbst, 2000).

As argued earlier, many of Africa's postcolonial states had peculiar, though not unique, challenges of citizenship whereby many inhabitants did not identify themselves with the state. This has been reflected not only in regional autonomous movements and irredentism, but also in fractured state structures and unstable regions. Classifying regimes has always been a difficult task in the comparative politics literature. Esman (1966) advances a classification scheme, mainly assuming that all regimes share common characteristics such as structure and behavior in their approach to nation building. He suggests five categories of regimes: (1) Conservative oligarchies, (2) authoritarian military reformers, (3) competitive interest-oriented party systems, (4) dominant mass-party systems, and (5) communist totalitarian system. Specific to Africa's regimes, Chazan *et al.* (1992) provided a six-fold classification: (1) Administrative hegemonic, (2) Pluralist, (3) Party mobilizing, (3) Party centralist, (4) Personal coercive, (5) Personalist coercive, and (6) Populist.

In most of the postcolonial African states the dominant regime type at independence was the dominant mass-party system. This trend resulted from two interrelated factors, the colonial state's inherent fear of political competition and party systems (Ferkiss, 1962; Berman, 1998; Clapham, 1985; Boahen, 1990; Young, 1988), and the leaders of the independence movements who viewed themselves as the embodiment of the nation. Opponents tended to be viewed as enemies of the nation (Shills, 1962; Emerson, 1963; Mazrui, 1967). As early as the mid-1960s the dominant-party regimes began to be replaced by a wave of military regimes that devastated the continent. This brought the second notable type of regime in: authoritarian military reformers, some of whom have been credited with more effective reforms than others. The two basic types of regimes that could be observed in the majority of African states were military or single-party dominant regimes.

For the purpose of this book two regime types were used military and civilian. The governance scores were initially averaged and then an independent sample test was created. The average governance score was –0.99 for civilian regimes and –2.29 for military regimes. The independent sample test found that military regimes had –2.1874 and civilian regimes had -.9892, a difference of -1.1982. There was, however, no difference found in variation or standard deviation. Also, regressing governance against regime type found it significant only at .10 (see Table 2.4 below). It can, therefore, be concluded that military governments were less likely to bolster development in their countries compared to non-military regimes (McCowan and Kposawa, 1998).

Table 2.3: Regime type and ICRG governance scores

Regime	N	Mean	Difference
Military	19	-2.1847	
Civilian	12	-0.9892	-1.1982
Sig.			.020 (2 tail)*

*P<.10   Source: Bratton and Van de Walle, 1996.

Leadership: Different types of personalist rulership have controlled many Sub Saharan postcolonial states.[12] Colonial powers set up states that were run single handedly by the appointed governors of the protectorate, and despite multi-party formation, especially during the 1980s, the same practice tended to continue after independence. There was autocracy with the systematic concentration of political power in the hands of a single individual who had a monopoly on all decision-making processes. These leaders projected themselves as benevolent father figures directly responsible for the people's welfare (Ayittey, 1998; Bayart, 1993). The new rulers eliminated any signs of political competition, including multiparty systems, and in some cases elections. Many African leaders embarked on policies that created large public bureaucracies that facilitated their wealth extraction through taxes and other rents (Abernathy, 1983). They also created large militaries and security apparatus designed to facilitate the rent seeking activities (Chabal, 1988; Young, 1994). Most of Africa's political leaders had concentrated on narrow political considerations related to their personalized power and corruption that undermined the process of creating responsive governance. Inequity in social, economic, and political systems has been a barrier to achieving good governance. This has resulted in notably increasing disparities between the rich and the poor in terms of income and capabilities.

In order to classify Africa's leaders, one must understand the ideological differences that they espoused. After independence, the nationalist leaders were in a hurry to develop Africa. They sought an alternative ideology as they uniformly rejected the colonial structures. Four distinct ideologies emerged. The first was African socialism, espoused by leaders such as Kwame Nkrumah of Ghana, Ahmed Sékou Touré of Guinea, Modibo Keita of Mali, Gamal Abdel Nasser of Egypt, Julius Nyerere of Tanzania, and Kenneth Kaunda of Zambia. These leaders advocated an egalitarian, just, and self-sufficient polity. The mechanism for the attainment of these goals was the state, which would furnish the pivot of critical identities and organize the economy. They installed a centralized political system and utilized societal mobilization as a vehicle for transformation (Chazan *et al.*, 1992).

The second ideology was political pragmatism, espoused by leaders such as Félix Houphouet-Boigny of Côte d'Ivoire, Abubakar Tafawa Balewa of Nigeria, and Hastings Banda of Malawi. They declared themselves non-ideological and claimed to concentrate on economic growth and prosperity. The state was charged with the task of fostering entrepreneurship, attracting foreign investment, and creating a climate conducive to material advancement. They were not, in fact, markedly less statist than the socialists, but they wanted to use the state more for the creation or preservation of wealth than for social or political transformation. Chazan *et al.* (1992, p.156) state, "Centralization therefore was delineated not in a social or political but in an administrative sense; it nevertheless was as deeply ensconced in the political attitudes of pragmatists as in those of self-proclaimed socialists."

The third approach was military nationalism, represented by the first group of military leaders who came onto the political scene in the late 1960s and early 1970s. These leaders include Idi Amin of Uganda, Jean-Bedel Bokassa of the Central African Republic, Mobutu Sese Seko of Zaire, Mohamed Siad Barre of Somalia and Gnassingbe Eyadema of Togo. These military strongmen installed dictatorial states purportedly to rectify the disorder that had followed independence. Since they had not been central to the independence struggles, they embarked on campaigns and at developing alternative ideologies to supplant the earlier leaders that they overthrew. They glorified the African warrior tradition, shunned foreign ideals, and revived certain traditional practices (even as they accepted foreign training and support, as in Israel's ties to Uganda, French ties to the CAR and U.S. ties to Zaire. In the economic arena they exercised full control over national resources, not only to deflect pressures from external creditors but also to account for statist monopolies. Chazan (1992, p.158) described the ideologies (or lack thereof) of these leaders:

> "They are by and large bereft of intellectual content, they are replete with contradictions they address key issues haphazardly. These orientations, at best, may be viewed as feeble attempts to legitimate their purveyors; in most instances, they have provided the cover for the exercise of brute force. Manifestations of this sort of military nationalism resurface periodically, as insecure leaders with dwindling support bases find refuge in cultural symbols in a desperate effort to gain some loyalty and legitimacy."

The fourth approach was Afro-Marxism, which was the official policy of Angola, Mozambique, Congo, and Ethiopia. This approach attributes Africa's economic malaise to the lingering effects of imperialism and continuing neo-colonialist practices. Accordingly, they embarked on the creation of a new social order, often in league with the former USSR, China, or Cuba (though mutual distrust persisted), in which private ownership of the means of production would be abolished, and the state would become the supreme patron of economic destiny.

Across these approaches, the most relevant and consistent ideology was always statism. State hegemony in most African countries was all-encompassing, although, as argued, different rationales were utilized based on the particular social, economic, and political conditions and response to dynamic internal and external pressures (Callaghy and Ravenhill, 1993). African countries generally operated a state system in which power was concentrated in the hands of the ruling elite and ultimately one individual. The above classification, with some modification, could provide an organizing schema for this book.

State stability: Power in the postcolonial states in Africa was also highly contested over the years, as indicated by the disproportionately high number of military coups d'état, both attempted and successful. As many as 80 violent changes of power occurred in Africa between 1960 and 1990 (Adedeji, 1999). These coups d'état have had a negative impact on economies reinforced by military rule and have severely damaged the quality of life for many Africans. Those countries that experienced less military intervention enjoyed fairly positive economic growth and improved quality of life (McGowan and Johnson, 1984 and 1985; Mbaku, 1992; Jenkins and Kposawa, 1990, 1992; Kposawa and Jenkins, 1993; Fosu, 1992).

Political instability has hindered the growth potential of many African countries and has led them towards poverty and violence. The seven war countries in this book experienced a total of 43 attempted and successful coups between 1960 (or independence date if later than 1960) and 1990 with an average of 6.14 coups per country for the whole period. In comparison, the 25 no-war countries experienced a total of 110 coups with an average of 4.4 coups per country (see Table 2.4).

Figure 2.5: Number of attempted and succeeded coups in the war (n=7) and no-war countries 1960-1990.

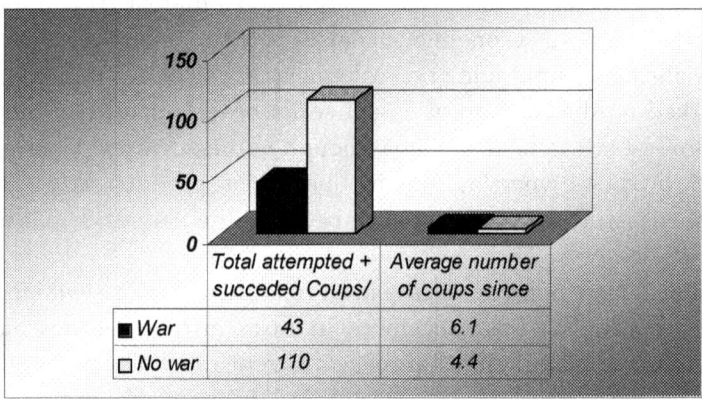

n=25) Data obtained from ICPSR collected by Bratton and Van de Walle (1996)

Size: The majority of African state leaders created large bureaucracies. This was also partly the result of the colonial legacy with bureaucracies expanding a great deal during the period of national movements after World War II. The colonial states imposed the Western style governance, but it was a style that lacked the state-limiting elements such as a functioning constitution, bill of rights, independent judiciary, civil liberties, and liberalism. The colonial states built governance systems intended to expand and reinforce their extraction potential. This expansion was accompanied by high state expenditure (Young, 1982). Colonial states immediately created marketing boards in many countries, strengthening the single crop dependency. The Tea Board of Kenya, for example, was established in 1950 and the Ghana Cocoa Board (Cocobod) was established in 1947. Growth in the size and costs of the colonial states during this period was accompanied by increased Africanization of the bureaucracy. For example, the number of Nigerian Africans who occupied higher posts increased from 26 individuals in 1938 to 172 in 1948, and by 1960, 62% of the senior bureaucracy was Nigerian.[13]

In the 1960s, a majority of the independent states inherited swollen state bureaucracies, which Chazan (1988) described as overestablished and underbureaucratized. There were fewer necessary functions to perform than individual bureaucrats to perform them. State bureaucracies kept growing in the following years. This was partially the result of the financial support that was provided by the international donors, who viewed states as the primary engine for development in the countries and, more importantly, as part of the board game between the superpowers during the Cold War. As a result, the majority of the development aid given to these countries went to the state, which in turn expanded the already large bureaucracies. As a result civil service in Africa grew an average of 7% annually (Schroeder, 2000).

A decade later, in the 1970s, public bureaucracies claimed more than 50% of government expenditures as salary, and in some cases nearly 80% of the state revenues were spent in supporting the bureaucracy (Chazan, 1988, p.55). Also the number of government agencies also increased. By 1970 Zambia had 134 state agencies; Nigeria had 250 agencies by 1974; and Tanzania had 400 agencies by 1981 (Abernathy, 1983). The swollen states in Sub Saharan Africa accounted for 55% of the countries' wage earners compared to 27% in Latin America and 36% in Asia (Ibid). The second largest employees in these states were the foreign firms. In Nigeria, for example, the state employs approximately 54% of the wage earners; foreign firms employ 38%, leaving less than 10% of wage earners to Nigerian owned enterprises (Diamond, 1987, p.74).

Sub Saharan African states also controlled the bulk of the consumption within their countries. This further consolidated state power and increased the economic inequality that began with the colonial state. In Zaire (currently the Democratic Republic of Congo) the state consumed 59% of GDP in 1974, and in Nigeria it was 35%

during the same year (Abernathy, 1983, p.14). The disproportionately large salaries of upper level bureaucrats further widened the social inequality gap. The average African bureaucrat makes a salary that is six times the GDP per capita, twice as high as in Latin America and Asia and four times that of OECD countries (Ibid). According to Abernathy (1983, p.17), top-level officials receive an even higher ratio above the GDP per capita:

> "As of 1963-4 the ratio of the former (salaries) to the latter (GDP per capita) was 73:1 in Malawi, 82:1 in Kenya…118:1 in Nigeria, 130:1 in Uganda. This pattern is in sharp contrast to that of the United States, where the ratio is under 10:1 – most likely under 8:1. If we translate African ratios at independence into contemporary American terms – admittedly a procedure of dubious validity – a top American civil servant earning one hundred times U.S. per capita income would receive a salary (in 1985 dollars) of $ 1.7 million a year."

Other factors of governance quality also include the role of kleptocracy, corruption and inequality play in dragging countries towards the occurrence of internal war. Despite the fact that these factors are difficult to measure and quantify, they need to be examined them briefly.

Kleptocracy: The postcolonial states in Sub Saharan Africa have been known for their corruption and embezzlement of public properties. Kleptocracy in this book is defined as the theft of state resources for the personal benefit of the leader and his cronies. Patrimonial states are noted for their leaders and subordinates routinely keeping large chunks of state funds to meet their own needs or wants.[14] In the patrimonial state, the net result is the creation of politics of exclusion, where the few who control the state are able to enrich themselves; many scholars argue that this is a primary cause of internal war in the region. Since independence, Sub Sahara African states have enriched only a very few, mostly upper level government officials and their relatives.

One late traditional ruler among the Yorubas, one of the three largest tribes in Nigeria summarized the corruption in Nigeria as, "Since the independence, our governments have been a matter of a few holding the cow for the strongest and most cunning to milk." This desire to control the state, coupled with Africa's abundance of autocratic weak states that: (1) lacked accountability and transparency, (2) practiced nepotism and favoritism, and (3) received moral and material support from abroad specifically the Cold War combatants Soviet Union and United States, created highly unstable governance in Sub Saharan Africa. Because of these factors, then it became practical for many individuals, mainly from the military, to either attempt overthrow the government (e.g. the numerous African military coups d'état) or to secede (e.g. the Biafran War of 1967-1970).[15] In many societies widespread and unchecked kleptocracy and corruption have led to the fall of the state in violence and internal wars. La Billon (2001, p.5) argues,

> "...corruption may influence the occurrence of conflicts involving large-scale organized violence. In the absence of political regime legitimating the use of public functions for private interests, such deviation is deemed to be conflictual. The more so when resource control is orchestrated along social identity fault lines defining sharp inequalities fueling both grievances among the marginalized groups and greed-driven jockeying within dominant ones."

Inequality: The structure and attributes of the postcolonial states created and enforced huge social inequalities and resentment that pushed many into war. Inequality occurs when one part of the society receives or holds more wealth or influence than other parts. Inequality is inherent in all human communities, whether this resulted from historical, geographical, situational, or psychological differences. The debate on inequality has been continuous and controversial for a long period of time. Karl Marx (1893) and many contemporary conflict theorists have viewed it as an evil that should be eradicated. Other scholars view inequality as given and indeed necessary and required for the successful operation of the society because it provides incentive.[16] In most cases in the industrialized world, inequality results from how much control one has over the mode of production, which mainly results from inherited wealth. In the developing world, however, the state plays this role.

In most African societies the state plays a vital role in consolidating the position of the dominant social group(s). Being close to the ruling elites determines the benefits one receives from the state. Berkhoff and

Hewett (2000) for example, surveyed ethnic inequality and its impact on infant mortality in 12 Sub Saharan African countries. Their results indicated that, despite claims of universal healthcare, levels of childhood death as well as immunization were highly correlated with a group's representation in the highest governmental levels. For example, in Ghana the children of Ashanti women are 20% less likely to die than other Ghanaian children, and in Kenya the Kalenjin (President Moi's clan) children are twice as likely to survive compared to other groups (Berkhoff and Hewett, 2000).

The issue of inequality, particularly in Africa, has been hotly debated over the years by scholars and politicians alike. Some scholars cite class-based inequality (Fatton, 1992; Kasfir, 1983; Sklar 1963); others argue that ethnic differences, rather than class, are the most important factors in the creation of inequality (Ayittey, 1998; Young, 1982). More recently, however, a number of scholars claim that class and ethnicity play the same role in determining who belongs to the privileged groups (Adedeji, 1999, 1985; Bayart, 1993; Bayart et al., 2000).

The early leaders of independent Africa, such as Nyerere, Nkrumah and Toure, also addressed the issue of inequality. Many adopted Marxism as an explanation and remedy for the inherent social inequality left behind by the departing colonial powers or engendered by foreign investors.[17] Many of the leaders who took power later, most of them from the military, also used the equality parlance to justify the illegal seizure of state power.[18]

In most African states, particularism has been the norm. They lack both the Weberian characteristics of modern nation-state and, more importantly, the ingredients necessary to promote development. Public officials in these states often serve their own interests rather than the public interest (Médard, 1996; Callaghy, 1984; Hydén, 1983; Bratton and van de Walle, 1997; Adedeji, 1995, 1999; Chabal, 2002). In these states there is a lack of distinction between public and private entities, and public services over the years took on particularistic, rather than universalistic characteristics. Corruption became endemic, which in turn hindered the state's ability to implement policies favorable to developmental economics.

In many societies elites consolidate their control over the modes of production by controlling the state. In most societies in Sub Saharan Africa, the state plays a vital role in consolidating the position of the dominant social group(s). Kasfir (1983, p.5) argues that, "...a socially dominant class controls the productive asset, the bulk of the distribution and most of all commands a socio-economic pre-eminence." Karl Marx also asserts that the state is instrumental in the creation and maintenance of this dominant class. Perhaps the most striking explanation has been offered by the Italian sociologist, Gaetano Mosca (1896), who argued that social inequality results when a small minority group within the society holds a monopoly over the instruments of power. In the African setting, as argued, the state determines who will receive benefits based on their tribe or clan affiliation, a pattern which emerged under colonialism and persisted or expanded thereafter.

It is difficult to measure inequality in African societies, mainly because there is a lack of quality data. Not all countries are fully represented; additionally these data assume the existence of wage earning economies where the tracking of the economic activities can be quantified. The reality, however, is that in many countries of the developing world there are large underground and barter economies. People faced high inflation and unemployment in the 1980s and turned to illegal or informal markets, specifically in the form of barter.

The most commonly used measure of inequality is the Gini Coefficient, collected by many international organizations, e.g. International Monetary Fund and World Bank. According to this indicator, Africa, along with Latin America, represents the greatest inequality among the world regions, while Eastern Europe has the lowest.[19] (See Table 2.4). The figure for Africa has been on the rise. In 2002, for example, the average Gini score for Africa is 0.47 whereas for Latin America it is 0.50; Africa's inequality has been worsening. The figure was 0.40 in 1999 and 0.30 in 1990 and 0.25 in the 1980s.[20] The highest Gini score in the world is found in Sierra Leone (0.63), which perhaps could explain why internal war occurred and persisted in that country after periods of earlier relative peace.

Table 2.4 Inequality in selected regions of the world

Regions	Gini Coefficient*
Asia	0.36
Europe	0.31
Latin America and Caribbean	0.51
Middle East and North Africa	0.38
North America	0.36
Oceania	0.43
Sub Saharan Africa	0.47
Average total	**0.40**

Data calculated from tables from http://www.wri.org/wri/wr-00-01/pdf/ei3n_2000.pdf *Gini Coefficients are measures for income distribution within the population, 0 = perfect equality and 1= perfect inequality.

In this section, the structural factors of Africa's political systems since independence were examined. Unlike the contextual factors the structural factors are influenced, at least partially, by the choices that rulers and their societies make. Several structural factors related to states can be examined: the nature of regimes, their strength, the behavior of leaders, the stability of regimes, the size of bureaucracies and most importantly, the social inequality that states created and sustained over a number of years. Once again, despite the overall finding of ineffective governance, there were still some countries that survived and indeed showed stability and growth (e.g. Botswana, Tanzania, etc.). The survival and growth of these countries can be explained by a combination of factors, most important of which could be leadership quality .Several preliminary patterns has been established between war and no-war countries. It can, therefore, be conjectured that war countries had more military regimes, military leaders, unstable political systems, income gaps, and large state sectors compared to no-war countries.

Policy factors

This book also examines some of the policies that states adopted since their independence. Policy is understood as the decisional output of a political system. From the normative perspective, policies should serve the society's interest in the sense of enhancing overall welfare (e.g. social surplus) and physical security. As stated in preceding sections, most of the African states did not enhance the overall social welfare and with increasing state breakdown, could not guarantee their security either. In this section, budgetary choices that these states have made since independence will be examined. The difference between investments in social capital (e.g. education, healthcare, housing, infrastructure and investment in security and social control such as military and military related activities) will be carefully scrutinized. Despite differing expenditures in these areas, there is still no guarantee that welfare and security will be achieved.

Budgetary allocations: Most of the postcolonial states in Africa have spent a great deal of time, money, talent, and other resources on acquiring weapons. By the 1970s, arms imports had risen (perhaps as a function of low previously low levels and as a function of liberation wars) faster in Africa than in any other region of the world, according to the Stockholm International Peace Research Institute (SIPRI). In that decade, SIPRI reported that African military spending increased by 6.6% a year, while the continent's economic growth rose only 0.4%. During the decade between 1975 and 1985, the government of Angola spent 60% of its revenues on the military in order to defend itself against UNITA rebels that were supported by South Africa and the United States. Angola invested only $49 per capita in educating its children but spent $133 per capita on its military (Barash, 1991, p.263).

At the heart of military expenditure is the issue of security. Hutchful (2000, p.211) argues that, among other things, the state is created as a "security racket." He says that,

> "The relationship between governance and security is at once intimate and obvious. First, governance is both about creating and the management of the instruments of violence necessarily underpins assuring conditions of security, and at the same time. Second, governance involves the effective administration, regulation and control of the instruments of violence."

Jackson (1992), however, argues that the security of the states in the post WWII era has generally been dependent on and guaranteed by external forces, e.g. former colonial powers, Cold War superpowers, international, and/or regional organizations (UN, NATO, ECOWAS, OAU etc.). The African state has thus been relatively secured from external threat. Despite this rather minimal external security threat, African militaries expanded tremendously. In 1963, the average African country's army had .73 soldiers per 1,000 people; by 1979 this figure jumped to 3.10 per 1,000 population (Herbst, 2000, p.105). Over the years, state militaries became palace guards and a tool for the ruling elite to dominate the rest of society or suppress local rebellions.

The rulers of Africa's patrimonial states also used the military as a reward for their patrons and supporters. In Kenya, for example, the Kamba and Kalenjin made up 34% of the military in 1961, while these tribes together accounted for only 9%-11% of the total population. In the same year in Nigeria, there were a total of 81 military officers, and of those 60 of them were Igbo (Odetola, 1982, p.138-9). During Mohamed Siad Barre's regime (1969-91), the Somali security force was controlled by three groups: the Marehaan, Barre's clan; Ogaden, his mother's clan; and Dhulbahante, his son-in-law's clan. All fall within a larger clan family of Darood, an alliance labeled among the Somalis as MOD (Laitin and Samatar, 1987). Over the years, these large and tribalized militaries created insecurity dilemmas,31 in which the average citizen was afraid of the military. This military expenditure also drove the economies of many Sub Saharan African countries into the ground. The result was that the responsibility for the security and welfare of individuals and groups, who were not part of military and bureaucracy apparatus, fell to other social organizations such as tribes, clans, and kinship groups.

During the 1980s, most African states experienced severe economic decline and became much weaker. In some cases, the security apparatus joined the informal economy. The police and the military fragmented and existed in name only (Keen, 1998, p.31). The economic decline of the 1980s led the military and police personnel to seek additional sources of income to supplement their low and often irregular salaries. They moonlighted in the private security industry and turned to racketeering and other predatory activities. In weakened African states, the police and the military no longer provided security and in some cases even impinged on the security of their own people. The police and the military acted locally on their own and came to be known, in some countries, as *pobers* (police-robbers) and *sobels* (soldier-rebels). Hills (1997), asserts that in many societies some kind of localized protection became necessary. This, in turn, pushed citizens to defend themselves from the military and police, and sparked an arms race among the groups. In countries where the state fails, as in Somalia,

Liberia, or Sierra Leone, the militia became totally responsible for the security (or insecurity) of local groups.

Most of the military hardware in Sub Saharan Africa was accumulated during the years of the Cold War; moreover, the available arms were also recycled from war to war or from soldiers to militias and civilian groups (Sislin and Pearson, 2002). Military spending led to economic slow down in many countries. As a country's economy declines, public safety deteriorates owing to the leakage of weapons through sale and theft into the hands of civilians, ethnic or personalist militia, and gangs. In places where a bad economic situation is coupled with the easy availability of arms, the state grows weaker and incapable of providing security both physically and economically. This may lead to chaos and possibly state collapse. As the state collapses, contending social groups must pay attention to their power relative to that of other groups. Balance of power races result as these groups prepare and pool their resources in order to survive. The groups must organize themselves, choose leaders, set up pseudo bureaucracies that collect taxes (or sometimes loot others), and organize security forces in order to enforce internal cohesion with military forces to insure external security (Posen, 1993, p. 110). The old regime's resources, especially materials (e.g. weapons, money, etc.) and contacts (e.g. diplomatic relations), then become spoils for the contesting groups. In the Somali internal war, the clans that had heavy representation in the military and the administration were best positioned to benefit from the disintegration of the state, gaining military and political power.

In this section, the policy output of the Sub Saharan African states has been examined. Policy entails a deliberate decision or set of decision rules that determine what is to be done (or not done) in specific circumstances. The budgetary choices these states made from 1960 (or year of independence if later) to 1990 are specifically examined. On the basis of the literature and preliminary findings it can be conjectured that the war countries had a pattern of higher military expenditure per capita than the no-war countries. The data in Figure 2.6 support this conclusion. This trend, coupled with the economic decline established earlier, evidently made the war countries more prone to violence.

Figure 2.6: The military expenditure in Sub Saharan African, war/no-war countries 1960-1990, as percentage of GDP.

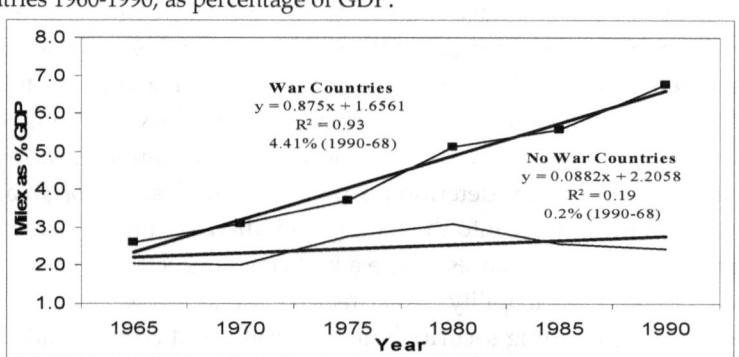

Data compiled from ACDA 1960-1990, war n=10, no war n=26 N=36

The countries differed greatly in the amount they spent in their social capital such as education and healthcare as opposed to military spending. Measuring these variables in the amount of per capita US dollars, the war countries were comparable at US $9.11 and the no-war spent US $10.20 in their militaries. The disparity, however, can be seen in the social expenditure specifically on education and healthcare. The war countries spent a combined amount of US $10.28 per capita in education and healthcare, whereas the no-war countries spent more than twice that amount at US $24.77 per capita (see Figure 2.7).

Figure 2.7: Per capita US $ spent on military, education and healthcare of the war and no-war countries between 1960 and 1990.

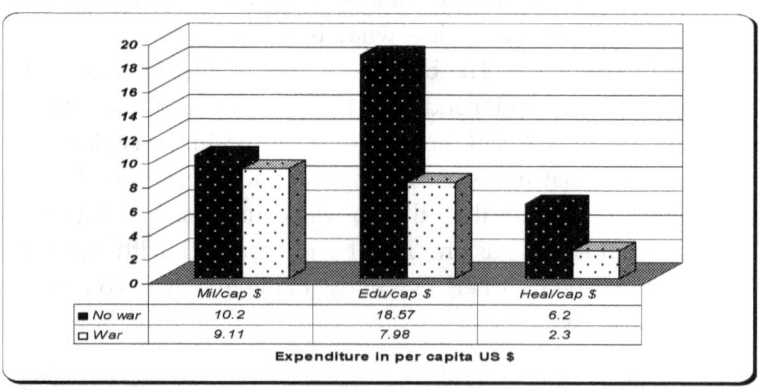

In this chapter the literature concerning general and its relation to Africa was surveyed. From the literature and available data, there appears to be vast difference between the war and no-war countries. Upon examination of the role of governance in sparking economic development, it was found that good governance is at the center of economic growth and stability (Englebert, 2000). After surveying governance in Sub Saharan Africa from context, structure, and policy perspectives several proposals can be advanced. First, contextually, war countries are overall poorer, economically more dependent, socially more fragmented, and highly tribalized than the no-war countries. Second, structurally, war countries' political institutions are more unstable, with kleptocratic and corrupt leaders than the no-war countries; third, the war countries comparatively give more attention and funds to military and military related interests, instead of social capital investments, such as education and healthcare, compared to the no-war countries. In the next section the methodology that we will be used to test the expected propositions advanced in this chapter will be introduced in more depth in the case studies to follow.

Conclusion

In closing, this chapter presented the theoretical framework of the study and established that the internal wars in Sub Saharan Africa are very likely the result of bad governance. I also established general patterns associated with governance qualities that were present (or absent) in the war and no war countries. I finally suggested specific propositions to be tested. The chapter advanced specific propositions, however, details on the methodology including unit of analysis, measurements and data sources are outlined in appendix one of this volume. In the next two chapters these hypotheses will be analyzed in greater depth against two sets of countries.

Notes

[1] For details on neo-patrimonial states and their behavior see: Michael Bratton and Nicholas Van de Walle (1997), La Billion (2001) Ayittey (1998). Sandbrook (1993).

[2] The ICRG index measures five factors that bolster development in a country during the 1990s. These include: (1) Enforceability of contracts and the risk of expropriation of investment; (2)

Corruption; (3) Quality of government institutions, including the trust of the citizens in them; (4) Quality of the bureaucracy; existence of civil liberties; (5) Degree of linguistic alienation from their government. Additionally, there are two other measures: (6) Homogeneity and (7) Civil liberties that Englebert added in the measure. The source for the governance data of this study came from: Pierre Englebert (2000). Rienner. p.29

3 The ICRG score goes from 1 to 10 and the higher the score the better the governance. Negative score indicates the total absence of the indicators. Other factors such as nearby foreign wars could have also sparked the violence in a state such as the DR Congo, but the low governance scores definitely seem to reflect the potential for violence.

4 In this study the words: ethnicity, tribalism and clanism are strictly used as an identity of a person and not as a cause of internal wars.

5 Many societies in Africa, including my own society of Somalia are suffering from invention of history and identity perpetrated mainly by the European anthropologists, historians and religious groups. For information on this particular dilemma see Mudimbe (1988), Clapham (1988), Iliffe, 1995, pp. 200-202. See also Ottaway (1999), Mamdani (1996), Davidson (1992).

6 http://www.ethnologue.com/

7. The African continent, with an approximate population of 800 million, has a land area four times that of the United States. It is a continent with immense natural resources: 40% of the world's potential hydroelectric power; 30% of its uranium; 50% of the world's gold and million of acres of unused farmlands. Africa also provides 70% of the cocoa, 60% of the coffee, and 50% of palm oil in the world. Angola alone has 11% of the known diamond reserves in the world. See George B.N. Ayittey (1999) pp.7-8.

8 9. World Bank (1981). Accelerated Development in Sub-Saharan Africa, Washington, D.C.: World Bank, 1981, p. 45. For details on Africa's food crises see: Jeffrey Herbst (1993). "The Politics of Sustained Agricultural Reform." In Thomas M. Callaghy and John Ravenhill (Editors). Hemmed In: Responses to Africa's Economic Decline. New York: Columbia University Press. pp.280-332.

9 In a 1989 report, the bank claimed that the overall economic performance improved since the SAP started in 1980's. The economic performance of the 19 African countries with strong reform programs is better than other countries that did not participate in the program. In 1993, however, the bank reported that among the 29 countries in their study, six had large improvements of almost 2%

growth between 1981-86 and 1987-91; another nine countries had medium improvement of 1.5%, and 11 countries actually had an economic decline of -2.6% during the same period (World Bank, 1993).

10 According to the UN Economic Commission for Africa (UNECA), the SAPs assert that poverty worsened in 1980s. The average annual growth rate of the per capita income between 1980 and 1986, for example, was either stagnant or negative in most of the countries, especially those countries that implemented SAPs. UNECA further argues that in the few cases where increase in the per capita income was recorded, it was largely at the expense of external debt and deterioration of social services. The report claims that by 1988, average real income in Africa, South of the Sahara was only 80% of the 1970 level.

11 For details on this topic see, Henry Bienen (1993). See also Apter (1963).

12 Franz Fanon in his 1961 book The Wretched of the Earth described the character of the elite class that the colonial powers left behind as, "...a sort of little greedy caste, avid and voracious, with the mind of a huckster, only too glad to accept the dividends that the former colonial powers hand out. This get-rich-quick middle class shows itself incapable of great ideas or of inventiveness. It remembers what it has read in European textbooks and imperceptibly it becomes not even the replica of Europe, but its caricature." (page 175) Fanon prophetically argued that this class is not capable of building industries: "The national bourgeoisie of the under-developed countries is not engaged in production, nor in invention, nor building, nor labour; it is completely canalised into activities of the intermediary type. Its innermost vocation seems to be to keep in the running and be part of the racket. The psychology of the national bourgeoisie is that of a businessman, not that of a captain of industry." (page 149) Today, this description remains accurate, as Africa's elites grew wealthy and powerful through patrimonialism, kleptocracy, corruption and predatory rule.

13 This trend also reflected somewhat improved educational opportunities for natives.

14 President Ahmadu Ahidjo (1960-82) of Cameroon kept a large portion of his country's oil revenues in a personal offshore bank account. President Felix Houphouet-Boigny (1960-1993) pocketed one-tenth of Côte d'Ivoire's cocoa exports; Mobutu Sese Seko (1965-97) controlled between 17% and 22% of the national budget for his personal use. Mobutu controlled a personal fortune roughly equivalent to Zaire's (now DR Congo) national debt. In 1982 his foreign assets were estimated at US $4 billion. In 1992, when the state could not afford to pay the army's salary, Mobutu was able to pay their wages from this personal fund. The former president of Kenya, Daniel Arap Moi, is alleged to have wealth estimated at $100 million of prime real estate, a transport corporation, an oil company, a cinema chain with monopoly over the distribution of films. Also the corruption and kleptocracy also

went to the lower levels of the bureaucracies. In 1993 Ghana's Auditor General released a report that estimated the corruption and embezzlement committed by the high officials at 401 billion cedis (about $400 million) between 1983 and 1993. Similarly, in Nigeria between 1988 and 1994, the military rulers misspent US $12.4 billion in oil revenue (Ayittey, 1998, p.5). See also Diamond (1987).

15 The Washington Times, 13 December 1998, A10.

16 The basis for this school is functionalism, for details of this school see Davis and Moore (1945), for contemporary writers see the World Bank group, especially Collier and Hoeffler (1999, 2000).

17 Among these leaders are: Julius Nyerere (1968), Kwame Nkrumah (1964).

18 General Siad Barre of Somalia after his military coup in October 1969 gave three reasons for his action: equality, justice and prosperity, yet only few years into his presidency the Somali state had become known as the Government of the Marehaan (Barre's sub-clan).

19 This is based on the mostly widely used measure of inequality the GINI Coefficients, where 0 represents perfect egalitarian society and 1 represents total inequality

20 http://www.imf.org/external/pubs/ft/fandd/1998/09/imfstaf1.htm

CHAPTER 3

PEACE-to-WAR COUNTRIES: RWANDA, SIERRA LEONE AND SOMALIA

This chapter addresses three Sub Saharan African countries that went from peace-to-war in the 1990s: Rwanda, Sierra Leone, and Somalia. This does not mean that these countries were without turbulence and conflict after their independence or before the 1990s. Rwanda, for example, had several conflicts and genocidal initiatives following independence in 1962.[1] The word "peace" must be understood in this context as signifying only the absence of an all out internal war, as defined by Regan. These countries were grouped based on the criteria detailed in Chapter 2. The selection of the cases may present several problems including biases (e.g. over-representation of former British colonies) and incomplete representation of the countries in the region, however, the selection was complicated by several reasons including availability of adequate data. The cases chosen represent sub-regions and provide enough details as to the nuances of why internal wars occurred.

The countries share several characteristics that led them to internal war in the 1990s after years of relative peace. Among these shared characteristics are historical backgrounds that include colonialism, neo-colonialism, Cold War and even post Cold War effects. There are also other social similarities that include tribalism and clanism as opposed to an integrated national identity.[2] These countries' economies were also dependent on outside powers such as Western nations and International Financial Institutions (IFIs). Since their independence, they have also all had unstable and oppressive military governments.

Each country does, however, have unique factors contributing to a particular war. In the previous chapters several explanations were proposed; these propositions relate to prediction of the occurrence of an internal war in a country. These explanations might not be true for all states at all times. There are differences in the type of social, environmental, economics and historical setting that each country possessed. Rwanda, for example, had an established system of governance that succeeded in creating a monocultural society before any European set foot on their land, whereas Somalis never experienced any political structure that ruled the entire territory prior to the arrival of the European powers in the late 1800s. Both descended into internal war, but with potentially different rationales, objectives, and scope (e.g. genocide).

This chapter analyzes differences and similarities among these countries and ultimately compares them to the no-war cases. Each country will be examined on the basis of the contextual, structural, and policy factors that were present in both the pre-colonial and postcolonial eras. For each country, the following general questions will be addressed: (1) What were the historical, social, economic, and political contexts that led to internal war? (2) What role did the structure of political institutions play in the experience of internal war? (3) What types of policies were adopted that dragged these countries into internal war? (4) What aspects of good (or bad) governance led to the wars? And (5) as during the 1980s many states in the Third World declined economically, socially and politically how did each state deal with this dilemma as crises emerged: confrontation or compromise?

The chapter will be divided as follows: (1) a summary of each country's historical setting; (2) each state's efforts to address the established questions; (3) comparison of the cases that will address similarities and differences that led to the internal war outcomes.

I. Rwanda

Rwanda is a landlocked country located in the Central African Great Rift Valley. It shares borders with Tanzania on the east, the Democratic Republic of Congo (formerly Zaire on the west, Uganda on the north, and Burundi on the south and east. With the exception of Tanzania, Rwanda's borders have been neither stable nor neutral. Burundi, for example, split from Rwanda in 1959, and it has a similar Hutu-Tutsi divide and has provided safe heaven for the Tutsi Rwandese. The political and military power brokers of Burundi came from the Tutsi ethnic group and have played direct and indirect roles in the Rwandan conflict. Uganda, also suffered its own internal war during the 1980s, but it too provided both military and political support to the Tutsi Rwandans. Zaire also played a large role in Rwanda's situation, specifically during the reign of Mobutu (1965-1997) who provided support to the successive Hutu regimes of Kayibanda (1962-1973) and Habyarimana (1973-1994).

In April 1994, a plane carrying President Juvenal Habyarimana along with President Ntaryamira of Burundi was shot down near Kigali, the capital city, triggering what appeared to be a coordinated attempt to eliminate the Tutsis and moderate Hutus. The subsequent Hutu-led genocide was conducted mainly in response to the military campaign launched by the Tutsi-led Rwandan Patriotic Front (RPF). For a period of 100 harrowing days, the world witnessed one of the most efficient killing systems in history. From April to July between 800,000 and 1,000,000 lives vanished. Philip Gourevitch (1998, p.133) estimated the killing rate as "three hundred-three and third murders an hour-or five and half lives terminated every minute." Gourevitch also stated that this killing surpassed three times the rate of the Nazi genocide in World War II and represented the largest mass killing since the atomic bombings of Hiroshima and Nagasaki in 1945; yet during this genocide, the world community played only the role of spectators.

The Great Lakes region of Africa is known for its ethnic and tribal hatred; both Rwanda and its neighbor Burundi had been the site of many ethnic disputes. In Rwanda these tensions had already exploded several times since 1959. The 1994 killing was mainly accomplished with "low tech" means (e.g. machetes) although it was backed by the threat of guns. This human disaster was shaped by several social, political, and economic factors that were, in turn, shaped by history and the environmental setting.

Approximately two million Hutus fled Rwanda to Zaire (now the Democratic Republic of Congo), and they included some of those responsible for the 1994 massacre. A portion of those who fled joined Zairean forces in order to attack local Tutsis. The Tutsi-dominated Rwandan government responded by invading refugee camps dominated by Hutu militiamen.

Historical Overview

The current borders of Rwanda were established through conquest and assimilation. By the 15th Century, the Tutsis established a strong and centralized monarchy headed by Mwami (king) and over time, Hutu-Tutsi[3] relations took the form of a patron-client contract called the *ubuhake*. At first, the agreement meant that a Hutu could use Tutsi cattle in exchange for personal and military service. Later, *ubuhake* became a feudal-type class system through which land and cattle, and therefore power, were in the hands of the Tutsi minority. Although the Tutsis make up only 14% of the population, they achieved a great political domination prior to the arrival of Europeans in the 19th century.

The 1885 Conference of Berlin assigned the current territory of Rwanda and Burundi to Germany. In 1894 the German Count von Götzen, who later became the governor of German East Africa, arrived in the area. By 1899, the Mwami submitted to indirect German rule, with the Mwami controlling the territory through his political structure. The Germans also helped militarily with the expansion of the Mwami's control over Hutu chiefs in the North. The Germans immediately ordered extensive coffee planting and began collecting taxes in cash rather than agricultural products. This forced many people to work at the coffee plantations since this was one of the only ways to earn cash.

With Germany's defeat in World War I, the League of Nations mandated that Belgium supervise the Ruanda-Urundi territory. The Belgian administration immediately began to reduce the Mwami's power. It modified the *ubuhake* system and eliminated the paying of homage to Tutsi nobles. The Belgian authorities, however, for political and practical reasons, continued to favor the Tutsi Mwami and his chiefs, and in 1935, introduced a discriminatory national identification system based on ethnicity. With this new system, Belgians arbitrarily assigned Tutsi and Hutu identities.[4]

Belgium retained control under UN Trusteeship after the end of World War II; however, it was mandated to integrate Rwandans into the political process. This allowed Rwandans limited representation in the government. In 1952, the Belgians implemented a ten-year plan designed to promote broad political, social, and economic reforms, but in the process and despite Belgium's stated goals, they still maintained the Tutsi supremacy (Melvern, 2000). During this period, the demand for independence began, pushed mainly by the Tutsi led Union Nationale Rwandaise (UNAR). Due to pressure from Hutus, the Belgians began helping the creation of a Hutu based party called the Hutu Emancipation Movement (Parmehutu). To complicate matters, in 1959 King Mutara Rudahigwa died a mysterious death and was replaced by his half-brother, Kigeri Ndahindurwa. The king's death sparked Tutsi violence against Hutus (Melvern, 2000).

In the first national elections of 1960 and 1961, the Parmehutu won political positions in large numbers. The Rwandans eventually voted to end the monarchy by an overwhelming majority of 80 percent and in the process, confirmed a January 1961 proclamation of Rwanda as a republic. The first president of the new republic was Grégoire Kayibanda, a Hutu and the head of the MDR party. This marked the beginning of the Hutu domination of Rwandan politics until 1994. During Kayibanda's presidency (1961-1973), frequent attacks and counter-attacks between the Hutus and Tutsis became a way of life for the Rwandan people, claiming innocent lives on both sides.

In July of 1973, Major-General Juvenal Habyarimana, a Hutu, the minister of defense and head of the Rwandan National Guard, overthrew President Kayibanda in a bloodless coup d'état. He declared himself president of a second republic and established a military government with a promise to restore civilian rule within a five-year period. In 1975, Habyarimana founded a new ruling party in Rwanda called the Mouvement Révolutionnaire National pour le Développement (MRND).

In 1983, Habyarimana was re-elected president, but not surprisingly, he was the only candidate. Though Rwanda was now nominally a republic, democracy was based on a demographic majority, namely the Hutus. Habyarimana, who enjoyed the backing of the military, exercised absolute power acting mainly on behalf of the Hutu people. Tutsis were excluded from positions of power in the government and the military (Learthen, 1994). As long as the Tutsi people understood this and did not aspire to positions of power or authority, they were able to live in relative peace.

At the end of the genocide and the RPF military occupation in 1994 the tables were turned and Tutsis began to govern Rwanda for the first time since the country's independence. The RPF government installed Pasteur Bizimungu, a Hutu, as president. In March 2000, President Bizimungu resigned, claiming that the Tutsi-led RPF marginalized him. One month later, Paul Kagame, the vice president, defense minister and the head of the RPF military wing, became president. Kagame's ascendance to power marked the first Tutsi presidency since independence.[5]

Contextual factors

Colonial: Much of the ambiguity surrounding the Hutu-Tutsi relationship is a result of an arrested social transformation that was consolidated at the time of colonialism and imposed in the late 19th century. In contrast to many African societies, an organized state ruled by a Tutsi Mwami existed when the German colonial state was established in the territory of Rwanda-Urundi. By the 19th century, Rwandans spoke one language, Kinyarwanda, and during the colonial period most came to practice the same religion, Catholicism. The colonial powers, Germany and later Belgium, opted to rule the country through the existing Tutsi dominated structure. As late as 1959, only three years before independence, 43 out of the 45 chiefs and 549 out of the 559 sub-chiefs were Tutsi. The power of the chiefs was increased, economic extraction was intensified, and the colonial authorities introduced forced labor mainly on state projects, such as building roads and forced cultivation of cash crops such as coffee. Further aggravating the situation, the Belgians promoted the Tutsis as the superior race (Gourevitch, 1998, Ottaway, 1982; Mamdani, 1996). This set the stage for a severe backlash of vengeance after independence, effectively barring Tutsis from power and hastening ethnic killing.

Ethnicity: About 80% of Rwanda's population is Hutu, and the rest are Tutsi, except for the small Pygmy group of Twa who make up about one percent of the population. Since independence in 1962, ethnic violence has led to large-scale massacres and the creation of perhaps as many as 3 million refugees. Kinyarwanda (*Kinya* means tongue), French, English, and Swahili are the official languages of the country. Rwanda is one of the most densely populated countries in the world with an annual growth rate of about 3%.

The relationship between the Hutus and Tutsis, one of domination prior to the European contact, was antagonized and intensified during the colonial period (1897-1962). The two groups were divided, and a vertical ethnic structure was enforced. Similar structures can be found in many parts of Africa. The fundamental social fact remains that Hutus and Tutsis are part of the same society sharing common language, religion, and culture (Mamdani, 1996). It would be even more accurate to call it a class or caste system, although, unlike the caste system of India, was not rigidly enforced by religious beliefs. The individual members of these groups generally associated with each other in the *ubuhake* (clientship) system, based on the lending of cattle by Tutsi patrons to the Hutu client; the relationship can thus termed feudal. The colonial administration used this already existing feudal system to increase its control of the territory. The result of this favoritism left behind an envious society, continually headed by a Hutu.

Economy: In 1998, the Rwandan population was approximately 8 million with a density of 302 persons per square kilometer. Most of Rwanda's population depends on subsistence farming, using mainly primitive tools such as hoes. The main cash crop since the colonial era has been coffee. The main staple foods include sorghum, cassava, plantain, sweet potato, and beans. The country also has a large number of livestock, namely cattle, goats, pigs, and sheep. By the 1980s, however, the country's ability to meet its food requirements diminished because of years of overgrazing and soil erosion coupled with years of political instability. Rwanda also suffered a severe decline in coffee prices in the late 1980s due to the collapse of the International Coffee Agreement (ICA).

The country attracted foreign aid, especially under the Habyarimana regime (1973-1994), becoming the darling of the aid agencies because of its good road and mail systems. Between 1970 and 1990, Rwanda received an average of US$67.21 million annually, with an average aid per capita of US $12 from the European Union and United States alone. (OECD.org)

Rwanda inherited a state that was prone to internal war. Practices in the colonial period created an envious, hierarchical, and - most important - highly politicized society. By 1962, the independence year, the country's first Tutsi-Hutu war was in progress. The country was eventually pushed to depend on a single commodity, coffee, whose price collapsed after 1989. The country also received a substantial amount in foreign assistance, which strengthened the Hutu controlled central state. As a result, Rwanda was more prone than most in the Third World countries to internal war.

Structural factors

Regime type and strength: Rwanda's leadership in the postcolonial era was the result of a dramatic shift of power in 1959. Several factors led to this shift, including the mysterious death of Tutsi King Mutara Rudahigwa III on July 24, 1959.[6] His death and the coronation of his younger brother King Kigeri V created great instability and led to a Hutu rebellion. The Hutus had become politically organized and created several political parties. The largest political party, the Parti du Mouvement de l'Emancipation Hutu (Parmehutu), was created in 1959, and in 1960 the Parmehutu won 70.4% of the seats in the municipal elections (Prunier, 1987). A final event, the *coup d'Etat de* Gitarama,[7] occurred on January 28, 1961, which sealed Rwanda's power shift. This coup d'état that occurred at Gitarama prefecture declared Rwanda a republic and suspended the monarchy (Learthen, 1994). In February 1961, the Belgian government, on a belated mission of Hutu empowerment, recognized the Gitarama coup and its republican declaration, in a clear violation of UN resolutions 1579 and 1580 (Prunier, 1995; Learthen, 1994; Newbury, 1998; Gourevitch, 2000).

These events sealed the shift in Rwanda's political power in favor of the majority, the Hutus. In the meantime, the Tutsis began to organize in neighboring Burundi and Uganda to recapture state power. In 1963, some 600 Tutsis attacked Rwanda from Burundi and came within 12 miles of the capital city of Kigali. They were, however, intercepted by units of Gendarmerie National Rwandaise (GNR) under the command of Belgian officers. These actions immediately led to Hutu revenge, and according to the World Council of Churches, between 10,000 and 14,000 Tutsis were hacked to death. The Kayibanda regime was a totalitarian, secretive, and ruthless, and it became even more pro-Hutu after the events of 1963. The Kayibanda regime also enjoyed the open support of the Catholic Church for its extreme Hutu nationalism (Melvern, 2000, pp.20-22).

In July 1973, Major General Juvenal Habyarimana seized power, as already recorded. Although Habyarimana's regime would end with one of the bloodiest genocides in human history, his general approach was overtly less Hutu nationalist. The regime actually appeared, at least rhetorically, to stress national unity and an end to ethnic killings. Habyarimana wanted to create a true agricultural society in Rwanda.

He glorified farming and the peasantry, but he believed that Hutus were the only real Rwandan peasants, while the Tutsis were considered feudal lords associated with colonial occupation.

On July 5, 1975, he founded his own party, Mouvement Révolutionaire National pour le Développement (MRND), and banned all opposition parties. In its manifesto, the MNRD laid out the political, economic, social, and cultural policies that would lead the country towards peace, unity, and progress. Habyarimana was very aware that the progress of Rwanda hinged upon the unity of its people: Hutu, Tutsi, and Twa.

The country was divided into 10 prefectures each run by centrally-appointed prefects. It was then divided into some 145 communes, and each was headed by a burgomaster. The communes were then divided into cells or *collines*. Each commune had an average of 40,000 to 50,000 residents. The burgomasters influenced citizens' lives in every aspect from mediating conflicts over property to hiring and firing commune staff, such as policemen. The burgomaster was the ultimate authority at the local level, and he could only be removed by the president (Prunier, 1987). This harsh dictatorship ruled with an iron fist and was not willing to share the rewards of prosperity. As a result, a majority of the population (including most of the Hutus) remained rural working poor. It is under this set of oppressive circumstances that the people of Rwanda experienced a relatively peaceful 17 years of coexistence. Strong divisions within the country, however, lay very near the surface only waiting to be awakened.

During the 1970s, Habyarimana installed a development-oriented dictatorship. At the center of his regime was agriculture and a goal of an agriculturally self-sufficient Rwanda. The regime targeted export crops, specifically coffee, as the largest source of the country's hard currency. Coffee growing, in fact, was so important that the state penal code listed penalties for stealing, destroying, or neglecting coffee plants (Little and Horowitz, 1988). During this period, farmers were obliged to sell their coffee to monopoly agencies for fixed prices per kilogram, a practice that mirrored that of Belgian colonial state (Newbury, 1987, p.152-4). The Habyarimana regime, like its Belgian predecessors, restricted peasant movement exclusively to agricultural areas, a policy that greatly benefited urban elites. As a result of this policy, between 1973 and 1993, 95% of the Rwanda's population consistently lived in rural areas.

The results of these policies were apparent immediately. The GNP per capita of Rwanda, for example, grew from $130 in 1977 to $180 in 1978, an increase of 38%; by 1988 this figure jumped to $320 (*World Development Report*, 1993). Rwanda jumped from 11th to 17th from the bottom of the World Development Ranking. This period of growth, however, came to an abrupt end in the 1980s with the introduction of Structural Adjustment Programs (SAPs). These programs pushed, among other policies, trade liberalization, currency devaluation, the lifting of subsidies to agriculture, the privatization of state functions, and a reduction in the number of state employees (Melvern, 2000). The collapse of the International Coffee Agreement (ICA) in 1989 further devastated the industry. This organization had been created in 1962 to manage the supply and demand of coffee. The organization floundered mainly as a result of pressure from the United States, which was pushing the ideology of the free market. As a result of these policies, the world's supply of coffee on the market increased and coffee prices dropped from an average of $ 1.20 per pound in the 1980s to $0.50 in the mid 1990s.

Politics in Rwanda, as in many parts of the continent, have always been intertwined with ethnicity. It is important to understand the connection between the power of the state and the ethnic identities of the people. One of the most notable of these groups is the Akazu and its role the country's politics. The Akazu is a power clique; the word means "little house" in Kinyarwanda. Although it is a clan-based group, outsiders can become members of the Akazu family through marriage. Akazu members are considered "insiders" and outsiders are immediately considered potential enemies. No one is considered neutral (Prunier, 1998; Keesing 1976). Resignation from the group is treated as high treason, and indeed several members have actually been assassinated in exile.

The Akazu has been central to Rwandan politics, at least since independence in 1962. During the Kayibanda regime (1962-1973), power was centered on the Southern Hutus near Kayibanda's birth place (Prunier, 1998). During the Habyarimana regime (1973-1994) the Akazu were also known as *"la Clan de Madame"*, signifying that power was centered around Habyarimana's wife, Agathe Habyarimana, whose family enjoyed significant privileges and occupied top posts during the regime (Melvern, 2000).

In the post-1994 era power shifted again, towards the Ugandan-Tutsis and the RPF. It focused specifically on the members of the Ugandan-Tutsis whose ancestors were those Tutsis who had escaped from Rwanda to Uganda during the 1960s as refugees. Although many Hutus held power positions, including the presidency of Pasteur Bizimungu (1994-2000), they were under the strict control of the Ugandan Tutsis and the RPF. Reyntjens (1999) says that non-RPF ministers were under constant surveillance in a period of intense Tutsification of the government machinery.[8] This process seems to be a reminiscent of the Tutsi revolution of the late 1950s and early 1960s.

Since its independence, Rwanda had military regimes that ruled for 21 years out of the 32 prior to the 1994 genocide. The state was relatively stable, considering the lack of recurring coups d'état, and from 1962 to 1994, there were only two presidents. The Habyarimana regime spent a large percentage of the economy on itself and employed the majority of the wage earners in the country. As a result of its political system, the country attracted little investment from outside. Although a short-lived economic improvement was experienced, during the 1970s, Rwandans remained one of the poorest societies in the world. The historical setting, a postcolonial regime that took advantage of the societal division, rampant poverty, and inequality made Rwanda prone to internal war.

Policy factors

Although Rwanda's level of poverty remained high, it showed great strides towards economic development from the 1970s to the mid 1980s. The country's quality of life improved, specifically under the regime of General Habyarimana. The country developed impressive infrastructure and communication, which made Rwanda a darling of the international aid agencies. International aid for Rwanda grew rapidly, from an annual average of US $35 million in 1974 to US$343 million by 1993. The Rwandan economy also grew impressively during much of this period. For example, the average annual growth of real GDP in Rwanda was 4.9% between 1965 and 1989 with an average inflation of only 4% (compared to the average for the Sub Saharan Africa region of 20%) during the same period (Melvern, 2000, p.49). After the collapse of the ICA in 1989, however, the country lost its revenue from coffee sales, which accounted for 70% of its income. This pattern fits the prediction of frustration-aggression or relative deprivation theory (Rapapport, 1995), which predicts violence in situations in which previously improving conditions did not continue to increase as expected.

Rwanda, unlike many parts of Africa, invested moderately in its military. The country invested an average of less than 2% of GDP in the military from 1962 to the early 1990s. The country's military expenditure, however, grew relatively faster during the early 1990s, mainly as a result of the reaction to Tutsi incursions in the Hutu dominated state. Tutsi incursions were a regular occurrence as early as 1963, 1966 and 1993 (Dorsey, 1994). Tutsi militants were not only envious of their loss of glory; they also reacted to the open discrimination of the successive Rwanda rulers (Melvern, 2000; Gasana et al., 1999). The Tutsi attack in the 1990s coincided with the severe drop in coffee prices in world markets and the effects of the adjustment programs. This pushed the Habyarimana regime to embark upon hypermilitarization activities.

The regime began expanding and equipping the military in the late 1980s as a result of the increased incursions of the Tutsi-based RPF. The regime obtained aid, both in equipment and training, from various sources, chief among them France and Egypt. The Rwandan army, which numbered only 5,200 poorly equipped soldiers, had to be supported by the French army in order to defeat the invading Tutsi-led RPF. Besides the political and moral support of the Habyarimana regime, France sent 600 soldiers in 1994, claiming the need to protect French citizens. French citizens, however, were few and not in danger, but the French began to train and modernize the Rwandan army. As a result, the army, which numbered only 5,200 in 1989, swelled to 28,000 by 1994 (Melvern, 2000).[9] These French-trained soldiers in turn trained the extremist Hutus genocide squad, locally known as the *Interahamwe* and *Impuzamugambi*.[10]

In addition to France, the Habyarimana regime enjoyed military support from Egypt and China, among others. Egypt sent massive amounts of small weapons during this period, coinciding with Rwanda's hypermilitarization. The two countries signed a military contract worth US $59 million, which included grenades, ammunition, assault rifles, rockets and rocket launchers (Melvern, 2000, p.32). Between 1990 and 1994, Rwanda spent over US $100 million on weapons, and in 1994 Rwanda was the third largest African weapons importer (Melvern, 2000, p.5).[11] The country's military expenditure grew from 2% of GDP before 1989 to 6.9% of the GDP, coinciding with a decline in the country's income by 6.8%.

Until the 1990s, Rwanda's political institutions did not adopt explicit policies that discriminated against sectors of the society (Prunier, 1987; Newbury, 1998). The country's military expenditure was relatively low. With the exiled Tutsi and RPF attacks, however, a massive militarization of the Habyarimana regime was sparked off at a time of sudden economic downturn. As for expenditure for social capital, the government did not invest heavily in education and healthcare, as evidenced by the relatively low Physical Quality of Life Index.

At the close of the 1980s, the Tutsi-led RPF attacks increased as a result of their increased military capabilities supported by Uganda. The Habyarimana regime opened a dialogue with the RPF rebels and several meetings were convened between the two groups in Arusha. While these negotiations continued the regime continued to arm and prepare militarily. During the time that Habyarimana's regime was sitting at the negotiating table, it was preparing its military and tribal militias. This suggests that the regime was more confrontationist than accommodationist. The death of President Habyarimana in April 1994 could, however, suggest that this conclusion is premature.

In the above section, the causes of Rwanda's conflict were surveyed from contextual, structural, and policy perspectives. The 1994 Rwandan genocide, which claimed more 800,000 lives, bought human cruelty to unprecedented depths. The warring factions were the Hutu extremists against Tutsi and moderate Hutus. As Gasana *et al.* (1999) suggests, this conflict was not purely ethnicity/identity based, nor was it political manipulation by the few, although clearly these factors were present. Rather, it resulted from complex multiple factors, including historical setting that sometimes played contradicting roles.

This history includes: a pre-colonial political consolidation; colonial manipulation siding first with the Tutsi Mwamis and later with the Hutu and Christian missionaries who sided with the Hutus; postcolonial modern elites which fostered hatred and fear in order to keep themselves and their supporters in power, backed by France, Egypt and others; economic decline that resulted from internal economic mismanagement; decline in commodity prices in international markets; effects of adjustment programs; opposition armed groups (e.g. Tutsi-RPF) who received support from neighboring countries (e.g. Uganda); and policymakers in France, Belgium, the United States and at the United Nations who knew about or witnessed the preparations for the genocide but failed to take the steps to prevent it.

II. Sierra Leone

Sierra Leone is located in West Africa. It shares borders with Guinea on the north and northeast, Liberia to the southeast, and the Atlantic Ocean to the south and southwest. In March of 1991 a group of armed rebels crossed the border from Liberia into the southeastern part of the country, attacking and subsequently occupying the border town of Bomaru in the Kailahun district. The attacking group was the Revolutionary United Front (RUF), a group supported by Liberia's Charles Taylor and Libya's Moammar Gadhafi and other countries in the region in cluding Burkina Faso, who had provided the training and weapons. The late Foday Sankoh, a Temne clansman and former corporal in the Sierra Leonean army, led the group. The war claimed approximately 75,000 lives between 1992 and 1998 and displaced nearly half of the country's population.

Even though the country is blessed with an excellent educational system, vast and diversified natural resources, including diamonds and other minerals, abundant agricultural and fishing industry, and potential tourist attractions, Sierra Leone is one of the poorest countries in the world and represents one of the most dramatic failures of development in Sub Saharan Africa. This section will explore why this well endowed country found itself in such a difficult situation. The Sierra Leonean disaster was shaped by several factors that included: a "curse" of natural resources, specifically diamonds, kleptocracy, repression, and ethno-regional rivalry.

Historical Overview

The Temne people lived along the northern coast of present-day Sierra Leone when the first Portuguese navigators reached the region in 1460. The Portuguese landed on the Peninsula and named the area

Sierra Leone (the Lion Mountain). In the early 1500s, European traders stopped regularly on the peninsula, exchanging cloth and metal goods for ivory, timber, and small numbers of slaves. In the mid-16th century, Mande-speaking people migrated into Sierra Leone from present-day Liberia and eventually established the states of Bullom, Loko, Boure, and Sherbro. By the early 17th century, British traders had also became increasingly active along the Sierra Leone coast.

Fulani and Mande-speaking persons from the Fouta Djallon region of present-day Guinea converted numerous Temnes of Northern Sierra Leone to Islam in the early 18th century. Sierra Leone also became a minor source of slaves for the transatlantic slave trade. At the end of 18th century, many attempts were made to resettle freed slaves in Africa. In 1787, 400 persons (including 330 blacks and 70 white prostitutes) arrived at the Sierra Leone Peninsula (Fyfe, 1962; Peterson, 1969; Wyse, 1989). They purchased land from local Temne leaders and established the Province of Freedom near present-day Freetown. The settlement, however, fell apart mainly because of the death of many of its residents in the first year. In 1792 a group of 1,100 freed slaves, led by the abolitionist Thomas Clarkson, landed on the peninsula and founded the current location of Freetown. They were joined by another 500 freed blacks from Jamaica a few years later (Wyse, 1989).

By 1807, Great Britain had outlawed the slave trade, and in early 1808 the British government took control of Freetown, using it as a naval base for antislavery patrols. Between 1808 and 1864, approximately 50,000 freed slaves settled in the area of Freetown (Wyse, 1989). In 1827 Protestant missionaries were active in the area and founded Fourah Bay College (now part of the University of Sierra Leone). The majority of its students were freedmen and their descendants. They became known as Creoles or Krios, largely became Christian, and were active missionaries, traders, and civil servants along the West African coast. They were, for example, active on Sherbro Island and among the Yorubas of present-day southwest Nigeria.

Between 1821 and 1874, the British holdings on the Gold Coast (present-day Ghana) were placed under the governor of Sierra Leone. In 1863, an advisory Legislative Council was established there. The British were reluctant to assume added responsibility by increasing the size of the colony, but in 1896 the interior was proclaimed a British protectorate in order to forestall French ambitions in the region. The

Colony and Protectorate of Sierra Leone was established. As usual with the British colonial system, the Protectorate was ruled indirectly. In 1898 the British imposed a hut tax, causing a great uprising among the African tribes. In the north Bai Bureh (ruler of a Temne clan) and in the south the Poro secret society staged a rebellion, but the British defeated them. Under British administration, there were few development activities until the 1950s, but a railroad was built and the production for export of palm products and peanuts was encouraged.

At the end of World War II, the British began to provide more jobs and educational opportunities to the locals. Mining activities, especially for diamonds and iron ore, also increased greatly. A new constitution was adopted in 1951, further allocating political power to the local communities. During the same year, an election was held, and the Sierra Leone Peoples Party (SLPP), under the leadership of Dr. Milton Margai, a Mende, won the election.

On April 27, 1961, Sierra Leone became independent with Margai as prime minister. In 1964, Dr/Sir Milton Margai died in office and was succeeded by his brother, Sir Albert Margai. The new regime was accused of corruption and mismanagement. In the general elections of 1967 Siaka Stevens of the All People's Congress (APC), a Temne-based party, became the new prime minister. His government, however, was prevented from taking office by military intervention under Brig. David Lansana, who supported Margai. Lansana was almost immediately displaced by a coup d'état led by Colonel Andrew Juxon-Smith, who formed a National Reformation Council (NRC). In 1968, an army rebellion overthrew the NRC and returned the nation to parliamentary government, with Stevens as prime minister. The following years were marked by considerable unrest, caused by severe poverty and unequal wealth distribution. This pushed ethnic disaffection from the central government.

In 1971, the parliament declared Sierra Leone a republic and Stevens as president. In the 1973 elections, Stevens and his APC won a majority of the parliamentary seats, but the country remained a *de facto* one-party state. In 1985, Stevens stepped aside and appointed Major General Joseph Saidu Momoh, a Limba (the same tribe as Stevens) as president. This transition was viewed as a Limba dynasty and further widened the inter-tribal rift in the country. As in Rwanda, this mistrust, coupled with the decline in the economy, heightened poverty and inequality creating the environment for the 1990s internal war.

In 1992, Momoh was overthrown in a military coup led by Captain Valentine Strasser and in turn Brigadier General Julius Maada Bio ousted him in another coup d'etat in 1996. General Maada Bio immediately promised a return to civilian rule, which he fulfilled later in 1996 when he passed the power to Ahmad Tejan Kabbah of the SLPP, who won a general election. In May 1997, Lieutenant Colonel Johnny Paul Koroma of the Armed Forces Revolutionary Council (AFRC) overthrew Kabbah's government. The junta soon invited the RUF to participate in a new government. This coup led to condemnation and sanctions by the United Nations in October 1997. The Economic Community of West African States (ECOWAS) also sent forces into the country in order to subdue the rebels (mainly the RUF) and reinstate Kabbah.

In July 1999, a peace accord was signed between President Kabbah, Foday Sankoh of the RUF, and Johnny Paul Koroma of the AFRC. Under this agreement, rebels were granted seats in a new government and a general amnesty from prosecution. In October 1999, the United Nations sent peacekeepers to help restore order and disarm the rebels. By May 2000, the process was disrupted amid clashes between UN troops and the RUF rebels. Some 500 peacekeepers were taken hostage at one point, and the peace accord effectively collapsed. But then British troops intervened, new talks were held, the disarmament of fighters was resumed, and the war was declared at an end in January 2002.[12]

This brief overview of Sierra Leonean history shows a great deal of political instability. Successive regimes were kleptocratic and led their country to severe economic decline and poverty, this, in turn, created an envious, suspicious, fragmented, and unequal social structure. These four factors were further exacerbated by external interventions, especially from Liberia and Libya. The interaction between these historical events and factors made Sierra Leone prone to internal war in 1992.

Contextual factors

Colonial: British colonialism amounted to indirect rule and left behind a society that was hierarchical. The main cleavage was between the locals and Krios descendants of the freed slaves living in the area of the capital city, Freetown. The declaration of the rest of Sierra Leone as a British protectorate in 1896 marked the beginning of a troubled society. The British authorities viewed the society as divided between Krios or non-natives and the rest who were seen as "aborigines, natives, savages, naked barbarians and many other epithets." (Kandeh, 1992, p.83)

The first problem of colonialism came with the immediate introduction of the Hut Tax, whereby Frederic Cardew, Governor of Sierra Leone, levied a five shillings tax per year on every house. As shown earlier, this tax caused a great uprising staged by the two largest clans, the Mendes and Temnes. Although the British suppressed the uprising, it left behind very angry chiefs who had lost their power and became subject to the new British system of indirect rule. These chiefs, who formerly had been kings and queens, now became subjects under the sovereignty of Queen Victoria.

There was also dissatisfaction among the locals with Krio traders, who held both political and economic power during British colonialism. Many Krios adopted English names and lifestyles, became highly educated, and rose to positions of authority within the colonial administration. Although they were largely Christian, many Krios still practiced traditional rites and ceremonies and belonged to secret societies (Wyse, 1989). During the second half of the 19th century, Sierra Leone became a shining example of the "civilizing influence" of the British over the African savages. During this time, the city of Freetown became known as the Athens of West Africa.

This made the Krios highly envied and their relations with the local groups were sometimes hostile. The Krio privilege came to an end, however, at the end of the 19th century. In the 1880s, many Lebanese and Syrian immigrants migrated to the area and pushed the Krios into subordinate positions in trade and business. Taking advantage of British favoritism, which coincided with the construction of the railway and the opening of the country's interior, the Lebanese and Syrians took over the commercial sector and immediately became successful traders. The Lebanese opened many businesses on the railways and feeder roads, and they soon extended their commercial interests throughout Sierra Leone. Many local people, particularly the Krios, became increasingly hostile to the Arab domination of the business sector. When independence came, the Krios who remained loyally pro-British did not dominate the postcolonial state.[13] Sir Milton Margai, from the Southern Mende tribe, became the prime minister.

Ethnicity: There are 17 ethnic groups; indigenous tribes make up 90% of the population (Temnes make up 30%, Mendes 30%, others 30%) and the Creoles or Krios 10%. The Mendes live mainly in the south and southeast and began moving into Sierra Leone from what is now Liberia in the 18th century. They created large chiefdoms, often by capturing and enslaving the original inhabitants. The Temnes, who occupy the central and western parts of the country, originally came from the Futa Jallon plateau in present-day Guinea. They set up trading empires before the 15th century. The Limbas live in the northern part of the country and form the third largest group; they claim to have always lived in the area.

The other ethnic groups include the Kono, Kuranko (or Koranko), Loko, Mandingo, Susu (or Soso), Vai, and Yalunka groups, who, along with the Mendes, belong to the Mande language group. The Gola, Kissi, Krim, and Sherbro peoples belong with the Temnes to the Mel language group, and the remaining groups are the Fula, Kru and Krio. The Krios inhabit the Freetown area and were formed as a result of the integration of the various groups who came together in the original colony. The first settlers were liberated slaves, Nova Scotians, Maroons, and recaptured slaves, mostly from Nigeria. These people came to form a distinct ethnic community with their own language and identity. The Krios have been the most Westernized group in Sierra Leone, many becoming highly educated and influential during the 19th and early 20th centuries (Wyse, 1989).

Ethnicity in Sierra Leone has always been politicized, especially since the early days of British contact in the area. The rift between the Krios and the native tribes occurred first. This antagonistic relationship was used as a tool to divide and conquer throughout the colonial era. As independence approached, the rift between the native tribes became more apparent, specifically between the two largest tribes, the Mendes and Temnes, each of which accounts for approximately 30% of the population. Although these two groups were united against the Krios, after independence they began competing against each other for political power. As Horowitz (1985, p.63) observed, this situation reflected the fact that "...discontinuance of a sin is always the commencement of a struggle."[14]

In the post independence era, Sierra Leonean politics has been dominated by suspicion and rivalry between these two groups, with others also involved. This ethnic rivalry carried over into political parties, of which the Sierra Leone People's Party (SLPP) was under the leadership of Milton A. S. Margai, a Mende, and the opposition All People's Congress (APC) was led by Siaka Stevens, a Limba, and many of its followers were Temne. The first seven years (1961-1968) of independence saw SLPP predominance, which was overwhelmingly supported by the southern Mendes. This was followed by the control of the APC, supported by the Temnes and Limbas to maintain power until 1992.

In addition to this political contest, the country suffered from a succession of bad and corrupt governments, both military and civilian. These successive governments were dependent upon the control of the country's diamond production trade, which attracted many from outside the country.

Economy: Sierra Leone's economy is based on mineral resources and agriculture, but neither sector has been managed effectively. Sierra Leone's resources include diamonds, gold, iron ore, rutile, and bauxite. Diamonds, however, have played the central role. They were first found in 1930 although large-scale mining did not begin until 1952. There was a diamond rush in the country especially in the Eastern Province. In the beginning, the diamond trade was dominated by the Sierra Leone Selection Trust; however, the government realized that it was losing a great deal of revenue owing to illegal smuggling and the government took over the diamond trade. Gold mining occurred on a smaller scale than diamond mining, but it also suffers from the smuggling problem, thus causing the official output figures to fluctuate widely. Since 1985, rutile, or titanium dioxide, has generated the greatest official export revenue, worth $66.5 million in 1989, but with long interruption due to the war.

Over the years, the majority of Sierra Leone's rich mineral resources were exploited by foreigners, specifically the Lebanese, while Sierra Leoneans were kept in absolute poverty. Governments lost revenue through smuggling and corruption while the diamond mine owners paid only low wages to mine workers.[15] Despite the existence of a rich mining sector, the country remained primarily agrarian. Agriculture provides around 65% of the employment and contributes to more than 40% of the GDP. The most dominant crop is upland rice, which is rain-fed and does not require high technology. In addition to rice, coffee, cocoa, and palm products are also grown as cash crops. The Sierra Leone Produce Marketing Board (SLPMB), established in 1949, has controlled the marketing and export of cash crops although it has, however, recently collapsed owing to low prices and large-scale smuggling into neighboring countries.

Independent Sierra Leone inherited a highly fragmented and suspicious society, and its politics reflected this fact, as evidenced by recurrent instability. Although the country was relatively less dependent on foreign aid and did not suffer greatly from decline in commodity (diamonds) prices, it still suffered the same fate as its counterparts on the continent. The abundance of diamonds, the tug of war for their control by both foreign and domestic groups, and a weakened, kleptocratic state pushed the country to internal war in 1992.

Structural factors

Regime type and strength: The first Prime Minister in 1960, Sir Milton Margai, promised equality for all and gained considerable support, on the basis of this rhetoric, especially from northerners who felt that the Mendes would dominate the government. When Milton Margai died and his brother Sir Albert Margai, a British trained lawyer, took power, he became dissatisfied with his brother's conservatism and instituted a more radical and aggressive leadership. In 1966, Sir Albert attempted to introduce a one-party system and began to strengthen international links within Africa and internationally. He negotiated many aid and loan agreements in order to finance several large-scale development projects. Under this regime, the number of Temne ministers was reduced by 50% from 4 to 2. This caused the opposition groups, mainly the Temne, dominated APC, to accuse the regime of extravagance and corruption (Kandeh, 1992).

In the March 1967 elections, as noted, the APC was deprived of its election victory by the coup which installed the National Reformation Council (NRC). The NRC's stated aims included the return to civilian rule, but as time passed and the military rulers' power grew, they became as corrupt as their predecessors (Kandeh, 1992, p.93). In April 1968, more lower-ranking army officers mutinied, overthrew the NRC, and reinstated the APC as the ruling party with Siaka Stevens, as Prime Minister.

Temne political power grew immediately. By 1973, the number of Temnes in the cabinet jumped to 10 (or 41.1%) up from 2 (or 14.3%) in 1964 (Kandeh, 1992, p.93). Siaka Stevens remained in power until 1985, but his term in office was at times unstable. In 1970, several government ministers resigned from the APC to form their own party, the United Democratic Party (UDP). This caused many periods of unrest; a state of emergency was eventually declared, and the UDP was banned. In March 1971, Brigadier John Bangura attempted another military coup, and two assassination attempts were made on Siaka Stevens. Stevens, however, remained in control, with the help of troops from Guinea, and Bangura and other army officers were executed.

In order to increase his power base, Stevens pushed legislation that declared Sierra Leone a republic and himself Executive President in April 1971. A general election was called in May 1973 under a state of emergency, but the SLPP did not contest any seats, declaring a fear of political violence. No opposition party was represented in parliament between 1973 and 1977.

During this period, the country's economy rapidly deteriorated. There were massive foreign debts and widespread smuggling of mineral resources (Kandeh, 1992; Hazelton, 2000). In 1976 the government-owned Marampa iron-ore mine was closed and the official revenue from diamond mining declined. This led to inflation and food shortages. Student demonstrations in 1977 led to general public protests, which forced the government to call another general election in May of that year. At this time, the SLPP gained 15 seats and once again became the official opposition party.

In the early 1980s, the country's economic situation further deteriorated, and many government ministers and civil servants became openly corrupt (Kandeh, 1992). There were sporadic public protests leading to another general election in May 1982. Despite the fact that Stevens declared his intention to retire, he continued as President. Finally in 1985, at the age of 80, Stevens announced that he was stepping down and named Major-General Joseph Momoh, the head of the army and a member of the House of Representatives since 1974, his successor. Momoh belonged to the same tribe as Stevens, the Limba (a sub group of the Temne people). Stevens bypassed the vice-presidents, Francis Minah and Sorie Koroma for the presidency, claiming that a military man would make a better president than a civilian.

Despite its abundant natural resources, a number of well-educated people and freedom from marked religious and ethnic strife, post-independence Sierra Leone has gone down a tragic path. It is one that was spoiled by bad governance, and gross economic mismanagement, eventually leading to internal war. During the 1960s, the economy grew 4% annually; however, in the following two decades, the economy sharply deteriorated because of rampant corruption, massive state intervention, concentration of state spending on the non-poor, dismantling of local government, economic policies that held back overall economic activity, heavily taxed agriculture, and the rural population (Hazelton, 2000). Real GDP per capita declined by 37% between 1971 and 1989, and by 1990, 82% of the population lived below the poverty line. By this time, Sierra Leone had the most unequal income distribution in the world (a Gini Index of .66).[16]

Structurally, the postcolonial state in Sierra Leone began with politicized, though not yet violent, ethnic divides. Temne versus Mende rivalry, specifically, shaped the country's politics and its subsequent collapse in 1992. This competition created an unequal society where controlling the state apparatus became an essential weapon. These two main groups had more complex sub-group minorities than in Rwanda and were more equally divided in population size. This ethnic split, coupled with the high demand for diamonds around the world, availability of weapons, aggrieved rebels, and foreign mercenaries, eventually weakened the state made the country vulnerable for the 1992 internal war.

Policy factors

The governmental institutions of Sierra Leone were not known for making sound policies that could help the country realize its potential to develop. Successive governments were headed by kleptocrats, who controlled the political institutions to execute predatory, wealth extracting policies. This created a society that ranked the lowest in the

Human Development Index in the 1980s, with a life expectancy of 33.6 years and adult literacy of 30.3%.[17]

After independence, Sierra Leone was not particularly highly militarized given the potential threat from coups. Between 1967 and 1988, military expenditure in Sierra Leone claimed an average of 4.96% of the central government expenditure and around 1.2 soldiers per one 1,000 population (ACD). President Momoh (1985-1992) further reduced the military to two ill equipped infantry battalions. This decline, however, lasted only until the 1991 attack by the RUF, under the leadership of Sergeant Foday Sankoh. The Momoh government then began to seek armaments from Britain and combat support from Nigeria (Gershoni, 1997, p.58).

Although the successive Sierra Leonean governments were not as highly militarized as their counterparts (e.g. Somalia), the country's potential to develop economically was still hindered by the tug of war between the local groups in concert with external groups, (e.g. Libya and Liberia), to control the state and the mineral wealth. Investment in social capital, such as education and health, was neglected, making Sierra Leone the lowest on the Human Development Index in the 1980s. These historical, social, political, economic, weapons, and foreign intervention, played heavily in hastening the 1992 internal war.

A complex history of settlements, colonialism, coups and counter coups, and most importantly corruption that is fueled by the ongoing struggle over the control of the diamond resources destroyed Sierra Leone and its people. In contrast to Rwanda, Sierra Leone's internal war was the result of greed (both local and external), although both states suffered from poor governance and severe economic decline. Since independence in 1961, Sierra Leone has endured a series of military and non-military regimes and rebellions, seeking to overcome economic and political deficits. The root cause of the internal war in Sierra Leone, however, lies beneath the ground in the diamond mines. As Ibrahim M. Kamara, Permanent Representative of Sierra Leone to the U.N. stated to the Council on July 5, 2000,

> The conflict is not about ideology, tribal, or regional differences. It has nothing to do with the so-called problems of marginalized youths or as some political commentators have characterized it, an uprising by rural poor against the urban elite. The root of the conflict is and remains diamonds. The conflict in Sierra Leone is not a civil war, but

a rebel war based on brutality, supported by regional, sub-regional, and international surrogates, and more importantly, financed by the illicit trade in Sierra Leone's diamonds.[18]

III. Somalia

Somalia is located in the horn of Africa. The country borders Kenya to the south, Ethiopia on the west, Djibouti to the northwest, the Gulf of Aden to the north, and the Indian Ocean to the east. Somalia's neighbors, specifically Ethiopia, have been a source of instability, providing weapons and military bases for numerous insurgent groups, an action commensurate to the Somali behavior. Other neighbors, specifically Djibouti, played less significant roles in the internal Somali conflict, but they have had territorial disputes affecting Somali security calculations.

In January 1991, rival clan militias chased the notorious regime of Siad Barre (1969-1991) from power. This gave way to chaos and anarchy, where all aspects of central government disappeared. The most notable disappearances were those of police protection, healthcare and education. Warlords and their armed gangsters, locally known as Mooryaans or Jirrey, ruled different enclaves of the country. The majority of the population lives under constant fear of robbery, rape, and senseless murders. Thousands lost their lives or those of loved ones and thousands more became refugees or internally displaced persons. Despite the fact that the international community has tried to end the conflict several times, the country remains anarchic and Somalia represents the ultimate failed state. No government has functioned since 1991.

In spite of this human catastrophe and suffering, the causes of the conflict remain highly contentious. Professor A.I. Samatar (1993), one of the leading scholars in Somali studies, asked the following question: "...why and how could this society, one of the few nations in the continent with one ethnic group, one culture, one language, and one religion, find itself in such parlous circumstances-verging on self destruction." For many years, Somalia was the envy of many African countries that were multi-ethnic and suffered ethnic fractionalization. Many scholars described Somalia as homogenous and explained the war as stemming from bad leadership, the end of the Cold War, the struggle for political and economic power, etc.[19] Other scholars, however, classified Somalis as heterogeneous, consisting of linguistically, economically and ecologically diverse groups. These scholars explain the war as stemming from an ethno-regional quest for domination.

Historical Overview

In contrast to Rwanda, the Somali people had never known any form of centralized state, in the modern sense of the word, before European colonialism at the end of the 19th century. Islam, which introduced a model of a central state system, did not succeed in establishing a viable central state in Somalia except in some isolated pockets on the coastal areas including Mogadishu, Merka, and Barawa. This did not mean, however, that there was an absence of other forms of traditional rule exercised within the framework of Somali kinship society.

British, French, Italian, and Arabic imperialism played an active role in the region in the 19th century. Great Britain was mainly concerned with the area in order to safeguard its port city of Aden in Yemen. The British moved in when Egyptian forces, which occupied the region, withdrew in 1884 to fight the Mahdist movement in the Sudan. The British penetration led to a series of agreements (1884-86) with local tribal leaders and, in 1887, to the establishment of a protectorate. France first acquired a foothold in the area in the 1860s. An Anglo-French agreement of 1888 defined the boundary between the Somali possessions of the two countries.[20] Italy first established its authority in Somalia in 1889 when it created a small protectorate in the central zone. Italy then expanded to the south and northeast, a territory abandoned by the Sultan of Zanzibar. In 1925, the Jubaland treaty was signed between Italy and Britain, detaching the area east of the Juba River from Kenya to become the westernmost part of the Italian colony.

In 1936, Italian Somaliland was combined with Somali-speaking districts of Ethiopia to form a province of the newly formed Italian East Africa. During the Second World War, Italian forces also invaded the British Somaliland; however, the British, operating from Kenya, retook the whole region, including Italian Somaliland in 1942, and ruled until 1950.[21]

In the early years of independence after 1960, the Somali government was faced with a severely underdeveloped economy and a vocal political movement that favored the creation of a Greater Somalia, encompassing the Somali-dominated areas of Kenya, French Somaliland (now Djibouti), and Ethiopia. The nomadic existence of many Somali herders and the ill-defined frontiers of the former colonial districts now united worsened the problem. Hostilities between Somalia and Ethiopia erupted in 1964 and 1977.[22] Kenya also became involved in the first conflict until peace was restored in 1967. The inhabitants of French Somaliland, meanwhile, voted to continue their association with France until they gained their independence as Djibouti in 1977.

On October 6, 1969, Somali President Abdirashid Ali Shermarke was assassinated and after 15 days, the civilian government was overthrown. The new ruler, Maj. Gen. Mohammed Siad Barre, dissolved the national assembly, banned political parties, and established the Supreme Revolutionary Council (SRC), a body that had absolute power. Barre immediately adopted "scientific socialism" and became good friends with the Soviets. This action resulted from the Soviet desire to gain a foothold in the region and Siad Barre's desire to gain Soviet favors in terms of military support.

From 1977 to1978, Somalia attacked Ethiopia in support of the Ogaden People's Liberation Front, a group of Somali speakers who wanted to separate from the Ethiopian government. Militarily, Somalia invaded most of the disputed territory; however, with Ethiopia's revolution in 1974, the Soviet Union unexpectedly sided with the Dergue rulers and helped them drive Somalis out of the territory in 1978. As a result, Somalia sought and received backing from the United States and Arab countries. Guerrilla warfare in the Ogaden continued until 1988 when Ethiopia and Somalia reached a peace accord.

In 1991, Siad Barre's regime was ousted from power by a popular uprising led by tribal militias. The country, however, descended into the internal war, chaos, and anarchy that continue today. During this period, the former British Somaliland also announced that it had seceded from the country and proclaimed itself the Somaliland Republic. In Mogadishu, Mohammed Ali Mahdi was proclaimed president by one group and Mohammed Farah Aidid by another, as fighting between rival clan factions continued. Civil war and the worst African drought of the century created a devastating famine in 1992, resulting in a loss of some 300,000 lives (Oberdorfer, 1992). A UN-brokered truce was declared, and UN peacekeepers along with food supplies arrived. The truce, however, was observed only sporadically and in December 1992, over 30,000 troops from the United States and other nations were deployed in the country in order to restore stability. Efforts to reestablish a central government were unsuccessful. In 1995, the United States and other nations withdrew their forces, and the last UN peacekeepers left with the country still suffering from anarchy. There were several attempts to mediate between the warring factions, but thus far, these efforts have not come to fruition.[23] The last attempt was the convening of the 14th reconciliation meeting held in Kenya between October 2002 and October 2004 when yet another president was elected. The new president is Colonel Abdulahi Yusuf Ahmed who will head a five year transitional government.

Contextual factors

Colonial legacy. Unlike its counterparts, Somalia had neither a long contact with colonial powers nor a viable indigenous political system. The country's history, at least in the modern sense of politics, is mainly the result of recent European contact, specifically with Italy. Somalia also attained high attention from the combatants of the Cold War, the United States and the former Soviet Union, because of its strategic location.

The seeds of Somalia's current suffering, especially in the southern part of the country, were planted at the end of the 19th century when the European colonial administrations of Britain, Italy, and France were established. Italy was especially crucial in setting up the current clan hierarchy. The end result was that the nomadic clans of Mudug and Majertinia regions ended up dominating the Somali political, economic, and cultural arena.

During its administration, Italy promoted the members of these clan families and groomed them to become local elites. One main reason was that the Italians needed agricultural products, which were available in the south. Italy, therefore, created a governing system that helped it to exploit the agricultural sector, and at the same time use as little Italian manpower as possible. Italy established a patrimonial state, and hired the inhabitants of the Mudug and Majertinia regions for lower and mid-level jobs.[24] The promotion of clan members from these chosen regions meant that the southern agrarian communities paid heavily as a result of the extractive policies of the colonial and postcolonial states.

The extractive nature of Somalia's post-independence government also created conditions for the anarchy that followed the collapse of the state in 1991. Many members of the Habargidir clan, for example, used weapons and violence to dominate the politics in Somalia and continue to occupy farmlands and extract wealth from the labor of the members of the southern agrarian community who were forced to work through intimidation and fear. Members of these clans have acquired the name of "Dawlad Ku-Nool" over the years, which literally means "to live on state property".

Ethnicity. According to some scholars, Somalis migrated from southern Arabia around 1000 AD and pushed the Galla, Borane, and Bantu groups out of the area.[25] Today, it is well documented that linguistically and archaeologically Somalis, along with the Oromos, originated from southern Ethiopia.[26] Somalis are divided into six major groups who speak two distinct languages. These are (a) Hawiye, Dir, Darood, and Isaaq, who are overwhelmingly nomadic and speak the Mahaa tiri language, and (b) Digil and Mirifle who practice agro-pastoralism (a mixture of dry farming and herding) and speak the Maay language. These two languages are not intelligible to each other. I.M. Lewis, founder of the Somali homogeneous school of thought, described the difference between these two languages as similar to the difference between "Portuguese and Spanish" (Lewis, 1980, p.5).

The southern settled communities make up the overwhelming majority of the Somali population. Based on the 1958 census[27] (the only available census of Somalia), roughly 82% of the population of the Italian Somaliland live in the area south of Shabelle River. The Italian colonial administration divided the country into six administrative regions. These regions remained intact until the Siad Barre regime (1969-1991) further divided them into eighteen regions. Siad Barre's regional division was mainly intended to create administrative enclaves for the Muduigan clans, specifically the Darood expansion into southern Somalia. The Upper Jubba region was divided into Baay, Bakool, Gedo,[28] and parts of Middle Jubba region.

Somalia's ruling elites are overwhelmingly from Mudug and Majertinia regions despite the fact that these clans are a minority.[29] From the transitional administration of 1955-60 to the collapse of the state in 1991, the domination of state institutions by the Mudugians can be clearly seen. During Siad Barre's regime (1969-91), the Somalia security apparatus was controlled by three groups: the Marehaan, which is Barre's clan; the Ogaden, his mother's clan; and Dhulbahante, his son-in-law's clan. All fall within the larger clan family of Darood, an alliance labeled among the Somalis as MOD (Laitin and Samatar, 1987).

The Darood domination of Somali politics is clear from the composition of Somali governments. Between 1960 and 1990 there were 26 governments that nominated a total of 567 posts. The Darood clan took 216 posts, Hawiye 125, Isaaq 102, and Digil and Mirifle 31 (Hagi and Hagi, 1992). The Darood domination has been visible throughout the existence of the Somali state from 1960 to 1990. During this period, the members from the Darood clan and their sub-clans made up 62 (or 40%) out of the 155 individuals who made up the ruling elite in Somalia's government including; president, vice-president, prime minister, and other ministers (ibid).

Economy: Somalia has an area of 638,000 square kilometers and a coastline of 3300 kilometers (the longest in Africa). The country has two permanent rivers, Jubba and Shabelle, which originate from the Ethiopian highlands. The area between these rivers provides almost all the farm products that the country produces. The World Bank has estimated that 13% (or 8.2 million hectares) of the land area of the country is cultivable, but only 1.6% (or 1 million hectares) of the land is farmed regularly. Most of these farmlands are located in the areas between the rivers of Jubba and Shabelle.[30]

Somalia's economy is a mixture of agriculture and livestock rearing or agro-pastoralism, which contributes 65% of the GDP. Although the country is blessed with the longest beach in Africa, fisheries contribute only 1%. Bananas are the main cash crop, providing nearly half of the country's export earnings; cotton, maize, sorghum, and other crops are produced for domestic consumption. Live animals and animal products, especially hides and skins, are another key source of revenue and are exported mainly to the oil rich Gulf States. Northern Somalia is also the world's largest source of incense and myrrh. In the 1980s, oil and gas reserves were explored but abandoned immediately mainly due to the weakened state capacity and increased violence and instability. The country has very little industry except small industries that barely meet domestic needs.

Over the years, Somalia had been favored by international donors. This was partly the result of the ideological war between the East and West during the Cold War. Somali ruling elites over the years received millions of dollars in foreign aid from various donors, which kept them in power for more than three decades. Between 1965 and 1987, despite the fact that the country's economy stagnated owing to kleptocracy, nepotism, and overall ineffective governance, Somalia still received over US $ 800 million from the U.S. alone (Ayittey, 1994, p.3). One main factor for the huge amount of aid was Somalia's strategic location. It was a magnet for the Cold War combatants. The port city of Berbera on Red Sea has been a point of contest, military bases, and a cash cow for the regime.

The former Soviet Union first established a naval base in the area and in return provided plenty of military hardware for the Siad Barre regime, making Somalia's military one of the strongest armies in Sub Sahara Africa, however, in 1977, during the Ogaden war between Somalia and Ethiopia, when the Soviets switched their alliance to Ethiopia, the regime then turned to the United States for help. In 1980, the Jimmy Carter administration promised support for Siad Barre on the condition that he severed his relationship with Moscow. During that same year, Washington and Mogadishu signed an agreement that allowed the U.S. Navy to use the Berbera naval facilities in exchange for military and economic assistance. The Carter administration provided about US $45 million, consisting of military, economic, and budgetary support (Ibid). Siad Barre's regime also received aid from the major former colonial power, the Italian government, through its aid agency Funda Aiuto Italiana (FAI). Italy invested more than one billion dollars in various projects, but a majority of these projects were wasteful and misguided. Among the many projects was a 450 km road in the sparsely populated and barren desert area between Garowe and Bosaaso (Ibid). The project cost US $250 million, and the funds were spent in a very wasteful and corrupt fashion. Ironically, the Italian government was aware of this fact (Ayittey, 1994, p.3).

Somalia did not have major ethnically politicized groups, but was a magnet for military and economic aid giving the central state the ability to discriminate among tribes in the country. The Somali economy in the 1980s still continued on a downturn spiral. Between 1980 and 1989 the Gross National Product (GNP) per capita declined by 1.7% per year (Marchal, 1996). The average per capita GNP declined from US $ 480 in 1980 by 29% to US $ 340 in 1991 (Mubarak, 1996, p.5).

Structural factors

Regime type and strength: Somalia's political leadership has always been highly polarized and tribalized. Between 1960 and 1969, Somalia had a parliamentary government. In 1960, a unitary government was established, with a parliament of 123 members from all the regions of the country (at the time there were 8 regions including two regions in former British Somaliland). The government had a president and a prime minister, who in turn appointed the cabinet. During the years between 1960 and 1969, the dominance of the Darood clan was clear; members of this clan held roughly two-thirds of government posts.

When Siad Barre took power, the SRC arrested and detained leading members of the democratic regime, including the recent prime minister the late Mohamed Ibrahim Igaal. The SRC banned all political parties, abolished the National Assembly, and suspended the constitution. With the adoption of Marxism, the regime promised, among other things, an end to tribalism, nepotism, corruption, and misrule. The new motto became: *maxaa taqaan* and not *ayaa taqaan* meaning "it is what you know, and not who do you know." In 1970, the new government organized a huge public rally in which a dummy symbolizing tribalism was burned and buried. Siad Barre, however, then established a totalitarian regime. His regime led to an even more polarized clan based polity. The 1969 cabinet, for example, consisted of 14 ministries, and of those Siad Barre's Darood clan held 7 seats (or 50% of the ministries) up from an average of 4 (or 28%). As time progressed, this domination became even more absolute.

In 1972, Siad Barre's regime introduced the Latin alphabet for the written Somali language. By 1973, all foreign language educational materials for primary and secondary schools had been gradually eliminated and the Somali script was introduced. Somalia's literacy rate, which was about 5% in 1972, increased tremendously. The regime adopted a literacy campaign with the goal to educate every citizen within two years. In 1974, the regime recruited 20,000 teachers, mainly from among government employees and secondary school students to carry out the literacy campaign in the rural areas. Despite this great effort, Somalia's literacy rate in 1990 was only 24% according to UN statistics.

Siad Barre renewed his border claims and attacked Ethiopia from 1977 to 1978, but he was defeated when the former Soviet Union backed Ethiopia. At the end of the war, the country's economy declined along with Siad Barre's popularity. Immediately, following the war, Siad Barre experienced the first attempted coup against his regime. In response, the regime carried out a reign of terror against the Majeerteen, the Hawiye, and the Isaaq. These terrors were carried out by the Red Berets (*koofi gaduud*), an elite unit recruited mainly from the president's Marehaan clansmen. This reign of terror gave the regime a short period of stability, which unraveled in May 1986, when Siad Barre was severely injured in a car accident. Although he recovered, a power struggle occurred among senior army commanders, members of his Mareehaan clan, and other factions, practically bringing the country to a standstill.

In 1988, the regime destroyed the second largest city, Hargeisa, with full military might. This attack was carried out to destroy the Somali National Movement (SNM), an Isaaq clan based organization dedicated to overthrowing Siad Barre's regime. The country went deeper into chaos, security declined, and clan based identity politics became even more pronounced. In January 1991, Siad Barre was finally chased out of Mogadishu, and his regime came to an end. A combination of lack of economic development, visible nepotism and favoritism, and easily available weapons led the country into the internal war, chaos, and lawlessness that it continues to experience.

Policy Factors

Somalia has not invested a great deal of money in social capital. The country's literacy increased from 5% to 24% during the 1970s, but all other social development stagnated mainly because of the obsession with hypermilitarization. Somalia spent an average of 20.45% of its budget on the military between 1960 and 1990 and had an average of

8.3 soldiers per 1,000 population. This figure was well above the regional average of less than 4 per 1,000 population. Between 1960 and 1990, Somalia's military grew steadily in spite of its being one of the poorest states in the world. The military expanded from 5,000 troops at independence in 1960 to 23,000 during the 1977-78 Ogaden War; by 1981 the armed forces had 50,000 personnel; by 1990 that number had increased to 65,000 (Lefebvre, 1991).

Somalia's hypermilitarization was greatly affected by its location, in an area of great geo-political and strategic interest to the world powers. It is proximate to the oil production centers of the Middle East, and it lies on the important trade routes through the Suez Canal and the Red Sea. Somalia, therefore, received large amounts of military aid from the Cold War combatants over the years, and aid from wealthy Arab states as well. During the early 1970s, the Soviets were allowed to establish the Berbera naval base on the strategic north coast at the entrance of the Red Sea, mainly in reaction to the large-scale American military assistance to Somalia's rival Ethiopia, then under the rule of the feudal emperor Haile Selassie.

In addition to the aid from superpowers,[31] the country received military support from Arab countries, China, West Germany, Italy and Apartheid South Africa (Ottaway, 1982; Lefebvre, 1991). Somalia became one of the most militarized countries in Africa and as a result, the Somali state, as in many countries in the Third World, became highly dependent on foreign handouts over the years, strengthening the central state at the price of indigenous economic development. As the decade of the 1990s began, Somalia suffered the same fate as its counterparts with a severe economic decline due to the end of the Cold War. Unlike its counterparts, however, Somalis had access to large supplies of weapons due to years of arms build-up. This hypermilitarization, coupled with the economic decline and the jockeying for political and economic control, made Somalia vulnerable to the 1991 internal war.

As with its counterparts, Somalia's troubles also began in the 1980s when armed opposition groups began challenging the regime of Siad Barre. The regime faced armed groups such as the Somali National Movement, predominantly from the Isaaq tribe of the former British northern Somaliland. The regime used its military might and killed thousands of civilians as well as destroying the second largest city of the country. In 1990 many prominent leaders suggested the resignation of Siad Barre from power, but he murdered some of the leaders of these groups, leading the country into the current chaos.

The ensuing Somali civil war developed over several years. It was caused by a combination of several factors, both local and international, and involved many different actors. At the national level, several years of continued frustration over basic human needs caused unrest in the midst of inequality due to lack of adequate education and healthcare. The government's ineffective economic policies also worsened economic difficulties, causing extreme poverty, intense government crises characterized by constant cabinet reshuffles, and the loss of state authority; a politicized army, coups and counter coups came to rule the day.

Between 1972 and 1989, the general population became poorer and gradually more desperate. The very difficult living conditions became an incentive for young men to join factional militia opposed to the government in office. A culture of violence and crime emerged as a strategy for ensuring livelihood. At a more general level, as with all developing countries, Somalia's economy was not integrated into the global market economy. The national economy was sustained by foreign financial and military aid from Europe, Middle East and North America. During the Cold War era, in the context of the prevailing ideological conflict, foreign economic assistance and development co-operation with Somalia were linked to the geo-strategic economic interests.

Comparing the cases

The three countries: Rwanda, Sierra Leone, and Somalia, all share a common trait of an all encompassing internal war occurring during the 1990s. There were, however, different factors that were uniquely present in each country that also accounted for these wars. In this section, the three countries will be compared and their similarities and differences examined. The contextual factors: historical, social, economic and political, will be examined first; then the structural factors: regime, leadership, stability and quality of life will be examined. Finally, policies that countries' political institutions produced and that created the war outcome will be scrutinized.

Contextual factors

Colonialism provided the arena for internal war; the postcolonial state is a potential source of internal wars (Blanton *et al.*, 2001; Herbst, 2000). Sierra Leone had the longest contact with European colonialism, first with the Portuguese and later with Britain. Both Somalia and Rwanda experienced a short and mixed colonial history: Germany and Belgium in Rwanda and Italy and Britain in Somalia. The effect of colonial history is inseparable from any analyses of war and conflict in Africa. Colonialism created stratified and politicized ethnicities in both war and no-war countries. Postcolonial political institutions implicitly or explicitly reflected this fact.

These countries did, however, differ in their ethnic politicization pattern. During the pre-colonial era, only Rwanda had a viable indigenous state in place, whereas Sierra Leone (with the exception of repatriated ex-slaves and later the Lebanese population) and Somalia did not have indigenous states that controlled the current borders. Rwanda's pre-colonial institutional structure was partially the result of high population density, which later provided the basis (Hutu and Tutsi) for the success of the colonial effort to divide and conquer (Melvern, 2000; Prunier, 1997). In the cases of Sierra Leone and Somalia, the division was mainly between exogenous forces, e.g. settling of the repatriated ex-slaves (Krios), and indigenous clans, specifically the Mendes and Temnes. In Somalia the division was based on socio-economic and familial structure. The nomadic clans of the central and northeastern part of the country were promoted as the colonial employees in charge of subjugating the southern agrarian communities. In Somalia, unlike Rwanda and Sierra Leone, war was not between the (southern) agrarians and (northern) pastoralist and urbanized groups, rather it was a power struggle between the central northeastern clans who ruled the country after independence (Kusow, 1998; Mukhtar and Kusow, 1998; Casenelli and Besteman, 1999).

Colonialism also created an export-based economic system, enforcing the production of a single primary crop such as coffee or sugar or the extraction of a specific resource such as diamonds, gold and other minerals. All three countries were economically dependent on the West, both as markets and sources of aid. By the late 1980s, the prices of many commodities declined in world markets. Rwanda faced the biggest problem when coffee prices plummeted (Melvern, 2000). Sierra Leone, dependent on diamonds, faced a different problem of smuggling and illegal marketing, eventually leading to the 1992 internal war (Reno, 2000). Somalia, on the other hand, did not have large commodity exports with the exception of bananas and livestock, exported to the Middle East. The most important asset for Somalia was its strategic location on the Red Sea and Indian Ocean, which produced military rents for successive Somali regimes. During the Cold War (1945-1990), both the former Soviet Union and the United States sought regional control and in return provided economic and military support for the successive Somali regimes. When the Cold War came to an end in 1989, Somalia did, however, suffer the same fate as its counterparts. The income from the Cold War combatants dried up.

By the late 1980s, however, all three countries, along with most of the countries in the Third World, faced severe economic decline. Africa suffered more than other regions.[32] Although economic decline was generally the trend, these three countries differed in their decline. Between 1960 (or independence year if later) and 1990 (or most recent available data), Somalia had the worst per capita GDP growth, approximately -1.25%, followed by Sierra Leone, -0.75%. Rwanda, on the other hand, experienced a positive growth of approximately 1.1% during the same period although its GDP figures were low in the first place (Englebert, 2000). War generally came after economic shocks, even to a country that showed some growth.

All three countries received substantial amounts of aid money from international donors, although Somalia received more aid, and certainly more military aid, than Sierra Leone and Rwanda combined. Between 1960 and 1990, it received more than US $ 121 million (or US $22.65 per capita), compared to Rwanda with US $ 72.58 million (or US $12.21), and Sierra Leone with US $26.24 million (US $7.58 per capita) during the same time period (OECD.org). In the mid 1980s, the international donors imposed adjustment programs that were mainly intended to generate loan repayment. Many countries faced economic hardship and witnessed declines in governmental performance. Looking at the period 1986 through 1989 as the peak years of Structural Adjustment Programs, the three countries experienced an average decline of US $ -21.15 million (or US $ -6.81 per capita) in ODA. This decline, however, came from Rwanda with ODA decline of US $ -5.94 million (or US $ -4.27 per capita) and Somalia with a decline of US $ -

71.36 million (or US $ 16.79 per capita). During this period Sierra Leone's ODA receipts remained positive at an average of US $13.84 million (US $2.53 per capita), although Sierra Leone received substantially less ODA than Somalia and Rwanda had received.

Table 3.1: Contextual factors 30 years average score for: ethno-linguistic groups, ODA (millions US $), ODA (1986-89), ODA (per capita US $), ODA (1986-89)*.

War Countries	#of ethno-linguistic groups	ODA/ Mill US $1960-90	ODA/ US $ Mill. 1989-86	ODA US $ Mil. 1960-90	ODA per capita US $ 1989-86
Rwanda	3	72.58	-5.94	12.21	-4.27
Sierra Leone	23	26.24	13.84	7.58	2.53
Somalia	13	121.3	-71.36	22.65	-16.79
Average	13.0	73.37	-21.15	14.15	-6.18

*Source respectively from: www.ethnologue.org; www.oecd.org

As the Table 3.1 shows, the war countries were ethnically relatively concentrated, making mobilization of political groups relatively easy; these states grew economically poorer as they marched towards the 1990s and were affected by the cuts of foreign aid in the post-adjustment period. These contextual factors compounded the political and conflict situations in these countries.

Structural factors

The three countries also had similarities and differences in their political institutions. These institutions were at the center of why these states came to the outcome of internal war in the 1990s. All three countries began with elected governments that were later transformed into autocratic regimes. In each case, opposition to these autocratic regimes helped spark the internal wars. Rwanda, after its independence of 1962, had an elected government headed by Kayibanda until 1973, the year he was overthrown by a military coup led by Juvenal Habyarimana. Similarly, Sierra Leone had its share of military regimes, as early as 1967. The country had 9 rulers after independence with an average life span of 3.4 years per regime. Of these rulers five were military and four were civilian, including the current president Kabbah. Somalia also had one of the few democratic transitions of power in Africa during the 1960s. In 1967 a democratic transition from president Adan Abdulle Osman to Abdirashid Ali Shermarke occurred; however, in 1969 the civilian government was overthrown by a coup led by General Siad Barre, who led the country towards its current failed state status.

These political institutions consumed the largest portion of economic production. The central governments spent an average 23.22% of the total consumption. The Sierra Leonean government spent the largest amount, 29.57%, followed by Rwanda with 22.91% and Somalia with 17.19%. This government consumption indicates the amount of the economy that is under the control of the state, providing the ingredients for mismanagement and corruption (Herbst, 2000; Schroeder, 2000). As a result, the political institutions of these countries led them into the depths of despair and poverty.

In all aspects of the physical quality of life, these countries were at the bottom of the human development index. They had an average GDP per capita of US $ 558.97; life expectancy of 42.33 years; an infant mortality rate of 151 per 1000/life births; and a literacy rate of 22.3% (Hardin, 1991; Adedeji, 1995). Because of political instability, poverty, and autocratic regimes, these countries were unable to attract investment. They had a negligible investment average of 4.8% of the GDP, Somalia actually topped the list at almost 9% and Sierra Leone occupied the bottom with 1.5%.

Table 3.2: Structural factors: number of successful coups, government consumption (% of GDP controlled by the government), investment in the economy (% of investment the economy attracts), infant mortality (death of children under one year/per 1,000 live births), literacy rate (% of adults that can read and write), life expectancy (average age between birth and death), and GDP per capita (US $)*.

War Countries	# of succ. Coups 1960-1990*	Gov. cons. (%) 1960-1990**	Invest. (% GDP) 1960-1990	Inf Mort. 1960-1990*	Life exp. 1960-1990*	GDP per capita US $ 1960-1990*
Rwanda	2	22.91	3.92	130.5	46	468
Sierra Leone	7	29.57	1.5	177.5	38	675.42
Somalia	2	17.19	8.98	145	43	533.5
Average	3.67	23.22	4.77	151	42.33	558.97

*Sources from: Bratton and Van de Walle, 1996
http://datacenter2.chass.utotronto.ca/pwt; www.wroldbank.org

As table 3.2 illustrates, the war countries suffered from unstable political systems, had large government consumption, and most importantly, suffered from low physical quality of life.

Policy Factors

The political institutions of these countries adopted policies that neglected the enhancement of their social capital, such as education and healthcare, as evidenced by the poor situation of the physical quality of life. The countries spent more on military and military related activities than on social capital (McGowan and Johnson, 1984; Adedeji, 1995). On social capital, the three countries spent, on average, from 1960 (or year of independence if later) to 1990, per capita amounts of US $5.90 on education and US $ 2.94 on healthcare. This amounted to an average of 14.21% of the central government expenditure. As a ratio, for every US $1 spent on the military only US $0.62 was spent on education and healthcare combined. Given the high poverty and poor quality of life in these countries, they tended to be militarized at slightly over the regional average with an average of 3.45 soldiers per 1,000 population. Somalia, which leads the group, had more than twice the number of soldiers as the other two countries combined with 8.3/

1,000 population, followed by Sierra Leone with 1.2/1,000 and Rwanda with 0.85/1,000.

Table 3.3: Policy factors 30 years average scores for: Military expenditure (% of GNP), military expenditure (% central government expenditure), military size (number of soldiers per 1000 population), educational expenditure (per capita US $), and healthcare (per capita US $)*.

War Countries	ME% GNP 1960-90	Mil. Exp (%/CGE) 1960-90	Soldiers per 1000 pop. 1960-90	Milex/ Cap (US $) 1960-90	Educ/ cap (US $) 1960-90	Health/ cap (US $) 1960-90
Rwanda	1.87	16	0.85	3.3	5.1	1.2
Sierra Leone	0.82	4.82	1.2	2.7	9.1	3
Somalia	4.98	21.82	8.3	16.2	3.5	1.7
Average	2.56	14.21	3.45	7.1	5.9	2.94

*Source respectively from: ACDA; SIPRI; Worldbank.org

Table 3.3 shows that Rwanda and Sierra Leone spent more on education than military compared to Somalia but were below the regional average. The war countries spent significantly more overall on the military and less on social capital (education and healthcare).

Chapter 3 also illustrated that the war countries had an average governance score of –2.30, with Rwanda scoring the highest score of -1.78, followed by Sierra Leone with –2.23, and Somalia being the lowest with -2.88 (see Table 4.4). It can be determined that the three war countries were not well governed even by regional standards. They did not handle their domestic unrest well and, unlike their counterparts, the no-war countries did not accommodate the demands for change that came from both local and international community during the 1980s. All three reacted to uprisings and insurgencies with military repression even as they negotiated with the opposition groups.

Table 3.4: ICRG governance scores for the war countries*

War Countries:	ICRG Score
Rwanda	-1.78
Sierra Leon	-2.23
Somalia	-2.28
Average	**-2.30**
Regional average	**-1.72**

*Source: Englebert, 2000

This chapter examined Rwanda, Sierra Leone and Somalia as the peace-to-war cases. The governance in these countries was examined from contextual, structural, and policy perspectives as well as factors that led to internal war in the 1990s. These countries were found to be economically poor, dependent on commodity prices as well as overseas assistance, politically ethnicized, unstable, highly or increasingly militarized, had poor quality of life, and failed to attract investment. The next chapter will examine the no-war countries: Ghana, Tanzania and Zambia to see if these same factors were present and if so, to what degree.

Notes

1 For details on the concept of insecurity dilemma see: Job (1992).

2 Prior to the 1994 genocide, Rwanda witnessed several genocidal attempts. 1959: Hutus rebel against the Belgian colonial power and the Tutsi elite and 150,000 Tutsis flee to Burundi.1963: Further massacre of Tutsis, as a response to military attack by exiled Tutsis in Burundi. Again more refugees leave the country. By mid-1960s approximately half of the Tutsi population lived outside Rwanda. 1967: Renewed massacres of Tutsis. 1973: Tutsi students were expelled from universities and again an outbreak of killings against Tutsis happened again. For more details see: Prunier, 1999.

3 Please be advised that these factors are not only unique only to the war countries, but all of these factors are present, as will be proven in the no war countries.

4 The word Tutsi, which apparently first described the status of an individual—a person rich in cattle—became the term that referred to the privileged group as a whole. The word Hutu originally meant a subordinate or follower of a more powerful person—came to refer to the mass of the ordinary people. The identification of Tutsi pastoralists as power-holders and of Hutu cultivators as subjects

was becoming general when Europeans first arrived in Rwanda at the end of the 19th century. Rulers of small states embedded in the larger nation, important lineage heads and some power-holders within the central state hierarchy exercised authority even though they were people who would today be called Hutu.

5 Alex Shoumatoff, "Rwanda's Aristocratic Guerrillas," New York Times Magazine, 13 December 1992, p. 44: "In 1926, [the Belgians] classified anyone with more than 10 cows as Tutsi and made everyone carry a 'tribal' identity card." African Rights, Rwanda: Death, Despair and Defiance (London: African Rights, 1995), pp. 8-9: "Despite the emphasis on height and straight noses, such was the slender basis of the racial categorization that, during the 1933-4 census, the Belgians were obliged to use ownership of cows as the key criterion for determining which group an individual belonged to. Those with ten or more cows were Tutsis--along with all their descendants in the male line--and those will less were Hutu."

6 Belgian doctors in Bujumbura, capital of Burundi, injected the 46 year old king with antibiotics. His death created great rumors in the country; the Tutsis believed that Belgian doctors deliberately murdered the king.

7 Gitarama is one of ten prefectures (or provinces) in the country. The prefecture was created in 1959 and is located in the central part of the country.

8 Ugandan-Tutsi domination, particularly in the army, police, and secret service was apparent. According to Dorsey (2000): "Within the army, of the 45 main positions – Ministry of Defence, RPA and Gendarmerie Chiefs of Staff, and unit commanders – 27 'belong' to the 'Ugandans', as against 10 to the 'Burundians', and 5 to ex-FAR members, 3 to the 'Rwandans' and just one to the 'Zairians'. Every on of the unit commanders of the RPA is 'Ugandan', as are three of the five Gendarmerie commanders. Among the five existing Intelligence Services in Rwanda, the same 'Ugandan' preponderance is present today. The head of the DMI [Department of Military Intelligence], following a temporary 'Burundian', is a 'Ugandan'. The head of the ESCO and his deputy are 'Ugandans'. The head of the Gendarmerie Intelligence Service was born in the Congo but educated in Uganda. There is also a 'Ugandan' at the head of Special Intelligence, with a 'Burundian' deputy." Michael Dorsey (2000). "Violence and Power-Building in Post-Genocide Rwanda." In Ruddy Doom and Jan Gorus (eds.) Politics of Identity and Economics of Conflict in the Great Lakes Region. Brussels: VUB University Press. p. 327. See also Mugabe, "The Killings Resume…", at

http://www.strategicstudies.org/crisis/rwanda.htm#Uganda-Rwanda

9 By 1999 the Rwandan military has reached, according to International Institute for Strategic Studies, a London-based organization, an estimated size of between 30,000 and 40,000 troops. Quoted in the Economist Intelligence Unit, EIU Country Profile 2000: Rwanda Burundi (London: Economist Intelligence Unit, 2000). In October 2000, the institute made an adjustment to this figure and estimated the military numbering between 49,000 and 64,000 troops. This figure does not include 7,000 paramilitary forces (so-called Local Defence Units) and 6,000 Gendarmerie officers, which were by then placed under the control of the Ministry of Interior. See Economist Intelligence Unit, EIU Country Profile 2001: Rwanda Burundi (London: Economist Intelligence Unit, 2001), p. 15

10 These trainees formed the Interahamwe militia, which means "those who attack together". They made up the core perpetrators of 1994 genocide. This militia was supported by the Impuzamugambi, meaning "those who have a single aim", of the Hutu Coalition pour le Défense de la République. The Impuzamugambi militia were trained, armed, and led by the Presidential Guard and other elements of the Rwandan government army.

11 In addition to military weapons the country imported, notably, a large number of machetes and other suitable equipment for genocide in 1993 and 1994 (the year of the genocide). Requests for import licenses from January 1993 through March 1994 show that 581,000 kilograms of machetes, each weighing one kilogram, were imported. A quantity that would equal some 581,000 machetes (or one for every third adult Hutu male in Rwanda) was imported as part of a larger quantity of 3,385,000 kilograms of metal goods including: hammers, picks, and sickles. The most significant was Félicien Kabuga, a businessman and friend of Habyarimana, who received seven licenses for a total value of 95 million Rwandan francs, or about US $525,000. One cargo of 987 cartons of machetes, weighing some 25,662 kilograms, was shipped to him from the Kenyan port of Mombasa on October 26, arriving in

Kigali in early November.

(http://www.hrw.org/reports/1999/rwanda/Geno1-3-11.htm).

12 General elections scheduled for early 2001 were postponed to February owing to the insecurity caused by the internal war. In May 2001 sanctions were imposed on Liberia because of its support for the Sierra Leonean rebels, and UN peacekeepers began to make headway in disarming the various factions. Disarmament of rebel and pro-government militias proceeded slowly and fighting continued to occur. By January 2002, however, most of the estimated 45,000 fighters had surrendered their weapons.

13 In many postcolonial states, one tribe dominates from the outset, sometimes having been favored by the colonial rulers before. For example, in Somalia the Italians preferred the Darood clan of central and northeastern regions. From 1960 to 1990 the Daroods occupied the presidency for 23 years.

14 One of the main reasons for the fallout between the Mendes and Temnes stems from the colonial educational system, which elevated the Mendes over the Temnes. Eighty percent of the schools and other infrastructural developments, including roads and railways were concentrated in the Mende lands. This created the basis for suspicion between the groups and Temne feelings of being relatively deprived. Kilson (1966, P.77).

15 In 1970 the country produced two million carats of diamonds. This figure of official production had declined to 95,000 carats in 1980 and further declined to only 48,000 carats in 1988. For details see Smillie, et al. (2000, p.5).

16 The Gini coefficient is a number between zero and one that measures the degree of inequality in the distribution of income in a given society. The coefficient would register zero inequality (0.0 = minimum inequality) for a society in which each member received exactly the same income, and it would register a coefficient of one (1.0 = maximum inequality) if one member got all the income and the rest got nothing.

17 UNDP (1999). Sierra Leone Human Development Report. p.18.

18 Quote obtained from:

http://www.ius.edu/SocialScience/ModelUN/SierraLeone.htm

19 For a similar idea see Latin and Samatar (1987), Samatar (1988) This line of thinking is the most accepted; however, it does not mean other lines of thinking were non-existent, rather it was never encouraged, or was ignored outright.

20 See: Lee V. Casanelli (1982), Mukhtar (1995a), Mukhtar (1995b). "

21 Italy renounced its claim to the rights and titles of the territory in 1947 under Article 23 of the 1947 peace treaty; however, on November 21, 1949, the General Assembly adopted a resolution recommending that Italian Somaliland be placed under an international trusteeship system for 10 years. Italy maneuvered politically and won this trusteeship, and the General Assembly granted Italy the authority to administer its former Somaliland territory. Italy established the Amministrazione Fiduciaria della Somalia (AFIS), which led to Somalia's independence on July 1, 1960. The northern British territory of Somaliland, which gained its independence on June 26, 1960, joined the South and formed the Somali Republic. This union has been broken since 1991 when the former British colony of

Somaliland declared its separation; however, this breakaway republic is yet to receive international recognition.

22 The area was first invaded by Emperor Menelik in 1890s. The Ogaden, a vast, ill-defined region occupied by Somalis, extends southeast from Ethiopia's southern highlands that includes a separate region east of Harar known as the Haud. Emperor Haile Selassie feared the possibility of British support in 1945 for a separate Somali state that would include the Ogaden, and Ethiopian officers took over administration in the city of Jijiga after the British evacuated the Ogaden in 1948. Upon the birth of the Republic of Somalia in 1960, the country proclaimed an irredentist policy. Within six months after Somali independence, military incidents occurred between Ethiopian and Somali forces along their mutual border. Confrontations escalated again in 1964 when the Ethiopian air force raided Somali villages and encampments inside the Somali border. Hostilities were ended through mediation by the OAU and Sudan, however, Somalia continued to promote irredentism by supporting the Western Somali Liberation Front (WSLF), which was active in the Ogaden, and there was a resurgence of fighting in 1977-1978.

23 The most notable of these efforts was the meeting at Djibouti in 2000 where most of the warring factions met for the 13th time in a major mediating conference. The conference lasted five months and succeeded in creating a national charter (interim constitution), and elected a national assembly and a president. Abdikassim Salad Hassan, a former official in Barre's regime, was elected as interim president. This interim government did not succeed in creating a viable state and did not even control the capital city. The warring factions currently built yet another transitional federal government as a result of the two-year meeting in Kenya. This meeting, which began October 2002, resulted in the creation of a 351-member parliament and federal system.

24 This system was used extensively during the colonial era. The Hausa political domination of Nigeria is an example of this. For details on this practice see Walter Rodney (1977.

25 Proponents of this argument include: I.M. Lewis (1961), Laitin and Samatar (1984), Cerulli (1957).

26 Proponents of this argument include: Fleming (1964), Turton (1975), Ali (1985).

27 Please note that in 1974 the Siad Barre government made another census, but its results were never published. For details on the 1958 census see Mukhtar, 1989, p.26.

28 This region was created for Siad Barre's Marehan clan; it is amazing that the capital city for the region was a town called Garbaharrey, a smaller, mountainous, and literally empty town, as opposed to Bardhere, a fledgling city with very long history that is estimated to be over 500 years old.

29 Please note that this is based on the 1958 census, the only census available. This census shows a total population of 1,263,584 and was based on the six regions of Majertinia (82,653 or 7%), Mudug (141,120 or 11%), Hiiraan (176,528 or 14%), Banadir (387,600 or 31%), Upper Jubba (362,234 or 29%) and Lower Jubba (113,449 or 9%). This makes the Southern regions the majority with 82% of the population. For details on the 1958 census see Mukhtar, 1989, p.26.

30 Somalia: Country Profile. The Economist Intelligence Unit Unit. 1992-93.

31 The Carter administration provided about US $45 million in a package consisting of military, economic, and budgetary support. See Ayittey (1994, p.3).

32 The average per capita growth between 1960 and 1992 was approximately 0.5%, compared to East Asia's 3.25% (Englebert, 2000).

CHAPTER 4

PEACE-to-PEACE COUNTRIES: GHANA, TANZANIA and ZAMBIA

This chapter addresses three Sub Saharan African countries that maintained relative peace from since the 1980s: Ghana, Tanzania and Zambia. Peace in this context signifies that these countries did not experience an all out internal war. This does not mean, however, that these countries were without turbulence or conflict. Adedeji (1999), for example, places Ghana and Zambia among countries that suffered from political turmoil and instability.

The selection of these cases may present problems such as biases and incomplete representation of the countries in the region. All three were former British colonies who experienced indirect rule and have strong tribal ties (Blanton et al., 2001). Several factors, however, are behind their selection such as the relative scarcity of peaceful countries in the region and availability of adequate data and literature.

As with the peace-to-war countries, these countries share several characteristics that helped them avoid the occurrence of an all out internal war in the 1990s. These include their historical background and particular experience of colonialism, neo-colonialism, the Cold War and even post Cold War events. Tribalism and ethnic factors must also be examined as with most African states. These countries' economies were dependent on outside powers. Finally, with the exception of Ghana, these countries have had more stable governance since their independence when compared to their counterparts. All three countries also had democratic political transitions during the 1980s and 1990s. The way these countries dealt with their internal opposition or uprisings will also be examined to see if factors of leadership or negotiations were more effective.

When examining different states, it is important to consider the differences in the type of environmental, social, political, economic, and historical setting for each country. Ethnic differences did not appear to become as politicized or militarized in these states as was seen in the war countries reviewed in Chapter 3. Similarly to the war countries, however, these three states varied in the degree of their political maturity and stability. Ghana had a tradition of well-established kingdoms in the area (e.g. the Ashanti kingdom prior to the establishment of British protectorate). Structurally, Ghana had six military regimes and three republics following its independence in 1957, whereas neither Tanzania nor Zambia ever had a military government.

This chapter analyzes the differences and similarities of these countries. Each country will be examined based on the contextual, structural, and policy factors that were present. In each country, the following questions will be addressed: What is the historical, social, economic, and political context that enabled them to avoid internal war?; What role did the political institutions play in their peaceful settlement of disputes?; What type of policies did they adopt that allowed them to avoid internal war, especially if one threatened?; and with the economic, political, and social capacity of many states in the Third World declining in the 1980s, how did each state deal with this dilemma and the rise of opposition: confrontation versus compromise?

The case studies will be arranged as follows: (1) each country's historical setting and conflict potential will be summarized. (2) questions for each country will be summarized. (3) the cases of this chapter will be compared, and similarities as well differences that led to the absence internal war will be addressed. In the next chapter, the war and no-war country patterns will be compared further.

I. Ghana

Ghana is located in West Africa and shares boundaries with the Atlantic Ocean on the South, Burkina Faso on the north, the Republic of Togo on the east, and Côte d'Ivoire on the west. Most of Ghana's neighbors have been relatively stable, but in 2002 rebel forces took over the northern half of Côte d'Ivoire, and internal war broke out. Efforts to resolve the Ivorian crisis have continued, with incomplete success so far. Although Ghana has avoided the occurrence of an all out internal war, it possesses many of the suggested patterns that were present in the war countries. Ghana has a multi-ethnic society and an economy that depends on a single crop, cocoa, with generally declining prices. Ghana also possesses one of the most unstable political structures in

Africa. Since its independence in 1957, it has had four republics and six military governments (for details see appendix 2). Although Ghana avoided an all out internal war, it experienced periodic civil unrest and several factors that might have led to war, including economic decline and political instability. In this section, how and why Ghana avoided the occurrence of an internal war will be examined.

Historical Overview

The present-day area of Ghana included a number of small independent kingdoms, including Gonja and Dagomba in the north, Ashanti in the interior, and the Fanti states along the coast. In 1482 the Portuguese established the first European fort at Elmina. Trade in gold and slaves began and led to intense competition among many European powers for trading advantages. With the decline of the slave trade in the 19th century, only the British, Danes in 1850, and Dutch in 1872 still maintained forts on the Gold Coast. The British, however, remained and allied themselves with the Fanti states against the Ashanti.

In 1874 the British defeated the Ashanti and organized the coastal region as the Gold Coast Colony. In 1901 the British declared the northern regions a protectorate. After World War I, part of the German colony of Togoland was mandated to the British, and they, in turn, were linked administratively with the Gold Coast Colony. By the end of World War II, nationalist activities had intensified. Kwame Nkrumah, one of the educated leaders of the Convention People's Party (CPP), emerged as the leading nationalist figure. In 1951 Britain granted a new constitution, and general elections were held. The CPP won overwhelmingly, and Nkrumah became premier.

In March 1957, Ghana became an independent country and the first postcolonial state in Sub Saharan Africa, with Nkrumah as its prime minister. In 1960 Nkrumah transformed Ghana into a republic and crowned himself as president. In 1964 all opposition parties were outlawed, and many critics of the government were imprisoned. Nkrumah, one of founders of the Non-Aligned Movement in world politics, followed an anti-colonial pan-African policy and grew increasingly less friendly to the West. Poorly financed large development projects coupled with falling cocoa prices also led to chaotic economic conditions.

In 1966, Nkrumah was overthrown by a military coup. The National Liberation Council (NLC) under Major General Joseph Ankrah was set up to rule until the restoration of civilian government. Relations with Western powers improved, and in 1969 the NLC transferred power to the government of K.A. Busia, who had been elected under a new constitution. Busia's government, however, was undermined by labor problems, an unpopular currency devaluation, and serious inflation. In 1972, Busia was overthrown in a coup led by Colonel I.K. Acheampong.

In 1978 Acheampong was forced out of office by a group of military officers. Low wages and high unemployment led to a series of strikes that further disrupted the economy. In 1979, Flight Lieutenant J.J. Rawlings overthrew the government and purged the country by having many people executed or jailed for offences such as corruption. He then turned the government over to an elected president, Dr. Hilla Limann. Rawlings seized power once again in 1981 and tightened his political control throughout the 1980s. He enlisted economic help from the International Monetary Fund (IMF) and the World Bank, and in the late 1980s, the economy finally began to show significant growth. In 1992 the government promulgated a new constitution and lifted the ban on opposition parties.

In February 1994, the country witnessed the death of 1,000 people and displacement of over 150,000 people in the conflict between Konkombas and Nanumbas in the northern part of the country near the border with Togo.[1] The conflict, which could have potentially become an all out internal war was curbed by Rawlings' government. In the 1996 elections, Rawlings was elected again, and Ghana's economic recovery continued into the late 1990s. In 2000 Rawlings stepped down, respecting the two term limit in the new constitution, and John Kufuor was elected as president.

Contextual factors

Colonialism: The British colonial states ruled indirectly and relied heavily on the divide and conquer system against traditional local authorities. Under the indirect rule system, ethnicity was politicized, and winners and losers were created in the country. Prior to 1948, politics in Ghana was pretty much an elite game; however, in 1948 the country witnessed large anti-colonial movements and political jockeying between two groups, the intelligentsia and traditional leaders. The intelligentsia, consisting of urban elites and rich merchants, preferred a system that was based on a Western parliament and constitution. The traditional leaders, supported by the British, on the other hand, preferred a traditional structure of government.

In 1948 a third group led by Kwame Nkrumah began to compete for control of the post-independence state. This group was characterized as petit bourgeois and was composed of teachers, small businessmen, clerks, and urban workers. Nkrumah, a great organizer and elegant speaker, won the 1951 election with the CPP as well as the subsequent postcolonial election of 1957. This victory, however, created an alliance between the intelligentsia and traditional leaders and formed the basis for the 1966 coup d'etat against him. It is important to note, however, that none of the war states reviewed in the last chapter had as charismatic a founding father as Ghana had in Nkrumah, who embodied the nationalist struggle for independence.

Ethnicity: There are at least 50 different ethnic groups living in Ghana, although some sources mention as many as 75, each with a distinct language or dialect. Regardless of how one calculates, Ghana is extremely ethnically and linguistically heterogeneous for its size. The largest group is the Akan speakers (Asante, Fante, Ahanta, Guan, Bono, Akyem, Akwamu, Kwahu, Akuapem, Sefwi, and Nzema) located in the southern and western sections and accounting for about 45% of the population. The Mole-Dagbani groups of northern Ghana account for about 16% of the population; the Ewes of the southeast have about 13%; the Ga-Adangbe (or Ga-Dangme) group in the area of Accra and the southeastern coast account for about 9%; the Gurma group, 3.5%; and other groups account for 11% (Chazan, 1997, p.462). Chazan (1997) further argues that the country's political control has been shifting among the different groups.

Economy: At independence, Ghana's economy was much better situated than most African countries. It had relatively well developed infrastructure, ample foreign exchange and among the best-trained civil services in Africa. In 1957 Ghana had the same per capita income as South Korea; however, by 1982 the average Ghanaian was significantly poorer. One main reason is that successive governments adopted questionable economic policies. In contrast, the South Korean per capita income during this period increased five fold (Martin, 1993).

Ghana remains primarily an agricultural society with more than half of its labor force engaged in farming. In 1957 Ghana was the world's leading producer of cocoa, supplying one-third of all cocoa in the world. In 1965 the country produced 500,000 tons of cocoa, but by 1984 production had sunk to 158,000 tons. From 1987 to 1988, cocoa production recovered somewhat, coinciding with the decline in world prices for cocoa, which fell from $2,603 per ton in 1980 to $999 per ton in 1989 (Reno, 2000; Chazan et al., 1999). Despite the decline in price, cocoa still provided about two-thirds of export revenues. In addition to cocoa, other cash crops include palm oil and palm kernels, oranges, tomatoes, sheanuts, and coffee, all of which are subject to the vagaries of international markets.

Ghana is also dependent on minerals, specifically gold, manganese, bauxite, and diamonds. The famous gold mining industry, which is central to the Ghanaian economy, is located in the Akan region of southern Ghana and has been active since the 13th century. Gold became a valuable trade item, reaching North Africa and as well as further lands. Muslim traders traveled across the Sahara. Four major mines (Obuasi, Tarkwa, Prestea, and Dunkwa) and a few lesser ones are currently in operation, but the Obuasi mine, operated by Ashanti Goldfields Corporation (AGC), accounts for the largest proportion of the total quantity of gold mined in the country. At independence, Ghana produced nearly one million ounces per year and was the world's fifth leading exporter of gold. It remains Ghana's most important mineral export, accounting for fifteen per cent of total export earnings in the 1980s.

In 1970 oil was discovered offshore near Cape Coast, and small amounts were produced by 1978. The country also has a timber industry with harvests from forests in the southwestern part of the country. The timber industry continues to meet the domestic demand with small amounts left for export. The country's industrial base was excellent by African standards at the time of independence in 1957. Nkrumah devoted considerable effort and expense to developing industry, at the expense of the agricultural sector.

The economic decline of the 1980s pushed the country to adopt many World Bank and IMF economic reform programs. Between 1983 and 1988, the government devalued the cedi (the Ghanaian currency) and significantly reduced subsidies as well as imposing strict monetary and fiscal controls (Reno, 2000). During the Structural Adjustment Programs of 1987-90, the government liberalized trade and reformed many state-owned companies. The government's strict observance of these recovery programs was highly praised by donor countries, and it earned Ghana the respect of the international community, and brought in millions of dollars in credit. Despite this "economic miracle", the country's economy is far from robust.

Ghana's present recovery is due largely to both the improved global economy of the 1990s and the determination and pragmatic skills of another charismatic leader, Jerry Rawlings. Although recovery is slow, there is a likelihood that it will endure. The economic recovery program was closely tied to significant levels of foreign loans and assistance, specifically from the World Bank and the International Monetary Fund. Between 1982 and 1990, foreign and multilateral donors disbursed a total of approximately US$3.5 billion in official development assistance (OECD.org). Although mentioning this aid seems to question the earlier argument that foreign aid can be harmful, in this context it is not controversial, because the quality of the leadership, specifically Rawlings, and the ability to accommodate the IMF and World Bank's conditionalities were high. Reasonable public use of the assistance coupled with democratic transition also helped create a favorable environment for continued stability.

Structural factors

Regime type and strength: Ghanaian politics have generally been unstable. Since independence, the country has had four republics and five military governments. Following independence, Nkrumah tried to create a modern industrialized socialist state. The CPP became the party of the nation as Nkrumah created a personality cult and adopted the title Osagyefo (meaning "he who is successful in war"). He developed an ideology of "Nkrumahism" as he led the pan-Africanist movement and sought to extend African socialism while increasingly leaning toward the Eastern bloc. Locally, however, corruption by government officials and administrators became rampant (Nugent, 1995). As he became more dictatorial, foreign debt grew, reserves shrunk, and living standards declined. These factors led to the erosion of Nkrumah's popularity and authority. While he was on a state visit to Beijing in February 1966, his government was overthrown by a military coup. Nkrumah went into exile in Guinea where President Sékou Touré named him co-president.

General Joseph Ankrah then established the National Liberation Council (NLC) and became the head of state. In April 1969, Brigadier General A.A. Afrifa, who led the country into elections and democratic government, replaced Ankrah. In August 1969, a new constitution was ratified, and Kofi Busia of the Progress Party (PP) won, but Busia's government also suffered because of economic hardship. In January 1972, while Prime Minister Busia was abroad, his government was overthrown in a military coup led by Lieutenant Colonel Ignatius Kutu Acheampong. Acheampong became the president and the chairman of the National Redemption Council (NRC) and quickly established an austere program of self-reliance. In 1975 government reorganization replaced the NRC with a seven-member Supreme Military Council (SMC), headed by General Acheampong. Gradually, Acheampong himself also succumbed to lingering and growing economic problems. In July 1978, his chief of staff, Lieutenant General Frederick Akuffo, arrested Acheampong and became president and the head of the SMC.

Akuffo initially made several popular gestures including the reopening of the universities and partially restoration of freedom; however, Akuffo still could not escape from the economic hardship that had haunted his predecessors. He devalued the cedi several times, which led to steep price increases of consumer goods, followed by strikes. As a result, he declared a state of emergency in November 1978.

Another coup occurred in June 1979 in which Flight Lieutenant Jerry John Rawlings deposed Akuffo. Rawlings and his colleagues immediately formed the Armed Forces Revolutionary Council (AFRC), which immediately executed Acheampong, Akuffo, General Afrifa, and five other senior military officers and imprisoned others amidst outbursts of populist anger against them. In September 1979, Rawlings permitted the scheduled elections and handed over the government to Dr. Hilla Limann of the People's National Party (PNP). Economic distress, however, caused the political downfall of Dr. Limann in 1981.

In December 1981, Rawlings, with popular backing, overthrew the government, suspended the 1979 constitution, dismissed the president, and dissolved the parliament. He then established the Provisional National Defence Council (PNDC), but with the reality of the economic hardship and pressure to democratize, Rawlings stepped down in December 2000 as mandated by the new constitution, which allows only two terms in office. In the 2000 election, John Kufuor from NPP won and is currently leading the country. These successive regimes, both military and civilian, created an unstable and corrupt political environment in the country and hindered the country's potential for development.

Policy factors

Ghana once had one of the most developed educational systems in Africa. By 1983, however, the country faced educational decline, as the quantity and quality of the infrastructure deteriorated. Primary enrollment and adult literacy dropped precipitously. The governmental expenditure on education declined to only 1% of the GDP in 1983 and 1984 (Armstrong, 1996, p.85).

Like most African armed forces, the Ghanaian military has depended on foreign military assistance since independence. Initially, Ghana looked to the West, especially to Britain, for equipment, training, and command support. As Ghanaian politics became radicalized, Ghana's military diversified its sources of aid by developing ties to radical states such as the former Soviet Union, China, the German Democratic Republic (former East Germany) and Libya. After the Cold War ended, Ghana again turned to the West for most of its military needs.

The Ghanaian military, numbering approximately 7,200[2] in 1993, was capable of maintaining internal security and preserving Ghana's territorial integrity. Improved military relations with the United States further strengthened the military; in 1995, for example, Ghana's armed forces and US Special Forces held a joint military exercise in the northern region. Throughout the 1980s, the generally pro-Western armed forces relied on a variety of sources for foreign military assistance including: the United States, Italy, Libya, and the Soviet Union. During the 1980s and early 1990s, the Ghanaian armed forces and some police personnel participated in United Nations peacekeeping operations in Cambodia, Croatia, Western Sahara, Iraq/Kuwait, Rwanda, and Lebanon. Ghana also contributed troops to the Economic Community of West African States Monitoring Group (ECOMOG) peacekeeping force in Liberia and Sierra Leone.

The fact that Ghana did not experience an all out internal war does not necessarily indicate that the country was entirely peaceful. Ghana possessed almost all the symptoms of war countries including political instability, successive military regimes, marked economic decline, and the existence of multi-ethnic society. At times various ethnic groups were conflictual (e.g. the Konkomba and Nanumba conflict of 1994). Although the casualties that resulted from this clash met the threshold of 1,000 battle deaths for civil war or internal war dataset, this conflict still did not make the list since the conflict was regionally contained.

With the decline of the economy and the general instability of the country, the Ghanaian state usually practiced an accommodationist policy. This is specifically true for the regime of Jerry Rawlings, who accepted the constitutional reforms. In May 1995, there were demonstrations in Accra that demanded democratic transformations; unlike Somalia's Siad Barre, Rawlings accepted the constitutional reforms and stepped down after his second term ran out in December 2000. Such conflicts could have engulfed the country and caused it to descend into chaos and all out internal war. It is believed that this was averted mainly because Rawlings' regime was able to respond to the conflict fairly quickly, using a contribution of force and negotiated agreements (e.g. agreements on the Northern ethnic disputes, some of which broke down, but most of which were pursued steadily).

II. Tanzania

Tanzania is located in East Africa and borders the Indian Ocean on the east, Kenya and Uganda on the north, Burundi, Rwanda, and Zaire on the west, and Mozambique, Zambia, and Malawi on the south. The country, also a former British colony, was the result of the union of Tanganyika and Zanzibar, which formed the United Republic of Tanzania in 1964. Once again, although many of the factors that could lead to internal war existed, including severe economic decline and a border war with Uganda in the 1970s, Tanzania has been one of the most stable countries in Sub Saharan Africa. If poverty and multiethnicity are accepted as necessary factors that cause internal war, Tanzania is an anomaly. According to the World Bank during the 1970s and 1980s, Tanzania was one of the poorest countries in the world, ranking only slightly above Mozambique. Additionally, Tanzania has one of the most fragmented societies in the world with over 130 ethno-linguistic groups present.

In this section the factors that saved Tanzania from internal war will be examined. Loftchie (1993) suggests that the ability of the state to respond to the twin problems of severe and prolonged economic decline and the external pressure for economic and political reforms by quietly building a local coalition, willing to support both economic and political reform, saved Tanzania from internal war. Tanzania's leadership, specifically that of the late President Julius Nyerere played the greatest role in managing potential conflicts that could engulf the country. Calaghy and Ravenhill (1993, p.7) argue that Tanzania

> "...illustrates the ability of a government to respond to the terrible costs of prolonged economic decline and external pressure to quietly build a new coalition willing to support major economic reform...this coalition appeared slowly, haltingly, and unevenly, with important consequences for the lurching quality of the implementation of new policies. And it did so despite the 'profound mistrust, deep misunderstanding, and fundamental dissensus' of the 'tortured,' 'politically charged,' and 'ideologically accusatory' relations between Tanzania and the IFIs. One of the factors facilitating this coalitional shift from the 'socialists' to the 'pragmatists' was the long-term stability of the government, a factor not yet tested by free electoral competition."

Historical Overview

Around 1000 BC, waves of small, organized Bantu-speakers moved into the interior of what is now Tanzania from the west and the south. In 1498 Vasco da Gama, the Portuguese explorer, became the first European to visit the Tanzanian coast, but in 1698 the Portuguese were expelled from the East African coast with the help of Arabs from Oman, and Islam spread in the region. In the 1880s, the scramble for African territory among the European powers intensified, and within a few years the German East Africa Company controlled the area. Over the years, the company clashed with local groups and coastal Arabs. In 1891 the German government took over the country and declared it a protectorate. Between 1905 and 1907, the Maji Maji[3] revolt against German rule engulfed most of southeast Tanzania. At the end of World War I, most of the German East Africa colonies were taken over by Belgium in the Ruanda-Urundi territory and Britain in Tanganyika; however, at the end of WWII a wave of freedom fighting swept Tanzania and many other parts of the continent.

In 1954 Julius Nyerere and Oscar Kambona founded the Tanganyika African National Union (TANU). TANU easily won the general elections of 1958–1960, and when Tanganyika became independent in December 1961, Julius Nyerere, a strong postcolonial leader, became its first prime minister and a year later, Tanganyika became a republic, and Nyerere was elected president. In April 1964 Tanganyika and Zanzibar merged and Nyerere became the first president. Abeid Amani Karume, the head of Zanzibar's government and leader of its dominant Afro-Shirazi Party (ASP), became the first vice president. In the meantime, several violent clashes between African and Arab populations in the Island of Zanzibar exploded during this period.

In February 1967, Nyerere issued the Arusha Declaration, a major policy statement that called for egalitarianism, socialism, and self-reliance. It promised a decentralized government and a program of rural development called *ujamaa* ("pulling together") that involved the creation of cooperative farm villages. Factories and plantations were nationalized, and major investments were made in primary schools and health care. In 1977 TANU and Zanzibar's ASP merged to form the Chama cha Mapinduzi (CCM, or the Party of the Revolution). A new constitution was adopted the same year.

In 1978 the Ugandan military forces, under the leadership of Idi Amin, occupied about 700 sq mi (1800 sq km) of Tanzania territory. One month later, Tanzanian forces and Ugandan rebels staged a counter-invasion. Tanzania captured the Ugandan capital of Kampala in April 1979 and drove Idi Amin from power; however, this campaign further worsened the country's already precarious economic resources. Tanzania maintained troops in Uganda after its victory but drew criticism from other African nations for its actions.

By the 1980s, it was clear that the economic policies set out in the Arusha Declaration had failed, owing to either local mismanagement or international pressures, and the economy continued to deteriorate through cycles of alternating floods and droughts. In 1985 President Nyerere resigned voluntarily and Ali Hassan Mwinyi, President of Zanzibar, became head of the state. In 1992 the constitution was amended to allow opposition parties. In 1995 the first multiparty elections were held in Tanzania and Benjamin William Mkapa, candidate of the ruling CCM, won and served as the head of state. In December 2005 Tanzania had its fourth peaceful transition of power where Jakaya Kikwete was elected as president.

Contextual factors

Colonial: Unlike some other parts of the continent, Tanzania did not have long contact with European colonialism. In the Zanzibar Islands, Arab influence was very strong and actually contended with the Germans for the control of the territory. The German colonial state came to an end during World War I, after which Britain ruled the territory as a Mandated and then a Trust Territory.

Ethnicity: There are approximately 130 ethnic groups in Tanzania. These groups differ culturally, socially, and linguistically. The largest ethnic group, the Sukuma, represents nearly 13% of the total population; the remaining groups represent fewer than 5% each. As in Ghana, the groups appear splintered and were not easily molded into full scale political movements.

The majority of the population belongs to the Bantu-speaking peoples, including the Sukuma (the largest ethnic group), Bena, Chagga, Gogo, Ha, Haya, Hehe, Luguru, Makonde, Makua, Ngoni, Nyakyusa, Nyamwezi, and Nyaturu peoples. The Maasais speak a Nilotic language; the Sandawe group speaks a language akin to Khoikhoi; and the Iraqw group speaks a Cushitic language. Swahili, however, is the *lingua franca* of the republic.

Economy: Agriculture is the foundation of the Tanzanian economy. It employs approximately 84% of the population and accounts for 61% of the GDP. The Tanzanian economy continues within its colonial structure and concentrates on the production and export of unprocessed agricultural commodities and minerals. With *ujamaa* as a policy, population growth, recurring floods and droughts, and war with Uganda in late 1970, the country faced a severe economic downturn. As in Ghana, GDP per capita fell during the early 1980s and is only now beginning to rise to the levels enjoyed in the early 1970s.

The trend of economic decline during the 1970s and 1980s resulted from the fact that producers were paid lower prices for their crops while the costs of production increased. By 1978 peasant producers were withdrawing from the cash crop market in large numbers. In that year coffee production dropped by 22% and cotton production by 23% when compared to the previous year. Industrial production levels also dropped to 40% capacity by the early 1980s owing to power failures, unreliable water supply, and shortages of raw materials. The result was a sharp rise in the prices of consumer goods with inflation skyrocketing to 40% by 1980. Lofchie (1993, p.418) describes Tanzania's economic difficulties thus,

> "...everything had gone wrong that could possibly go wrong. Gross domestic product and per capita income had declined disastrously; production of exportable agricultural commodities had fallen sharply causing a major deficit in the country's balance of payments; excessive expansion of public services in the face of severe revenue contraction had led to excessive budget deficits and these, in turn, had contributed directly to spiraling inflation, declining per capita food production and corruption in the public sector."

According to the 1992 World Bank *World Development Report*, Tanzania's GNP per capita in 1990 was the second lowest in the world, topping only that of Mozambique, a country devastated by more than two decades of civil war. This led to falling living standards for all classes and the threat of a collapse of social services. The fall in living standards in this period severely eroded popular mass support for CCM and socialism. Worse yet, the economic hardship brought an increase in corruption and a proliferation of illegal business deals by government officials. Nepotism, smuggling, and the abuse of public property became common. As a result, Nyerere pushed anti-corruption campaigns between 1981 and 1983. During this period, several highly visible and symbolic actions were taken. In 1981 the Finance and Planning Minister in Zanzibar was dismissed, and in 1982 the Minister of Agriculture was fired after investigation confirmed nepotism in the state sugar enterprise. In 1985 Nyerere stepped down from the presidency and was replaced by his handpicked successor President Ali Hassan Mwinyi.

By 1986 increasing indebtedness and economic decline forced the Tanzanian government to accept a series of agreements with the World Bank. Tanzania became yet another African country forced by economic realities to abandon the socialist ideology of self-sufficiency and accept structural adjustment. As a result of this move and Nyerere's statesmanship, the country was saved from collapse. Tanzania is one of the few states in the region that experienced an increase in its ODA receipts. Between 1986 and 1989 ODA receipts increased by US $149 million, translating to almost US $14 in ODA per capita (www.OECD.org).

Structural factors

Regime type and strength: Julius Kambarage Nyerere, locally known as Mwalimu (teacher), was born in 1922 in Butiama village, near Lake Victoria, as one of the sons of the polygamous Chief Nyerere Burito of the Zanaki-speaking people. At the heart and center of Nyerere's political values was the fundamental equality of all humankind; he was committed to the building of social, economic, and political institutions, which would reflect and ensure this equality.

In 1967 Nyerere introduced idea of *ujamaa*, an African socialist family-hood, which was for many years the official political philosophy of Tanzania. He was genuinely dedicated to the liberation struggle in southern Africa, and he consistently supported movements such as the MPLA (Movimento Popular de Libertação de Angola) in Angola, Frelimo (Frente de Libertaçao de Moçambique) in Mozambique, ZANU (Zimbabwe African National Union) in Zimbabwe, and ANC (African National Congress) in South Africa.

By the early 1980s, Tanzania was facing a serious economic crisis, the result of a combination of a several internal and external factors. This crisis was a true test of the idealism of *ujamaa*. Mawlimu Nyerere's leadership proved to be effective, especially after he accepted the flaws of his vision. The president stepped down voluntarily and with dignity in 1985, and he continued to serve the country as a respected elder politician. Unlike many of his fellow African leaders, Mwalimu Nyerere did not steal his country's meager resources and stayed true to his conviction of equality. Tanzanians for more than four decades had a leader of unquestionable integrity who, despite his policy errors, was deeply committed to their welfare.

After Nyerere left office, the country's leadership shifted to Ali Hassan Mwinyi and after ten years to Benjamin Mkapa, and in December, 2005 the country went through its third election where Jakaya Kikwete was elected. Both of Mwinyi and Mkapa guided the country towards well-planned reform both politically in the form of multi-party democracy and economically in the form of stable growth.

Policy factors

Most of Tanzania's policy has been geared towards social development, first under *ujamaa* and later with market reforms. Unlike most of the African countries, Tanzania put greater efforts towards producing food commodities rather than cash crops (Callaghy and Ravenhill, 1993). The country also maintains a policy of increasing the literacy rate, which stands at nearly 50%. Primary education is compulsory and free. Although the enrollment is not 100%, by 1993 it was 82%, well above the average of 72% for Sub Saharan Africa. The healthcare policy in the country has also shown some results. By the 1990s the infant mortality rate had declined from 92 per 1000 live births to 72 per 1000 live births. Military expenditure in Tanzania has been low compared to many countries in the world; however, by 1978 such military expenditure jumped from 4.1% of GNP (or 14.7% of central government expenditure) to 9.1% of GNP (or 24.5% of central government expenditure) mainly on account of the Ugandan border attack in 1978 and the subsequent campaign.

Like other Third World countries, Tanzania faced severe economic decline and political instability (though less intense than other countries) that could destabilize the country. The fact that Nyerere stepped down in 1985 suggests that the state has been accommodationist towards the demands for change, and the nomination of President Ali Mwinyi of Zanzibar gave comfort to the more troubled half of the Tanzanian union. Although Tanzania has had a longstanding tradition of civil peace, the country has had its share of instability, specifically in the Zanzibar Archipelago.[4] Zanzibar has a history of civil violence, and the current political atmosphere in Zanzibar is one of profound tension and mistrust. Zanzibar's tense political environment represents a stark contrast to the Tanzanian mainland, which is characterized by a tradition of civil peace owing principally to the low saliency of ethnicity specifically in the political process. In Zanzibar the tension is specifically between the Shirazis and native Africans.[5] For the past 150 years, Zanzibar politics has been driven by intermittently violent tensions between ethno-political groups. Political violence in Zanzibar, for example, erupted in 1961 and 1964. These conflicts have the potential to spill over to the mainland, as evidenced by the Tanganyika Army mutiny that immediately followed the Zanzibar revolution in 1964; however, so far, like Ghana, these disputes have generally been regionally contained.

III. Zambia

Zambia is a landlocked country located in Southern Africa, which shares borders with Angola to the west, Namibia to the south, Zimbabwe and Mozambique to the southeast, Malawi to the east, Tanzania to the northeast and the Democratic Republic of the Congo (formerly Zaire to the northwest. With the exception of Tanzania and Malawi, Zambia's neighbors have been engaged in many conflicts, mostly struggles for independence and later civil wars (Mozambique and Angola), and borders were in turmoil from the 1960s to 1980s.

Zambia's former ruler Kenneth Kaunda (1964-1991), along with some other Africa's leaders, was very active in supporting the independence struggle against the Portuguese (Angola and Mozambique) and the apartheid regime of South Africa. Like Tanzania, Zambia also faced both fragmented ethnic groups and economic decline. Unlike Tanzania, however, Zambia is landlocked and depends on other states for its import and export activities. The country is dependent on copper as the primary commodity and source of hard currency. Zambia was badly hurt by the collapse of world copper prices in early 1970s, and by 1978 the country faced severe shortages in basic food (Pottier, 1983). Although Zambia resembled Rwanda in this respect, it still avoided the occurrence of internal war. The state, under President Kenneth Kaunda, also a giant figure among the early leaders, played the critical role of simultaneously dealing with the economic and political demands both locally and regarding the IFIs.

Historical overview

Bantu-speaking peoples reached the region and replaced the Khoiby around A.D. 800, but the ancestors of most modern Zambian ethnic groups arrived from present-day Angola and Congo (Kinshasa) between the 16th and the 18th century. By the late 18th century, traders (including Arabs, Swahili, and other Africans) penetrated the region from both the Atlantic and Indian Ocean coasts. They traded in copper, wax, and slaves. In 1835 the Ngoni, a warlike group from South Africa, entered Eastern Zambia. At about the same time, the Kololo penetrated Western Zambia from the south; they ruled the Lozi kingdom of Barotseland from 1838 to 1864.

The Scottish explorer David Livingstone first came to the area in 1851. He visited Victoria Falls in 1855 and was near Lake Bangweulu when he died in 1873. In 1890 Cecil Rhodes of the British South Africa Company (BSAC) signed treaties with several tribal leaders and began to administer the region. The area was divided into the protectorates of Northwestern and Northeastern Rhodesia until 1911 when the two were joined to form Northern Rhodesia.

The mining of copper and lead began in the early 1900s. In 1909 the central railroad from Livingstone to Ndola was completed. In 1924 the British took over the administration of the protectorate, and by the late 1920s extensive copper deposits were discovered, giving the area the nickname the Copperbelt. In the early 1950s, under the leadership of Harry Nkumbula, local groups fought against the establishment of the Federation of Rhodesia and Nyasaland (1953–63), which combined Northern Rhodesia, Southern Rhodesia (now Zimbabwe), and Nyasaland (now Malawi).

In 1959 Kenneth Kaunda, a militant former schoolteacher, took over the leadership of the independence movement and formed a new party, the United National Independence Party (UNIP). On October 24, 1964 Northern Rhodesia became independent as the Republic of Zambia, with Kaunda as its first president; he was reelected in 1968 and 1973. Kaunda's administration immediately faced the twin tasks of uniting Zambia's highly diverse population and gaining control over the economy from the Europeans, while steering the state in the midst of nearby, continuing freedom struggles.

As a landlocked country, Zambia had to depend on other states for exports and imports. Tanzania filled this gap, and the two countries cooperated on several projects. Trade items were transported to and from the Tanzanian port city of Dar-es-Salaam by plane and by truck. In 1968 an oil pipeline between Dar es Salaam and Ndola was opened. The crowning project, however, was the completion of the Great Uhuru (Tanzam or Tazara) Railway in 1975 that connected Dar es Salaam and Lusaka, Zambia. Throughout the 1970s, Kaunda supported the liberation movements in Rhodesia, Angola, Mozambique, and South Africa, mainly by advocating diplomatic solutions, an approach favored by the West. Beginning in the late 1960s, Kaunda faced formidable opposition from political and student groups protesting the growing concentration of power in his hands. In July 1964, Alice Lenshina, head of the Lumpa church, led a rebellion that was later crushed by government soldiers. In 1972 all political parties except UNIP were outlawed, and Zambia became a one-party state.

During the 1970s, the economic sanctions against Rhodesia and a drop in copper prices put Zambia's economy under severe strain. In the 1980s, as a condition for future aid, Kaunda was forced by creditors to introduce economic austerity measures. Shortages of basic goods, cuts in food subsidies, and unemployment led to rioting and strikes. Meanwhile, the country began to institute a multiparty political system. In 1990 another round of austerity measures sparked more unrest and an attempted coup against Kaunda. In the same year, the constitution was amended to allow opposition parties.

In 1991 Frederick Chiluba of the Movement for Multiparty Democracy party (MMD) won the majority of seats in the parliament. Chiluba's economic reforms, including plans for privatizing the copper industry, initially resulted in better relations with foreign aid donors, and economic conditions improved somewhat. Under Chiluba, however, corruption and nepotism were practiced openly. He filled all key positions in the administration and army with his fellow Bemba tribesman (Edgerton 2002, p.178). In 1996 Chiluba was reelected although the economic downturn worsened. Following a 1997 coup attempt, Chiluba declared a state of emergency; numerous opposition leaders and military officers were arrested, including Kaunda, who was freed in 1998 and announced his intention to retire from politics.

In 2002 Levy Mwanawasa was sworn in as the new president, facing a grave situation that includes the high presence of AIDS and a severe shortage of food. In 2006 Mwanawasa was reelected for another four year term.

Contextual factors

Colonial. The colonial history of Zambia began after Cecil Rhodes and his BSAC signed a treaty with some local groups in the late 1800s. The area had minerals, especially copper, and mining began in the early 1900s. In the 1930s, 4,000 European skilled workers and some 20,000 African laborers were engaged in the mines. The Africans protested the discrimination and ill treatment to which they were subjected by staging strikes in 1935, 1940, and 1956. Zambia's colonial legacy resulted in a highly diverse society and a tradition of union and labor movements that brought together persons of diverse ethnic backgrounds.

Ethnicity: Zambia's ethnicity must be categorized by region, as sections of the country have their own individual histories. Similar to the other two no-war countries, Zambia is highly diverse, and its ethnic divisions have sometimes been highly polarized in political parties and institutions. There are 72 different ethnic groups or tribes in Zambia, all with their own languages. Main groups and languages include the Bemba (31%), who live in the north and center around the Luapula provinces. Other groups associated with the Bembas include the Bisa, Mambwe, and other smaller groups. The Nyanja group (19%) inhabits the east near the Malawi border. There are also the Chewe, Timbuku, Ngoni, and other groups. The Tongas (13%) live in the south and are associated with Ila and other smaller groups. The Lozis (13%) are live in the west and are associated with the Lundas and other groups. (Rotberg, 1967; Dresang, 1974; Rasmussen, 1969).

Economy: Some 85% of Zambians work the country's relatively infertile soil as subsistence farmers. Commercial agriculture is mostly confined to a small number of large farms. The leading crops are corn, sorghum, rice, peanuts, sunflower seeds, tobacco, sugar cane, and cotton. Cattle and other livestock are also raised, and there is a small fishing industry. The mining and refining of copper, however, constitutes the largest industry in the country and is concentrated in the cities of the Copperbelt. Cobalt, zinc, lead, gold, silver, gemstones, and coal are also mined. There is very little manufacturing capacity, with the exception of small industries that include food products, beverages, textiles, construction materials, chemicals, and fertilizer. Hydroelectric plants supply most of Zambia's energy, more particularly the plant at the Kariba Dam.

From 1965 to 1976, Zambia enjoyed steady growth. Real gross domestic product (GDP) increased at an average of 4.3% annually. The price of copper, however, collapsed in the mid-1970s, and this, coupled with economic mismanagement, ushered in a long period of economic decline, ultimately undermining the government. Real GDP growth rates for the 1976-86 period averaged only 0.07% per year, and GDP per capita in this period declined at a rate of 3.5% per year. The sharp decline in GDP per capita is explained in part by a population growth rate of 3.9% per year in the 1980s.

The country's economy also suffered from the lingering effects of colonialism. When white-ruled Southern Rhodesia (Zimbabwe) unilaterally declared its independence from Great Britain in 1965, Zambia found it necessary to cut off all links with the territory that had been its most important trading partner and the principal outlet for Zambia's copper exports. Zambia began to look toward its northeast neighbor, Tanzania to replace this loss. The TAZARA railway neared completion in 1974 and promised a safe outlet for copper, but in that same year, world copper prices reached a peak and then began to plummet to new lows. In addition to the copper price drop, the country faced the added pressure of helping the independence movements in the south including southern Rhodesia (Zimbabwe), which became independent in 1980. These two factors threw the country into a downward spiral.

Structural factors

Regime type and strength: At the 1967 UNIP General Conference, Bemba politicians, led by Simon Kapwepwe, mounted a challenge for the leadership positions of the party held by Kenneth Kaunda. Their success provoked an anti-Bemba backlash among UNIP members, which led to removal of Kapwepwe, the Vice President of the republic, at the 1969 conference. In 1969 President Kaunda announced sweeping economic reforms, including nationalization of the copper mines. At the end of 1972, Kaunda signed into law a constitutional amendment outlawing all political parties but UNIP.

In 1973 Kaunda was reelected without any opposition; the voters were only given the choice of voting yes or no: for or against the candidate. It was clear that serious challenges to Kaunda would not be tolerated. During the Second Republic, national elections were held in 1973, 1978, 1983, and 1988. President Kaunda consistently won each of these elections with over 80% of the vote (Rasmussen, 1974). Kaunda used strong arm tactics, limiting freedom of the press and using the state of emergency repeatedly. He also had a strong presence in the selection of parliamentarians. In addition to the control of politics, Kaunda controlled the economy. For the first five years or so after independence, Kaunda extended his control over industries, including mines, banks, industrial and commercial enterprises, and agricultural marketing and pricing. All were put under the control of government parastatals.

By the late 1970s, the need for economic liberalization to correct the faults of statism and socialism became paramount. The country's economy began to decline in the 1980s, creating political unrest in the country. Kaunda's government was criticized for its poor economic performance. He was also criticized for the costs of standing against the minority regimes in Rhodesia and South Africa. As the economy grew weaker, Kaunda faced strong opposition. He used more desperate tactics by closing newspapers and jailing many prominent opponents, including Frederick Chiluba, who later became president in 1991.

Overall, Kaunda's policies were allied to Nyerere's Ujamaa, and he coined his own version of the policy named Humanism (Shaw, 1976). Kaunda, however, faced a different reality than his colleague Nyerere. The social make up of Tanzania and Zambia differed significantly. In Tanzania ethnic groups are highly fragmented and difficult to mobilize, whereas in Zambia, there are four major groupings, the largest being the Bemba. This made mobilization much easier. Frederick Chiluba, a Bemba, was elected in 1991 and reelected in 1996 despite the country's economic recession, open corruption, and nepotism. In 2002 Zambians elected Levy Mwanawasa president and he was reelected in 2006 for another term.

Policy factors

Zambia was created out of various groups and represents the careless borders created by the colonial powers, rampant in much of Africa. The country began its independence with unrelated ethnic communities. Rampant tribalism has thus been the cornerstone of the country's policy making. As noted, Kaunda's regime had close ties with Tanzania's Nyerere, and many of his policies, both domestic and foreign, matched policies in Tanzania's. In local politics, Kaunda spent less money on social policies, and this led to the country's high illiteracy and poor healthcare. Kaunda's Zambia was ethnically less fragmented and generally had a poorer economic base than Tanzania. Zambia also depends more on a single commodity, copper. In the foreign policy arena, the two were matched in their support of the freedom fighters in Angola, Zimbabwe, Mozambique, and Apartheid South Africa (Shaw, 1976). As a result, the country's military expenditure jumped from 1.9% of the GNP in 1970 to 16.7% by 1975 (ACD).

Like its counterparts, Zambia avoided an all out internal war. This does not, however, mean that the country has been peaceful. As Northern Rhodesia became the independent republic of Zambia, the country saw its first conflict. At the time of independence, there were frequent outbreaks of violent conflicts between competing liberation and interest groups. In July 1964, after Kaunda's election victory, Alice Lenshina, head of the Lumpa church, led a rebellion. Kaunda used force to suppress it, and about 1,000 people were killed. Kaunda's regime faced additional economic decline in the 1980s and political instability that has potentially shaken the stability of state. Although it took five years, after Nyerere, Kaunda too stepped down - in his case by accepting an election defeat - and he accommodated many of the local as well as international demands. Unlike Tanzania, the country witnessed several aborted military coups, the assassination of President Kanuda's son, and labor strikes that could have dragged the country into internal war. All three of the no-war countries had strong leaders who were willing to make way peacefully for successors at a time of economic stress and difficulty. This contrasts sharply with the ways leaders in the war states dealt with their opponents and uprisings.

III. Comparing the cases

The three countries, Ghana, Tanzania, and Zambia share a common trait in that they all avoided the occurrence of an all out internal war despite internal tensions during the 1990s. In this section, the three countries will be compared and relevant differences and similarities examined regarding conflict resolution or violence control. First, contextual factors including their historical, social economic, and politics will be considered. Second, structural factors including their regimes, leadership, stability, and quality of life will be examined. Third, the policies that the countries' political institutions produced that created the no-war outcome will be examined.

Contextual factors

All three countries experienced British colonialism, which created and enforced the arena of the state along with attendant institutions such as the bureaucracy, the military, the judiciary, and many more. Unlike Rwanda, none of these countries had a viable indigenous structure that ruled the entire present territory prior to the arrival of European powers. Ghana had the best developed pre-colonial state, the longest contact with the European powers, and bears the scars of divide and conquer colonialism. At independence the country possessed one of the most divided and ethnically politicized societies on the continent. That division has been the basis for subsequent state instability in the form of coups and intermittent ethnic violence. Comparatively, both Tanzania and Zambia had shorter colonial experiences. Tanzania was a mixed colony of first Germany and later Britain, specifically in Tanganyika and Zanzibar (which was earlier ruled by the Kingdom of Muscat, present day Oman). Today, Zanzibar represents the highest violence potential of the areas studied, both in the form of internal turmoil and secessionism. As for Zambia, Cecil Rhodes and his British South Africa Company (BSAC) created the current borders mostly to control the copper mines. This mixed and late colonial experience, coupled with the lack of pre-colonial divisions as in Rwanda (and to some extent in Ghana), gave Tanzania and Zambia relatively more stable societies than the others studied.

As argued, colonialism created and enforced export-based economies that pushed the production of cash crops and minerals. In Ghana cocoa played this role and provided the largest portion of the country's hard currency. For Zambia copper played this role. Both countries, however, faced the painful impact of declining prices in the 1970s (Zambia) and 1980s (Ghana). The governments of these countries often dedicated large portions of the fertile land and labor to commodity production. Once the prices collapsed, they faced the daunting issues of unemployment and economic decline (Callaghy and Ravenhill, 1993). With the exception of coffee, Tanzania relied on commodity exports to a comparatively lesser extent. Nyerere's adoption of *ujamaa* during the 1960's and 1970's made the country more oriented towards food production based on small farm holders. *Ujamaa* entailed policies of self-reliance and included extensive compulsory villageization, nationalization, and price controls. As a result, about 84% of the GDP and 61% of the country's exports came from agriculture. Although it faced economic decline during the 1980s, Tanzania, unlike many African countries, had covered its basic food needs (Loftchie, 1993).

The 1980s, also known as Africa's lost decade, brought severe economic decline in the region, and most of the countries, both war and no-war, faced severe unemployment (Adedeji, 1985, 1999; Callaghy and Ravenhill, 1993, Englebert, 2000). Although economic decline was the general trend, our three no war states differed in their decline. Between 1960 (or independence year if later) and 1992 (or most recent available data), Zambia had the worst per capita growth of the three, approximately −0.9%, followed by Ghana with 0.3%; Tanzania, however, though very poor, enjoyed a substantial growth of almost 2% during the same period (Eglebert, 2000).

On foreign aid, all three countries received a substantial amount of money from international donors. Tanzania received twice as much ODA as Ghana and Zambia during this period. Between 1964 and 1990, Tanzania received an average of US $287.1 million (or US $13.9 per capita), followed by Zambia with US $121.1 million (or US $21.3 per capita), and Ghana with US $ 66.5 million (US $5.6 per capita) during the same period (OECD.org). The adjustment programs of the mid 1980s devastated many economies in the developing world as many governments failed to meet basic governmental functions or their debt servicing requirements. 1986 is accepted as an arbitrary year when adjustment programs were imposed and 1989 as the end year of the decade. During these years, the no-war countries experienced an average gain of US $83.8 million (or US $0.80 per capita) in ODA. This gain, however, came for Ghana and Tanzania, which received a net gain of US $137 million (or US $9 per capita) and US $149.6 million (or US $4.2 per capita) respectively; Zambia on the other hand experienced a decline of US $ -35.07 million (or US $ -10.8 per capita).

Table 4.1: Contextual factors: 30 year averages for: ethno-linguistic groups and ODA (millions US $), ODA (1989-86), ODA (per capita US $), ODA (1989-86).

No-War Countries	Number of ethno-ling.	ODA (Mill US $) 1960-90	ODA (mill US $) 1989-86	ODA per cap (US $) 1960-90	ODA per capita (US $) 1989-86
Ghana	79	66.5	137	5.6	9
Tanzania	135	287.1	149.6	13.9	4.2
Zambia	41	121.1	-35.1	21.3	-10.8
Average	85.00	158.2	83.8	13.6	0.80

*Source came respectively from: www.ethnologue.org; www.oecd.org

As the Table 4.1 shows, the no-war countries were ethnically very diverse, making political and economic mobilization somewhat difficult; economically, however, they fared better than their counterparts as they marched towards the 1990s and received considerably more foreign assistance in the post-adjustment era. Their economies stressed self-help to a significant degree, as they absorbed this aid, and their governments were not known for high degrees of open civil corruption.

Structural factors

Structurally, the three no-war countries had both similarities and differences in their political institutions. The institutions explain why these states avoided internal war in the 1990s. All three countries had begun with charismatic, socialist leaning leaders during the peak of Africa's independence. Ghana's Kwame Nkrumah was at the center of Pan African movement and the creation of the Organization of Africa Unity (OAU) in 1963. Unfortunately, owing to serious ethnic divisions within Ghana and the geo-political reality of the day (e.g. the Cold War, Nkrumah was deposed by a military coup in 1966. As a result, the country developed an unstable political system, and since 1966 it has had eight presidents, of which five came to power through military takeovers. Flight Lieutenant Jerry Rawlings played a significant role in saving Ghana from the brink of collapse. As a leader, Rawlings saw his role as that of a watchdog for ordinary people, and he addressed problems of injustice and corruption (Nugent, 1995). Rawlings, unlike many other Ghanaian leaders, led the country through the difficult years of economic recovery and more importantly, gave Ghanaians back their national pride. Chazan (1983, p.75) argues that, "...without Rawlings' strength of character and unwavering determination, Ghana would not have survived the Economic Recovery Programs (ERPs) of the 1980s put in place by the ruling Provisional National Defence Council (PNDC)."

The postcolonial leaders of Tanzania and Zambia, on the other hand, were in power for longer periods until they stepped down. All three of these states produced instances of Africa's rare peaceful power transitions. The late president Nyerere's rule lasted for 21 years, and he relinquished power to Ali Hassan Mwinyi in 1985. He was then accepted as a dignified elder statesman and teacher, not only in Tanzania but in other countries as well, until his death in 1999. After Kenneth Kaunda stepped down in 1991 after losing a contested election, unlike Nyerere he faced problems including house arrest, the murder of his son, and many mistreatments from his successor Frederick Chiluba. All three states have witnessed periods of authoritarianism and ethnic conflict in politics; however, levels of corruption and kleptocracy have generally been lower than in the warring states and examples of attempted political accommodation more frequent.

In these countries, like their counterparts, the largest portion of the economy was consumed by the state institutions and bureaucracies. The states in the no-war countries consumed an average of 26.7% of the GDP. The Kaunda and Nyerere governments functioned in a somewhat similar fashion. Tanzania's government, for example, consumed 32% and Zambia 31.3% of the GDP. This was a result of the socialist-like policies of *ujamaa* in Tanzania and Humanism in Zambia. Ghana, on the other hand, had a relatively more market-oriented economy; the government consumed around only 17% of the GDP. As argued, high government consumption might provide the basis for mismanagement and corruption (Herbst, 2000; Schroeder, 2000). The no-war countries, however, continued to fare better in the Physical Quality of Life Index, reflecting better social services, than warring countries. They had an average GDP per capita of US $595; life expectancy of 51.3 years; an infant mortality of 91.3 per 1000/live births; and literacy rate of 42% (Hardin, 1990; Adedeji, 1995). Despite coups or attempted coups, these countries attracted more investment than the war countries owing to their relative political stability. The no-war countries had an average investment of 11.6% of the GDP; Zambia topped the list with almost 18%, Tanzania with 10.3%, and Ghana with the lowest at 6.2% of their GDP.

Table 4.2: Structural factors 30 year averages for: Coups, government consumption (% of GDP controlled by the government), investment in the economy (% of investment the economy attracts), infant mortality (death of children under one year/per 1,000 live births), literacy rate (% of adults that can read and write), life expectancy (average age between birth and death), GDP per capita between 1960 (or independence if later) to 1990*.

No-war Countries	# of Succ. Coups 1960-90	Gov. con. (% of GDP) 1960-90	Inv. (% GDP) 1960-90	Inf. Mort 1960-90	Lit. rate 1960-90	Life Exp. 1960-90	GDP per capita (US $) 1960-90
Ghana	6	17	6.2	99.2	39	51	554
Tanzania	0	32	10.3	77	44	51	594
Zambia	0	31.3	18.1	97.5	43	52	635
Average	2	26.7	11.5	91.3	42	51.3	595

*Sources respectively from: Bratton and Van de Walle, 1996
http://datacenter2.chass.utotronto.ca/pwt; www.worldbank.org

In Table 4.2 the no-war countries had relatively more stable political systems than the war countries; their governments consumed more than their counterparts; more importantly they helped to ensure that their people had a relatively a better physical quality of life

Policy factors

These countries' political institutions adopted policies, over the years, that paid relatively higher attention to social capital such as education, healthcare and other areas than the countries that experienced wars. The no-war countries spent less on military and military related activities than on social capital (McCowan and Johnson, 1988; Henderson and Singer, 2002).The three no-war countries spent an average per capita US $13.57 on education, US $5.87 on healthcare between 1960 and 1990, and per capita US $7 on the military. These countries spent 9.8% of the central government budget on the military, leaving a favorable percentage of the budget free for education and healthcare. For every US $0.50 spent on the military, the combined education and healthcare spending was US $ =1. These countries have also been comparatively less militarized that their warring counterparts, and have an average of 1.98 soldiers/100,000 population. Zambia led the group with 2.6 soldiers/100,000 population, followed by Tanzania with 2 soldiers/100,000, and Ghana with 1.35 soldiers/100,000.

Table 4.3: Policy factors, 30 year averages for: Military expenditure (% of GNP), military expenditure (% central government expenditure), military size (number of soldiers per 1,000 population), military expenditure (per capita US $), educational expenditure (per capita US $), healthcare (per capita US $)*.

No-war countries	ME(% GNP) 1960-90	ME (% CGE) 1960-90	Soldiers (1000 pop) 1960-90	Milex per Capita $ 1960-90	Educ. Exp. per Cap. (US $) 1960-90	Health exp. Per cap. $ 1960-90
Ghana	1.87	7.5	1.35	3.4	8.8	3.2
Tanzania	2.8	9.6	2	9	9.3	3.4
Zambia	4.9	12.3	2.6	8.8	22.6	11
Average	3.2	9.8	2	7	13.6	6

*Source respectively from: ACDA; SIPRI; Worldbank.org

Table 4.3 shows that the no-war countries spent comparatively less money on the military and more on social capital (education and healthcare) compared to regional averages and the war countries.

When comparing governance scores, the no-war countries had an average score of –1.53 (table 4.4), which is below the regional average governance score of –1.72 and significantly below the score of the war countries' –2.30. Tanzania scored the highest on governance at –1.23, followed closely by Ghana with –1.25, and Zambia, the lowest, with –2.1. Even Zambia's score was above the mean score for the war countries. Although the three no-war countries were not especially well governed by general international standards, unlike the war countries, they handled their domestic unrest more effectively by being accommodating to the demands for change from both local and international groups.

Table 4.4: ICRG governance scores for the no-war countries*.

No-War Countries	ICRG Score
Ghana	-1.25
Tanzania	-1.23
Zambia	-2.11
Average	**-1.53**
Regional Average	**-1.72**

*Source: Englebert, 2000

This chapter examined the circumstances whereby the sample states - Ghana, Tanzania and Zambia - avoided an all out internal war in the 1990s. The governance of these countries was examined from contextual, structural, and policy perspectives, and it was found that these countries were relatively better off economically (despite downturns) and less dependent on aid although they did receive relatively higher ODA than the war countries. They were also politically more stable and less militarized, and delivered relatively better quality of life to their citizens than their warring counterparts. In the next chapter, these two categories of countries will be compared in more in-depth.

Notes

1 On February 2, 1994 fighting in the north near the border with Togo broke out between Konkomba and Dagomba ethnic groups. The incident began with a dispute over prices in a market, but quickly accelerated to large-scale violence. The two groups have been at loggerheads for many years because the Konkombas, who are not Ghanaian natives, are denied chieftainship and land. Only 4 of 15 ethnic groups in the region have land ownership. One thousand people were killed and a further 150,000 displaced. Immediately, the government issued a state of emergency in the northern region (the districts of Yendi, Nanumba, Gushiegu/Karaga, Saboba/Chereponi, East Gonjo, Zabzugu/Tatale and the town of Tamale). About 6,000 Konkombas fled to Togo as a result. The government also closed four of its border posts to prevent the conflict from spreading.

2 Organized into a 5,000-member army; a 1,200-member air force; and a 1,000-member navy.

3 The conflict of the Maji-Maji Rebellion (1905–1907) originated in 1902 when German Governor Count Adolf von Götzen ordered that cotton be grown throughout southern German East Africa. The word maji in Swahili means water, and the revolt resulted from two coinciding factors: one mythical and magical and the other arising from colonial economic hardship. First, a young man named Kinjikitile Ngwale claimed that he had special powers and provided blessed water (maji) that could protect his followers from European bullets and drive the unwanted Germans from East Africa. Kinjikitile's reputation quickly spread. The second factor was the German decision to push the cultivation of cotton in the area. German colonial forces responded harshly to this revolt by unleashing a reign of terror against the locals. Using European, New Guinean, Papuan and

Melanesian troops, the Germans killed between 75,000 and 120,000. For details see: Thomas P. Ofcansky, Rodger Yeager and Laura Kurtz (1997).

4 The term Zanzibar refers to the islands of Unguja and Pemba and numerous smaller adjacent islands that comprised the formerly separate country of Zanzibar.

5 The majority of the population of Zanzibar identify themselves as "Shirazi", a term that is Persian in origin, not African. Most Shirazis believe that they are not an African society and tend to make a distinction between themselves and "mainland Africans." They argue that mainland Africans are more recent arrivals who came to Zanzibar as slaves, squatter farmers, or workers. Despite Zanzibar's physical proximity to the coast of Tanzania, Shirazis regard Zanzibar as a political entity whose most important cultural ties are with the region of the Persian Gulf. This sentiment explains why so many Zanzibaris were skeptical about the union with Tanganyika in 1964.

CHAPTER 5

FINDINGS, IMPLICATIONS AND CONCLUSION

This book set out to answer the question: how and why did some African countries south of the Sahara manage to avert internal wars in the 1990s while others did not? The book also set out to identify factors that contributed to the increased number of internal wars in Sub Saharan Africa during the 1990s (El Badawi and Sambanis 1999). It was that at the center of these wars was a complex set of factors reflecting bad governance. Governance allows an examination of multiple causes of internal wars. Since independence, many African states have been a source of unchecked power and wealth accumulation for those who control them and, in turn, became a source of suffering and poverty for the masses (Schroeder, 2000; Braathen *et al.* 2000; Herbst, 2000).

While the casualties from internal wars piled up, and refugees streamed inside and outside their home countries, there were still some states that enjoyed relative growth and stability. Botswana, for example, began at the same level as most of its African counterparts, but it also had the fastest growing economy in the world between 1960 and 1985 (World Bank, 1993). Despite the existence of such success states, overpowering images of death, destruction, starvation, refugees, gun and machete toting young men and their equally brutal leaders around the continent overshadow them.

A specific set of contextual, structural and policy factors support the argument that internal wars in Sub Saharan Africa occurred because of bad governance (Braathen *et al.,* 2000; Herbst, 2000; Adedeji, 1999). Context is defined as the historical, social, and environmental factors that the postcolonial states inherited or were forced to confront from exogenous circumstances. Structural factors are defined as the governmental institutions and their interaction with the political, economic and social settings. Policy factors include the specific trade off in decisions and budgetary allocations. In short, context entails the givens, structure entails institutions, and policy entails the choices the postcolonial states made since their independence.

Methodologically, descriptive-explanatory analysis was used, mainly on account of the open-ended nature of the research question. A qualitative case study design was chosen because the occurrence or non-occurrence of internal war is already a known fact and cannot be separated from its context (Patton, 1990; Strauss and Corbin, 1990; Yin, 1989). The six countries were chosen on the basis of geographical location, selecting two countries from each region (East, Central, and West Africa), and whether or not an internal war occurred in the country. The countries selected were: Somalia and Tanzania from East Africa, Rwanda and Zambia from central Africa and Sierra Leone and Ghana from West Africa. A series of questions were systematically designed to be asked about each country (George, 1987). After a study of the literature and prevailing theories several patterns have recognized. This chapter provides conclusion to the book and is divided into two parts. First, the war and no-war cases will be compared and the findings summarized. Second, some concluding remarks will be provided.

I. Findings

Contextual factors

Contextual factors are defined as the givens of the postcolonial states. Although several contextual factors were examined, colonialism was the most central; however, because all the countries in the region went through some form of European colonialism, it was adopted as a control variable, and distinctions were made among the colonial experiences where pertinent.

On the ethnicity/culture variable, many studies suggest that the existence of multi-ethnic groups in a country may cause internal war (Geertz, 1973; Haas, 1974; Rummel, 1977). In proposition 1a, we set out the following: The larger the number of ethnic groups, the less likely that the country will experience internal war. After counting the number of ethno-linguistic groups that existed in the six countries, it was determined that the peace-to-war countries (Rwanda, Sierra Leone and Somalia) had a total of 39 ethnic groups between them, an average of 13 groups each. The peace-to-peace countries (Ghana, Tanzania and Zambia), had a total of 255 groups, an average of 85 groups each. Thus, the proposition is not supported in this sample, although the degree of ethnic political mobilization appeared greater in the war countries. In Ghana and Tanzania, for example, stronger social groupings, such as labor organizations, tended to link the smaller ethno-linguistic groups in ways that were missing in states such as Rwanda and Somalia.

Table 5.1: Comparing the Number of Ethnic Groups Between the No-War and War Countries

War Countries:	Ethnic groups
Rwanda	3
Sierra Leon	23
Somalia	13
Total	39
Average	13.0
No-War Countries	
Ghana	79
Tanzania	135
Zambia	41
Total	255
Average	85.0

*Source: www.ethnologue.org

It was argued that foreign aid heightened debt levels and made many countries dependent on handouts, further supporting corruption and nepotism (Bayart, 1993; Bayart et al. 1999; Adedeji, 1999). Proposition 1b hypothesizes that: The greater the amount of Official Development Assistance a country received before SAP, the more likely the country will experience internal war. Two figures, ODA in million US $ and ODA per capita in US $ were examined. Between independence year and 1990, the no-war countries received an annual average of US $158.3million, whereas the war countries received US $73.4 million. The per capita ODA for the no-war countries was US $13.58 and for the war countries was slightly higher at US $14.15. It seems that ODA does not correlate with greater war propensity; therefore proposition 1B is not supported. One can argue, however, that if properly absorbed and put to social investment, such assistance may actually help avert warfare.

As the Structural Adjustment Programs (SAP) were imposed in the mid 1980s, the picture became quite different. The year 1986 was chosen as an arbitrary year for the start of SAP, and the two ODA figures was deducted from 1989, which is the last year of the decade. In this way, the picture was more revealing. The no-war countries fared better overall in attracting more ODA and investments mainly because of their acceptance of the donor economic and political reforms that the IFI's imposed. The no-war countries had a net gain of US $ 83.8 million between 1986 and 1989, whereas the war countries actually had an average ODA loss of US $ -21.2 million. The pattern could also be seen in the ODA per capita decline between 1986 and 1989. In the no-war countries, there was a slight gain of US $0.80, but the war countries experienced a huge loss of US $ -6.18. Although it was argued that aid was an overall contributor to internal wars, it seems that it has helped save our no-war countries from collapse, especially in the years between 1986 and 1990. There are still exceptions, as in Zambia's declining aid receipts and Sierra Leone's increase in the late 1980s.

Table 5.2: Contextual factors 30 year average of: ODA in US $ Millions, ODA per capita in US $, ODA 1989-86 in US $ Million, ODA 1989-86 per capita in US $ for war and no-war countries between 1960 and 1989*.

War Countries:	ODA (Mil. US $) 1960-90	ODA (Mil. US $) 1989-86	ODA per cap (US $) 1960-90	ODA per cap. (US $) 1989-86.
Rwanda	72.6	-6	12.2	-4.3
Sierra Leone	26.2	13.8	7.6	2.5
Somalia	121.3	-71.4	22.65	-16.8
Average	**73.4**	**-21.15**	**14.15**	**-6.2**
No-War Countries				
Ghana	66.5	137	5.6	9
Tanzania	287.1	149.6	13.9	4.3
Zambia	121.1	-35.07	21.3	-10.
Average	**158.3**	**83.8**	**13.6**	**0.80**

*Source from: www.oecd.org

Structural factors

Structure was defined as the form of a state's governing institutions after independence. The type of state institutions that were established and their relationship to the society was specifically studied. Several variables were looked at including: stability, physical quality of life, size of the state, levels of corruption, and the ability to attract investment.

In proposition 2a, the following hypothesis was set: The higher the Physical Quality of Life Index (PQLI) in a country, the less likely a country will experience internal war. Three indicators: life expectancy, literacy rate and infant mortality rates were examined. In all three indicators the war countries were worse off compared their no-war counterparts. Life expectancy, between 1960 and 1990, in the war countries averaged 42.3 years, whereas the no-war countries averaged 51.3 years. As for the literacy rate (percentage of people who can read and write), the war countries had an average of 22.3%, whereas the no-war countries averaged 42%. The infant mortality indicators (number of babies dying before age one per 1,000 population) revealed that the war countries had an average of 151/1,000 live births, whereas the no-war countries 91.3 per 1,000/live births. Thus the proposition is supported. It appears, that unlike ethnicity and international dependency, social service performance clearly distinguished war from no-war states

In proposition P2b, the following economic hypothesis was set: The greater the decline in GDP per capita, the more likely the country will experience internal war. Once again, the war countries had a worse economic situation when compared to their counterparts. Between 1960 and 1990, the war countries had an average per capita income of US $ 559, whereas the no-war countries had an average of US $ 595.

In proposition P2c, the following hypothesis was set: The more coups d'état a country experiences since independence, the more likely the country will experience internal war. War countries fared worse than their counterparts again. Military coups have been a normal occurrence in Africa especially during the Cold War era (1945-1990); however, the war countries were more unstable than the no-war countries. In this category only the number of successful coups since independence (until 1990) was measured. The war countries had a total of 11 coups (3.7 coups per country), whereas the no-war countries had a total of six, all occurring in Ghana.

In proposition P2d, the following hypothesis was set: The larger the portion (of the national economy) the state consumes, the more likely the country will experience internal war. In this category the average percentages of GDP consumed by the government between 1960 (or year of independence if later) and 1990 (or the last available figure) were measured. The no-war countries actually had a slightly higher percentage, 26.7% compared to the war countries' 23.2%. This difference could be insignificant, but also could partially be explained by the poorer economies or utter mismanagement in the war countries. In no-war states, such as Tanzania, government services, leading to better PQLI index scores, showed that it is the relatively higher government spending on social issues and lower corruption levels that count most.

In proposition P2e, the following hypothesis was set out: The smaller the external and internal investment in the economy, the more likely the country will experience internal war. Testing this, we note that the war countries indeed attracted less investment than their counterparts. The war countries attracted 4.8% of their GDP, whereas the no-war countries attracted more than twice that percentage at 11.6%. Investment, adding to economic growth, appears to help protect against the occurrence of internal war. Investment is likely to be affected over time by relative political stability, educational level and the overall political stability of the country (Englebert, 2000). All these have been shown to be superior in the no-war states.

Table 5.3: Structural factors, 30 year average of: number of successful coups d'état, % of the GDP government consumes; % investment in the GDP, Infant mortality per 1,000 life births, literacy rate (% of adult population that can read and write), life expectancy (years) GDP per capita in US $ for war and no-war countries, average between 1960-1990*.

War Countries	# of succ. Coups 1960-90	Gov. con. (% GDP) 1960-90	Invest. (% GDP) 1960-90	Infant mort. 1960-90	Lit. rate 1960-90	Life expect. 1960-90	GDP per cap (US $) 1960-90
Rwanda	2	22.91	3.92	130.5	24	46	468
Sierra Leone	7	29.57	1.5	177.5	19	38	675.
Somalia	2	17.19	8.98	145	24	43	534
Average	3.67	23.22	4.80	151.00	22.33	42.33	559
No-War Countries							
Ghana	6	16.93	6.23	99.25	39	51	554.
Tanzania	0	31.94	10.31	77	44	51	594
Zambia	0	31.31	18.1	97.75	43	52	635.
Average	2	26.73	11.55	91.33	42	51.33	595.

*Sources respectively from: Bratton and Van de Walle, 1996; http://datacenter2.chass.utotronto.ca/pwt; www.worldbank.org

Policy factors

Policy is defined as the choices states made after their independence. Several indicators, mainly governmental expenditures, were examined including military and military related activities, education and healthcare. In proposition P3a, the following hypothesis was set out: The lower the social expenditure (education and healthcare) as a percentage of the government expenditure, the more likely a country will experience internal war. This was true for this sample. The war countries spent an average of US $5.90 per capita and US $2.94 per capita on education and healthcare respectively; the no-war countries spent US $13.57 and US $5.87 respectively, despite their own poverty levels.

In proposition P3b, the following hypothesis was set out: The larger the military expenditure as a percentage of the budget, the more likely a country will experience internal war. This hypothesis was not supported. The war countries spent an average of 2.6% of their GNP on the military, whereas the no-war countries spent 3.2%. This figure does not reflect, however, the amount of military assistance the country received from various sources. Between 1980 and 1989, Somalia received US $194.4 million military aid from the US alone (Africa News, 1992). When military expenditure as percentage of central government expenditure was looked at, it was found that the war countries had spent an average of 14.2% compared to the 9.8% spent by the no-war countries. The level of militarization does seem to be a driving force for internal wars. One main factor is that the large number of trained soldiers and armaments becomes a highly destabilizing force, spurring activities such as private security schemes or even robbery during the period of economic decline (Reno, 2000; Chabal, 1988; Bayart, 1993).

Also related to the militarization factors in proposition P3c, the following hypothesis was set out: The larger the size of the military personnel, the more likely the country will experience internal war. This hypothesis appeared to be true. The war countries were more militarized with an average of 3.5 soldiers per 1,000 population, compared to the no-war countries, which averaged 2.0 soldiers per 1,000 population.

Table 5.4: Policy factors, 30 year averages for: Military expenditure as percentage GNP, military expenditure (percentage central government expenditure–CGE), number of soldiers per 1,000 population, Military expenditure per capita (US $) Education expenditure per capita (US $), Health expenditure per capita (US $) average between 1960 and 90*.

War Countries:	Mil. Exp. (%GNP) 1960-90	Mil. Exp (% CGE) 1960-90	Soldiers per 1000 pop. 1960-90	Mil. Exp. Per cap (US $) 1960-90	Edu. Exp. Per cap(US $) 1960-90	Healht Exp per cap (US $) 1960-90
Rwanda	1.87	16	0.85	3.3	5.1	1.2
Sierra Leone	0.82	4.82	1.2	2.7	9.1	3.0
Somalia	4.98	21.82	8.3	16.2	3.5	1.7
Average	2.56	14.21	3.45	7.4	5.9	2.9
No-War Countries						
Ghana	2.0	7.47	1.35	3.4	8.8	3.2
Tanzania	2.8	9.6	2	9	9.3	3.4
Zambia	4.9	12.28	2.6	8.8	22.6	11
Average	3.2	9.8	2.0	7.1	13.6	5.9

*Source respectively from: ACDA, SIPRI, www.worldbank.org

In proposition *Pgov* the following hypothesis was set out: The lower the governance score a country has, the more likely the country will experience internal war. This hypothesis was also true. The war countries scored lower than their counterparts with an average score of -2.30 and -1.53 respectively. The regional average was -1.72.

Table 5.5: The ICRG score for war and no-war countries*.

War Countries:	ICRG Score
Rwanda	-1.78
Sierra Leon	-2.23
Somalia	-2.28
Average	**-2.30**
No war countries	
Ghana	-1.25
Tanzania	-1.23
Zambia	-2.11
Average	**-1.53**
Regional Average	**-1.72**

*Source: Englebert, 2000

In summary, the study explored multiple factors related to attributes of governance in postcolonial African countries and how these factors impacted the outcome variable of internal war. With respect to contextual factors, the war countries were ethnically less fragmented, but they experienced higher levels of ethnic polarization. Also the overall level of ODA appeared to foster stability. Between 1986 and 1989, war countries also experienced a greater shock of decline in the amount of ODA both in total and per capita terms, whereas their counterparts, no-war countries fared better (see figure 5.1).

Figure 5.1: ODA receipts between 1986 and 1989 of war countries and no-war countries

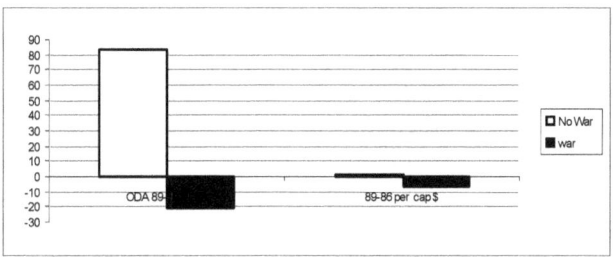

Source: www.OECD.org

The war countries had to deal with two interrelated dilemmas simultaneously. First, their economies were already severely weakened by the decline in commodity prices and/or end of the Cold War. Secondly, they lacked the effective leadership that saved their counterparts, the no-war countries, from economic shocks. Because of weakened economies mixing with weakened state power in relatively a bloated government sector, these countries were more vulnerable to the occurrence of an all out internal war, especially since these wars degenerated into struggles for the spoils of power. The sample countries have dealt with these difficulties differently. While the no-war countries were generally accommodationist,[1] the war countries have taken the opposite path and have generally been confrontationist.[2]

Structurally, the war countries tended to be poorer, had a poorer quality of life, were unstable, and attracted less investment. The states in the no-war category, displayed "better" governance with less overt corruption, and spent higher percentages of their GDP on education and healthcare than the war countries. In the structural and policy areas, the war countries relied more on the military (measured as a % of government expenditure), suffered more coups, and were more militarized compared to the no-war countries. Overall, the findings of the study support the hypotheses that the quality of governance brings or averts the occurrence of internal war in a country.

II. Conclusion

This book examined the relationship between governance and internal war. The study found that much of the literature that proposed variables such as ethnicity, economic decline and political factors as the culprits for Africa's increased conflict in the post Cold War era. Each of the explanatory variables previously advanced provided a partial causal link at best. Governance, on the other hand, encompasses much of these theories and provides a larger and more inclusive explanatory variable as to why conflicts occurred in certain countries and not in others. The word governance provides an important explanatory ability; however, one has to mindful of certain pitfalls that may mislead many analyses. These are even more prevalent in the African context, where since independence of many countries, there has not been a shortage of externally imposed governance styles, development programs, and cures for ailments that had very little to do with the reality on the ground.

During the 1950s and 1960s, Keynesian theorists preached the strengthening of the state, and it was accepted as the propeller for the society's development. This perspective, however, came at the expense of the development of a strong civil society and other entities, including the private industries. These policies, along with the reality of the precedent autocratic colonial state and the Cold War, were the basis for the flourishing of neo-patrimonial states run by kleptocratic leaders such as the late Presidents Mobutu of Zaire and Siad Barre of Somalia. By the 1980s, as the Keynesian based policies created highly bureaucratized and bloated states that showed many signs of failure. The donor states and agencies introduced yet another cure in the form of privatization and market-based economies, which preached, among other things, weakened the state capacities to effectively provide basic services including adequate education and healthcare.

This study identified several patterns that could provide both early warning of the occurrence of internal war and suggest possibilities for their resolution, creating implications for both scholars and policy makers. The main finding of the study is that internal war in the African continent resulted from bad governance specifically in economic mismanagement, inability to deliver political goods, and militarization. These hindered the overall quality of life of the society in these states. The study finds that the war countries lagged behind the no-war countries in all of the development indicators and consistently scoring lower in governance indicators and higher in corruption. The conclusion of this study needs to address two factors effectively. First is how governance has been conceptualized must be identified. Second, the lack of rebuilding efforts of the failed states must be noted.

Governance and Africa's reality: The issue of governance in Sub Saharan Africa has been conceptualized and enforced primarily by external entities that understand very little about these societies. It is imperative to understand two historical factors. First, most African countries were established through colonialism and maintained through neo-colonialism, the highly intrusive Cold War (1945-1990), and international financial institutions (e.g. IMF and World Bank). These were states but not yet fully nations; they remained economically dependent (though to varying degrees). Second and more importantly, outsiders supported the illicit commodity trade and provided the weapons with which they fought. As argued, most of the governance in these countries has been driven by outside groups that imposed conflicting remedies, such as strengthening the state during the Cold War era or strengthening the private sector in the post Cold War era.

The concept of good governance was introduced and enforced by institutions such as the World Bank, not because it is good in itself and deserved by the African people, rather, the object of the World Bank good governance project was mainly to provide favorable political environment for the markets to function properly and benefit, in most cases states and companies that are primarily in the West. As Tandon (1996, p.27) states,

Whose governance? It is certainly not governance on behalf of the common people. It is a governance on behalf of a couple of hundred industrial and banking trans nationals who are draining Africa's natural resources at enormous profit for themselves, a couple of thousand African billionaires who have tucked away their ill-gotten gains in Western banks, a couple of million white settlers who still own farm lands, mines and tourist resorts in Africa, and a couple of million black intermediaries who are acting on behalf of their foreign companies. That is the rough arithmetic of those who benefit from the rich resources of Africa.

Currently good governance is being marketed as possible only under democracy, hence the push for democratization since mid 1980s. The donor states and agencies made democracy the main condition for the support and legitimization of the African states. This push towards democratization, however, came at the expense of the states' effectiveness. Although democracy and state effectiveness are needed for the proper function of any governance, they still produce a controversy of their own. Democratization and its intricacies produce a rather confusing environment where first there are multiple definitions of the concept. How it should be set up and practiced is another hurdle. Despite the fact that democracy is increasing in Africa, much of what is being instituted are, in the words of Zakaria (2003), illiberal democracies where there are elections but not much rule of law or transparency and corruption looms high. Incumbents remained the sole candidates in recent elections in Burkina Faso, Djibouti, Egypt and Uganda.

The prevalence of poverty in Sub Saharan Africa also proves to be an obstacle in the formation and strengthening of democracy.[3] Despite the fact these confusions exist, democratic governance has still been paraded as the only way to achieve peace and economic growth. The reality, however, remains that stability and state effectiveness are often the result of the state's ability to enforce laws within its borders. Enforcing these laws is sometimes deemed by the donor states and agencies, most of the times selectively, as violations of human rights, and hence the states are then punished. Overall, many studies find that there is no correlation between economic growth and democracy. States like China, South Korea, Singapore, and Hong Kong did not have democratic systems, yet their economies have experienced high rates of growth. In closing, effective governance must be separated from democratic governance (Tardon, 1996).

Post conflict reconstruction: The continent has faced many internal conflicts, but their greatest challenge is the reconstruction of state institutions and establishment of rule of law in their territories. Many countries including Liberia, Somalia, and Sierra Leone are recovering form years of internal strife, and the new states often require strong support to rebuild the collapsed state institutions. In addition to the disappearance of law and order, the trust among the combating groups and legitimacy of the political institutions is often destroyed is. In the past few years, international efforts have been mainly focused on cessation of hostilities and signing of peace agreements, while neglecting other more pressing factors. As a result, many conflicts settlements are aborted (e.g. Somalia). In order to increase the success of peace agreements, the settlements must be accompanied by favorable political and economic conditions.

There is usually a lack of international finance and capital for humanitarian disaster and, more important, reconstruction after peace settlements. The conflicts in Sub Saharan Africa tend to be longer and deadlier due to the lack of support from the donor states and agencies.[4] This inaction is totally opposite to the response of these entities when disaster strikes in areas near Europe. Perhaps Vidal (1999) best summed up this issue and argues:

> Western governments, the IMF and the World Bank trumpet their generosity and speed of response in the Balkans; the world's rich countries, who largely dictate to the nominally independent UNHCR where international humanitarian aid should go, say $475m, or almost half the UNHCR's projected spending, should assist 3.4m refugees in Kosovo, Bosnia and other parts of the former Yugoslavia. A covert racism, too, may be developing. Have the Kosovans received help because they are white and are more identifiable to the 14 (almost all white-dominated) governments which provide 97% of UNHCR funding?

Many conflicts in this region usually restart after a peace deal has been reached and a government is installed. The donor agencies and countries continue their abandonment and the critical help needed to reconstruct its political and economic institutions is usually never provided. It is not a coincidence that many wars linger for decades and then suddenly find solutions of one form or another. It is important that policymakers, both Africans and non-Africans, understand the relationship between governance and internal wars and avoid sudden political and economic shock policies that exacerbate conflict.

Notes

1 Nyerere's 1985 stepping down from power, Kaunda's acceptance of election defeat in 1991, and Rawlings' acceptance of the term limits imposed by the constitution and his stepping down of 2000.

2 Habyarimana and the hyper-militarization after the attack by the Tutsi-led RPF; Siad Barre's military attack against the rebels and his refusal to accept the suggestion to step down; and finally Sierra Leone's Stevens handing over power to Gen. Momoh and the successive military regime that refused to compromise.

3 As Seymour Martin Lipsett pointed out way back in 1959, the more well-to-do a nation, the better its chances of transforming itself into a democracy. As a rule of thumb better-off countries with a GDP per capita of between US $3,000 and 6,000 a year are able to make the transition successfully - India being a notable exception to the rule. In Africa, only Mauritius, Botswana and South Africa fall into this economic bracket.

4 For example, the OECD aid allocation for Liberia is 0.2% of the GNP, far below the U.N. target of 0.7%. Moreover, the United States, which was formerly the largest donor to Liberia, is now the lowest rank among the donor countries.

APPENDIX 1

NOTES ON METHODOLOGY AND DATA SOURCES

In this section we consider the methods used in this study. Hypotheses are identified, along with the unit of analysis, the rationale underlying the selection of the cases, variables, measures and source of data, and method of analyses. The main research question is: How and why did some African countries manage to avert internal wars, while others did not? The study will compare countries that had relative peace in prior to 1990 and continued at peace with countries at peace before 1990s, which went to war in the 1990s. The study will examine the attributes of the postcolonial states and whether or not they contributed to the occurrence of internal war. Specifically, context, structure and policy variables will be identified and surveyed as potential pre-cursors of internal war. I will gauge the effects of independent variables from these three categories, according to the hypotheses generated, analyzing their separate and joint effects, trying to explain the occurrence of internal war in the 1990s.

In-depth focused case studies will be employed to compare these two categories of countries. The process of governance since independence is analyzed in relation to internal war. Yin (1984) suggests that the case study is particularly suited for situations where an event is inseparable from its context. Therefore, this study examines the "causes" of events by looking carefully at contexts (McMillan and Schumacher, 1984; Meriam, 1988). Yin (1994) suggests that in case study design there must be a clear link between the data and the propositions. He suggests the use of pattern matching, a technique introduced by Campbell (1975) in order to enhance construct validity. In addition to the above-described methodology, I will utilize the structured, focused comparative case study method (George, 1979). This method is appropriate for it involves asking the same set of structured questions in all the cases.

The following are specific propositions:

Propositions: the three main hypotheses established in chapter three are deconstructed into working propositions as follows:

Contextual

P1a: The larger the number of ethnic groups, the less likely the country will experience internal war
P1b: The greater the amount of Official Development Assistance a country received before SAP the more likely the country will experience internal war.
P1c: The greater the decline in GDP per capita, the more likely the country will experience internal war
P1d: The higher the Physical Quality of Life Index (PQLI) in a country, the less likely a country will experience internal war
Pde: The smaller the investment in the country the more likely the country will experience internal war

Structural

P2a: States with military regimes are more likely to experience internal war than those with non-military regimes
P2b: The more coups d'état a country experiences since independence, the more likely the country will experience internal war.
P2c. The larger the portion the state consumes of the GDP, the more likely the country will experience internal war

Policy

P3a. The lower the social expenditure (education and healthcare) as a percentage of the government expenditure, the more likely a country will experience internal war.
P3b: The larger the military expenditure as a percentage of the government expenditure, the more likely a country will experience internal war.

P3c: The larger the number of the military personnel, the more likely the country will experience internal war.

Finally, we will compare ICRG scores as a separate proposition since it encompasses all three variables and we propose that:

Pgov. The lower the quality governance score a country has, the more likely the country will experience internal war

Selection of Cases

The selected countries for the peace-to-war scenario are Somalia, Rwanda and Sierra Leone. The cases selected for the peace-to-peace scenario are Tanzania, Zambia and Ghana. A number of criteria were used to select these cases. In 1990s the peace-to-war cases must have experienced an all-out internal war as defined by Regan (2000, p.21), "...an armed combat between groups within state boundaries in which there are at least 200 fatalities." These cases as compared to those staying peaceful all experienced state collapse. This was a common phenomenon in Africa, e.g. Somalia, Sierra Leone, Liberia, etc. According to Zartman (1995, p.1) state collapse "refers to a situation where the structure, authority (legitimate power), law and political order have fallen apart and must be reconstituted in some form, old or new." Gros (1996, p.462) adds five attributes associated with failed states: "...economic mal-performance, lack of social synergy, authoritarianism, militarism and environmental degradation caused by rampant population growth."

It should also be noted that all is not hopeless and lost in Sub Saharan Africa. In the 1990s two different realities existed. Some countries experienced internal wars and in some cases state collapse after years of stability, e.g. Somalia, Liberia and Sierra Leone. In some peace-to-war countries wars have continued beyond the 1990s; e.g. Sudan and Angola. Even as the continent shoulders the largest burden of internal wars in the world, however, some countries show signs of development, democracy and positive change in the 1990s e.g. Botswana, Tanzania, etc.

Third and finally, cases were selected based on geographic criteria, from East, Central and West Africa, in order to broaden the scope of the analysis and enhance the generality of the study. The scourge of these conflicts has affected all the sub-regions of sub-Saharan Africa. Therefore, it is appropriate to have cases include all regions. Six countries were selected to represent the three sub-regions (east, central and west). Two for each region: one which experienced internal war, and the other which did not.

Variables, Measures and Sources of Data

Dependent variable: Internal war is defined as "...an armed combat between groups within state boundaries in which there are at least 200 fatalities." (Regan, 2000, p.21).

Independent variable

I. Contextual factors

Economic factors: Gross Domestic Product is the total goods and services produced in the economy. GDP per capita is an indicator of the GDP divided by the population converted into US $ on the basis of Purchasing Power Parity (PPP) exchange rates. The data come from University of Pennsylvania World Tables: http://datacentre2.chass.utoronto.ca/pwt/

Foreign aid officially known as Official Development Assistance (ODA) is defined as the money flows to the developing countries and multilateral institutions provided by official agencies including states and local governments. This fund is intended to promote development and improvement of the welfare of the developing world. The data will consist of: (1) the total US $ from ODA figures from the U.S.A. and EU countries from 1965 to 1990 and (2) the amount in per capita aid in US $. The data for this variable comes from: oecd.org

Physical quality of life (PQLI): Physical Quality of Life Index is a composite of several indicators (Life expectancy, Infant mortality, and Basic literacy), obtained from World Quality of Life Indicators, prepared and compiled by Schumacher *et al.* (1989 and 1990); the United Nations Population Fund (UNFPA: 1984, 1988, 1996, 1998), The World Bank (1986, 1990, 1994, 1998); The *African Development Yearbook*

(1986, 1990, 1994); The *Handbook for African Development* (1995, 1997); The *World Development Report* (1987, 1989, 1995, 1997), and The *Statistical Yearbook* (1987, 1995, 1998).

Ethnicity: Ethnicity is defined as: "...large or small group of people, in either backward or advanced societies, who are united by common inherited culture (including language, music, food, dress, and customs and practices), racial similarity, common religion, and belief in common history and ancestry and who exhibit a strong psychological sentiment of belonging to the group." (Ganguly and Taras, 1998, p.9). One measure will be the number of ethnic groups that exist in the country. Another measure will be the size of the ethnic group measured as percentage of the total population. Data come from: http://www.ethnologue.com/

II. Structural factors

Stability: Government transition from one regime to another. The measurement is the number of coups d'état since independence. Data come from the Inter-University Consortium for Political and Social Research (ICPSR), prepared and compiled by Bratton and Nicholas Van de Walle (1996), for the period 1910-1994.

State size: The states in Sub Saharan Africa are large, which affects the creation of viable private sector. Measurement is the percentage of the economy under the control of the state. Data come from http://datacentre2.chass.utoronto.ca/pwt/

Investment: The states in Sub Saharan Africa have difficulty attracting such investment. Measurement is the percentage of investment share of the GDP. Data come from
http://datacentre2.chass.utoronto.ca/pwt/

III. Policy factors

Budgetary choices: social vs. *military expenditure*
Social expenditure is measured because of its ability to increase the country's social capital. Measurement will be limited to education and

health. Measured as per capita US $. Data come from UNDP and World Bank.

Military expenditure is looked at both because of potential for security and because of its hindrance to investment in social capital. Measurement: (1) the percentage of GDP spent in the military, and (2) military personnel per 1,000 population. Data come from ACDA.

Governance score: qualities of governance scores were consistently low in the war countries. Measurement is the score provided by the ICRG index, which is a composite of six factors that indicate good governance. Data come from Englebert, 2000.

Method of analysis

The method of analysis is the qualitative, comparative case-study design. As George (1987) suggests, several preset questions relevant to the dependent variable and propositions are designed to provide uniformity, focus and organization to the study of the cases. The following are the questions that will be addressed as the case studies evolve, particularly, as connected to the outbreak and escalation of political violence.

First we will consider the general history leading immediately to the outbreak of political violence or to potentially violent situations where violence was averted in the 1990s Then we will consider the preceding contextual, structural and policy factors that were plausibly connected these outcomes.

Contextual factors
- What role did the colonial powers play in setting the particular political system of the country?

Ethnicity
- What is the number and proportion of the total population?
- Who is the dominant ethnic group?
- What is their percentage of the total population?
- How was ethnicity related to violent or non-violent outcomes?

Economy
- What is the basis of the country's economy?
- How did the economic trend fared over the years?
- How much ODA did the country receive both pre and post SAP era?
- What was the pattern of overseas in relations to violence potential?

Structural factors
Regime type and strength
- What type of regimes did the country have since independence?
- What methods of political transition did the country experience since independence?
- How was contestation over regimes related to the outbreak or non-emergence of violence?

Policy factors:
- What is the dominant policy (military or non-military) of the country?
- How much did the country spend on economic (i.e. food production, infrastructure, etc.) or social (i.e. education, health, etc.) activities since independence?
- How much did the country spend on military or military related activities since independence?
- Did military expenditure increase or decrease internal security?

APPENDIX 2

PRESIDENTS OF AFRICA SINCE INDEPENDENCE

Country, capital city, colonial power and date of independence	Ruler/ title/ method of ascendance	Years
Algeria Algiers France July 3, 1962	1. Ahmed Ben Bella, president. elected 2. Col. Houari Boumedienne, president, coup 3. Col. Chadli Bendjedid, president, elected 4. Abd al Malik Benhabiles, Chairman, Constitutional Council 5. High Committee of State appointed as collegiate president 6. Liamine Zeroual, president, elected 7. Abdelaziz Bouteflika, president, elected	1962-1965 1965-1978 1979-1992 1992-1992 1992-1994 1994-1999 1999-pres
Angola Luanda Portugal November 11, 1975	1. Antonio Agostinho Neto, president, elected 2. Jose Eduardo dos Santos, president, elected	1975-1979 1979-pres
Benin Porto Novo France August 1, 1960	1. Hubert Maga, president, elected 2. Col. Christopher Soglo, president, coup 3. Sourou-Migan Apithy, president, elected 4. Tahirou Congacou, president, elected 5. General Christopher Soglo, president, coup 6. Lt Col Alphonse Alley, president (Head of State), coup 7. Emille-Derlin Zinsou, president, coup 8. Lt.Col. Paul emille DeSouza, president, coup 9. Hubert Maga, president, elected 10. Justin Ahomadegbe, president, elected 11. Col. Mathieu Kerekou, president, coup 12. Nicephore Soglo, president, elected 13. Gen. Mathieu Kerekou, president, elected 14. Yayi Boni, president, elected	1961-1963 1963-1964 1964-1965 1965-1965 1965-1967 1967-1968 1968-1969 1969-1970 1970-1972 1972-1972 1972-1991 1991-1996 1996-2006 2006-pres
Botswana Gaborone Great Britain September 30, 1966	1. Sir Seretse Khama, president, elected 2. Quett Masire, president, elected 3. Festus Mogae, president, elected	1966-1980 1980-1998 1998-pres
Burkina Faso Ouagadougou France August 5, 1960	1. Maurice Yameogo, president, elected 2. Lt.Col. Songuele Lamizana, president, coup 3. Col. Saye Zerbo, president, coup 4. Maj. Jean Baptiste Ouedraogo, president, coup 5. Capt. Thomas Sankara, president, coup 6. Capt. Blaise Campaore, president, coup	1959-1966 1966-1980 1980-1982 1982-1983 1983-1987 1987-pres
Burundi Bujumbura Germany, Belgium July 1, 1962	1. King Mwambutsa IV 2. King Mwami Ntare V 3. Capt. Michel Micombero, president, coup 4. Col. Jean Baptiste Bagaza, president, coup 5. Maj. Pierre Buyoya, president, coup 6. Melchoir Ndadaye, president, elected 7. Cyprien Ntaryamira, president, elected 8. Sylvester Ntibantunganya, president, elected 9. Maj. Pierre Buyoya, president, coup 10. Domitien Ndayizeye, president, elected 11. Pierre Nkurunziza, president, elected	1915-1966 1966-1966 1966-1976 1976-1987 1987-1993 1993-1993 1994-1994 1994-1996 1996-2003 2003-2005 2005-pres
Cameroon Yaounde Germany, France, Britain January 1, 1960	1. Ahamdu Ahidjo, president, elected 2. Paul Biya, president, elected	1960-1982 1982-Pres

Country / Capital / Colonizer / Independence	Leaders	Period
Cape Verde Praia Portugal July 5, 1975	1. Arestide Pereira, president, elected 2. AntonioMascarenhas Montero, president, elected 3. Pedro de Verona Rodrigues Pires, president, elected	1975-1991 1991-2001 2001-Pres
Central African Republic Bangui France August, 13, 1960	1. David Dacko, president, elected 2. Field Marshal Jean Badel Bokasa, president, coup 3. David Dacko, president, coup 4. Gen. Andre Kolingba, president, coup 5. Ange Felix Patasse, president, elected 6. Gen. Francois Bozize, president, coup	1960-1965 1965-1979 1979-1981 1981-1993 1993-2003 2003-pres
Chad Ndjamena France August, 11, 1960	1. Ngarta Tombalbaye, president, elected 2. Gen. Felix Malloum, president, coup 3. Goukouni Oueddei, president, elected 4. Hissene Habre, president, coup 5. Idriss Deby, president, coup	1960-1975 1975-1979 1979-1982 1982-1990 1990-pres
Comoros Moroni France July 6, 1975	1. Ahmed Abdullah, president, elected 2. Said Mohammed Jaffar, president, coup 3. Ali Soilih, president, coup 4. Ahmed Abdullah, president, coup 5. Bob Denard, president, coup 6. Said Djohar, president, elected 7. Bob Denard, president, coup 8. Caabi Elyachroutu, interim president, elected 9. Mohamed Taki Abdulkaim, president, elected 10. Tadjidine Ben Said Massounde, president, elected 11. Col. Assoumani Azzali, president, coup 12. Ahmed Abdallah Mohamed Sambi, president, elected	1975-1975 1975-1976 1976-1978 1978-1989 1989-1989 1989-1995 1995-1995 1995-1996 1996-1998 1998-1999 1999-2006 2006-pres
D.R. of Congo **(Formerly Zaire)** Kinshasa Belgium June, 30, 1960	1. Joseph Kasavubu, president, elected 2. Col. Joseph Mobutu, coup, 3. Gen. Mobutu Banga, president, coup 4. Laurent Kabila, president, coup 5. Joseph Kabila, president, elected	1960-1965 1960-1961 1965-1997 1997-2001 2001-pres
Congo Brazzaville France August, 15, 1960	1. Fulbert Youlou, president, elected 2. Alphonse Massamba-Debat, president, coup 3. Capt. Marien Ngouabi, president, coup 4. Col. Joachim Yhombi-Opango, president, coup 5. Col. Dennis Sassou Nguesso, president, elected 6. Pascal Lissouba, president, elected 7. Col. Dennis Sassou Nguesso, president, coup	1959-1963 1963-1968 1968-1977 1977-1979 1979-1992 1992-1997 1997-pres
Djibouti Djibouti France June 27, 1977	1. Hasan Gouled Abtidon, president, elected 2. Ismail Omar Guelleh, president, elected	1977-1999 1999-pres
Egypt Cairo Britain February 28, 1922	1. King Fu'ad 2. King Faruq 3. Gen. Muhammad Najib, president, coup (led by Col. Gamal Abdul Nasser) 4. Col. Gamal Abdul Nasser, president 5. Col. Anwar Sadat, president, elected 6. Lt. Col. Hosni Mubarak, president, elected	1922-1936 1936-1952 1953-1954 1954-1970 1970-1981 1981-pres
Equatorial Guinea Malabo Spain October 12, 1968	1. Francisco Macia Nguema, president, elected 2. Lt. Col. Teodoro Obiango Nguma Mbasogo, president, coup	1968-1979 1979-pres
Eritrea Asmara	1. Issaias Afewerki, president, elected	1993-pres

Italy, Ethiopia May 24, 1993		
Ethiopia Addis Ababa Italy 1941	1. Emperor Haile Selassie 2. Lt. Col. Aman Andom, chairman, coup 3. Brig. Gen. Teferi Beanti, chairman, coup 4. Col. Mengistu Haile Mariam, chairman, coup 5. Meles Zenawi, president, elected 6. Negasso Gidada, president, elected 7. Girma Wolde-Giorgis, president, elected	1930-1974 1974-1974 1974-1977 1977-1991 1991-1995 1995-2001 2001-pres
Gabon Libreville France August 17, 1960	1. Leon M'Ba, president, elected 2. Omar Albert-Bernard Bongo, president, elected	1961-1967 1967-pres
Gambia Banjul Great Britain February 18, 1965	1. Dawda Jawara, prime minister/president, elected 2. Capt. Yahya Jammeh, president, coup	1965-1994 1994-pres
Ghana Accra Great Britain March 6, 1957	1. Kwame Nkrumah, prime minister/ president, elected 1. Lt. Gen. Joseph Ankrah, chairman, coup 2. Brig. Gen. Akwasi Afrifa, chairman, elected 3. Kofi Busia, prime minister, elected 4. Lt. Col. Ignatius K. Achaempong, chairman, coup 5. Gen. Frederick Akuffo, chairman, coup 6. Flight Lt. Jerry Rawlings, chairman, coup 7. Dr. Hilla Liman, president, elected 8. Flight Lt. Jerry Rawlings, president, coup 9. John Kufuor, president, elected	1957-1966 1966-1969 1969-1970 1969-1972 1972-1978 1978-1979 1979-1979 1979-1981 1981-2000 2000-pres
Guinea Conakry France October 2, 1958	1. Ahmed Sékou Touré, president, elected 2. Col. Lansana Conte, president, coup	1958-1984 1984-pres
Guinea Bissau Bissau Portugal September 10, 1974	1. Luiz De Almeida Cabral, president, elected 2. Gen. Joao Bernardo Vieira, president, coup 3. Malam Bacai Sanha, interim president, coup 4. Kumba Yala, president, elected 5. Henrique Rosa, interim president, coup 6. Gen. Joao Bernardo Vieira, president, elected	1974-1980 1980-1999 1999-2000 2000-2003 2003-2004 2005-pres
Ivory Coast Abidjan (de facto) Yamoussoukro (official) France August 7, 1960	1. Felix Houphouet-Boigny, president, elected 2. Henri Konan Bedie, president, elected 3. Gen. Robert Guei, president, coup 4. Laurent Gbagbo, president, elected	1960-1993 1993-1999 1999-2000 2000-pre
Kenya Nairobi Great Britain December 12, 1963	1. Jomo Kenyatta, prime minister/president, elected 2. Daniel Arap Moi, president, elected 3. Mwai Kibaki, president, elected	1963-1978 1978-2002 2002-pres
Lesotho Maseru Great Britain October 4, 1966	1. King Motletlehi Moshoeshoe II 2. Chief Joseph Leabua Jonathan, coup 3. Maj. Gen Justin Metsing Lekhanya, chairman, coup 4. Col. Elias Phisoana Ramaema, chairman, coup 5. Dr. Ntsu Mokhehle, prime minister, elected 6. King Letsie III (as head of state) 7. King Moshoeshoe II (as head of state) 8. King Letsie III (as head of state)	1966-1970 1970-1986 1986-1991 1991-1993 1993-1994 1994-1994 1995-1996 1996-pres
Liberia Monrovia USA Territory July 26, 1847	1. 18 Presidents between 1847-1944 2. William Taubman, president, elected 3. William Tolbret, president, elected 4. M. Sgt. Samuel Doe, president, coup	 1944-1971 1971-1980 1980-1990

	5. Amos Sawyer, interim president, elected	1990-1994
	6. David Kpomakpor, chairman, elected	1994-1995
	7. Prof. Wilton Sankawulo, chairman, elected	1995-1996
	8. Ruth Perry, chairwoman, elected	1996-1997
	9. Charles Taylor, president, elected	1997-2003
	10 Moses Blah, interim president, elected	2003-2003
	11 Gyude Bryant, interim president, elected	2003-2005
	12 Ellen Johnson-Sirleaf, president, elected	2005-pres
Libya Tripoli Italy December 24, 1951	1. King Idris al-Sanusi 2. Col. Muammar Qaddafi, president, coup	1951-1969 1969-pres
Madagascar Antananarivo France June 26, 1960	1. Philbert Tsiranana, president, elected 2. Gen. Gabriel Ramanantsoa, president, coup 3. Col. Richard Ratsimandrava, president, coup 4. Gen. Gilles Andria Mahazo, president, coup 5. Lt. Comdr. Didier Ratsiraka, president, coup 6. Prof. Albert Zafy, president, elected 7. Norbert Ratsirahonana, interim president, elected 8. Lt. Comdr. Didier Ratsiraka, president, elected 9. Marc Ravalomanana, president, elected	1960-1972 1972-1975 1975-1975 1975-1975 1975-1993 1993-1996 1996-1997 1997-2002 2002-pres
Malawi Lilongwe Great Britain July 6, 1964	1. Hastings kamuzu Banda, prime minister/president, elected 2. Gwanda Chakuamba, chairman, elected 3. Bakili Muluzi, president, elected 4. Bingu wa Mutharika, president, elected	1964-1994 1993-1993 1994-2004 2004-pres
Mali Bamako France September 22, 1960	1. Modibo Keita, president, elected 2. Lt. Moussa Traore, president, coup 3. Lt. Col. Amadou Toumani Toure, acting head of state, coup 4. Alpha Omar Konare, president, elected 5. Amadou Toumani Toure, president, elected	1959-1968 1968-1991 1991-1991 1992-2002 2002-pres
Mauritania Nouakchott France November 28, 1960	1. Mukhtar Ould Daddah, president, elected 2. Lt. Col. Mustapha Ould Mohamed Salek, chairman, coup 3. Lt. Col Mohammed Mohamoud Ould Louly, president, coup 4. Lt. Col Mohamed Khouna Haidalla, president, coup 5. Col. Maawiya Ould Sid Ahmed Taya, president, coup 6. Col. Ely Ould Mohammed Vall, chairman, coup	1961-1978 1978-1979 1979-1980 1980-1984 1984-2005 2005-pres
Mauritius Port Louis Britain March 12, 1968	1. Seewoosagur Ramgoolam, prime minister, elected 2. Anerood Jagnauth, prime minister, elected 3. Veerasamy Ringadoo, president, elected 4. Cassam Uteem, president, elected 5. Karl Hoffman, president, elected 6. Anerood Jagnauth, president, elected	1968-1982 1982-1995 1992-1992 1992-2002 2002-2003 2003-pres
Morocco Rabat France March 2, 1956	1. King Mohamed V 2. King Hassan II 3. King Mohamed VI	1956-1961 1961-1999 1999-present
Mozambique Maputo Portugal June 25, 1975	1. Samora Moises Machel, president, elected 2. Joachim Alberto Chissano, president, elected 3. Armando Guebuza, president, elected	1975-1986 1986-2002 2005-pres
Namibia Windhoek Germany, South Africa March, 21, 1990	1. Sam Nujoma, president, elected 2. Hifikepunye Pohamba, president, elected	1990-2004 2004-pres

Appendix 2: Presidents of African countries

Niger Niamey France August 8, 1960	1. Diori Haman, president, elected 2. Maj. Gen. Seyni Kountché, president, coup 3. Col. Ali Seybou, president, coup 4. Lt. Col. Mahamane Ousmane, president, elected 5. Lt. Col. Ibrahim Mainssara Barre, president, coup 6. Maj. Daouda Malam Wanké, president, coup 7. Mamadou Tandja, president, elected	1960-1974 1974-1987 1987-1993 1993-1996 1996-1999 1999-1999 1999-pres
Nigeria Abuja Great Britain October 1, 1960	1. Sir Abubakar Tafawa Balewa, prime minister, elected 2. Benjamin Nnamdi Azikiwe, president, elected 3. Gen. Johnson Aguiyi- Ironsi, chairman, coup 4. Gen. Yakubu Gowon, chairman, coup 5. Gen. Murtala Ramat Muhammad, chairman, coup 6. Lt. Gen. Olusegun Obasanjo, chairman, coup 7. Alhaji Shehu Shagari, president, elected 8. Maj. Gen. Muhammadu Buhari, chairman, coup 9. Maj. Gen Ibrahim Babangida, president, elected 10. Ernest Shonekan, interim president, elected 11. Gen. Sani Abacha, chairman, coup 12. Gen. Abdulsalami Abubakar, head of state, elected 13. Olusegun Obasanjo, president, elected	1960-1966 1963-1966 1966-1966 1966-1975 1975-1976 1976-1979 1979-1983 1983-1985 1985-1993 1993-1993 1993-1998 1998-1999 1999-pres
Rwanda Kigali Germany, Belgium July 1, 1962	1. Grégoire Kayibanda, president, elected 2. Maj. Gen. Juvénal Habyarimana, president, coup 3. Dr. Théodore Sindikubwabo, interim president, elected 4. Pasteur Bizimungu, president, elected 5. Gen. Paul Kagame, president, elected	1961-1973 1973-1994 1994-1994 1994-2000 2000-pres
Sao Tome and Principe Sao Tome Portugal July 12, 1975	1. Manuael pinto da Costa, president, elected 2. Miguel Trovoada, president, elected 3. Fradique de Menezes, president, elected	1975-1991 1991-2001 2001-pres
Senegal Dakar France August 20, 1960	1. Leopold Sedar Singhore, president, elected 2. Abdou Diouf, president, elected 3. Abdoulaye Wade, president, elected	1960-1981 1981-2000 2000-pres
Seychelles Victoria Great Britain June 29, 1976	1. James Mancham, president, elected 2. Albert Rene, president, elected 3. James Michel, president, elected	1976-1977 1977-2004 2004-pres
Sierra Leone Freetown Great Britain April 27, 1961	1. Sir. Milton Margai, prime minister, elected 2. Lt. Col. Andrew Juxon-Smith, chairman, coup 3. Siaka Probyn Stevens, prime minister/ president, elected 4. Maj. Gen. Dr. Saidu Momoh, president, elected 5. Capt. Valentine Strasser, chairman, coup 6. Brig. Gen. Julius Maada Bio, president, coup 7. Ahmad Tajan Kabah, president, elected 8. Maj. Johnny Paul Koroma, chairman, coup 9. Ahmad Tajan Kabah, president, elected	1961-1967 1967-1968 1968-1985 1985-1992 1992-1996 1996-1996 1996-1997 1997-1998 1998-pres
Somalia Mogadishu Italy, Great Britain July 1, 1960	1. Aden Abdulle Osman Daar, president, elected 2. Abdirashid Ali Chirmarke, president, elected 3. Maj. Gen. Mohamed Siad Barre, president, coup 4. Ali Mahdi Mohamed, president, elected 5. Abdiqaasim Salaad Hassan, president, elected 6. Abdulahi Yusuf Ahmed, president, elected	1960-1967 1967-1969 1969-1991 1991-1997 2000-2004 2004- pres

South Africa Pretoria Great Britain 1961	1. Dr. Hendrik Verwoerd, president, elected 2. B.J. Vorster, president, elected 3. Peter W. Botha, president, elected 4. Chris Heunis, president, elected 5. Frederik de Klerk, president, elected 6. Nelson Mandela, president, elected 7. Thabo Mbeki, president, elected	1958-1966 1966-1978 1978-1989 1989-1989 1989-1994 1994-1999 1999-pres
Sudan Khartoum Great Britain, Egypt January 1, 1956	1. Ismail al Azhari, prime minister, elected 2. Abdullah Khalil, prime minister, elected 3. Lt. Gen. Ibrahim Abboud, prime minister, coup 4. el-Khatim el-Khalifah, prime minister, elected 5. Muhammad Ahmad Mahgoub, prime minister, elected 6. Sayed Sadiq el-Mahdi, prime minister, elected 7. Muhammad Ahmad Mahgoub, prime minister, elected 8. Abubakr Awadallah, prime minister, elected 9. Field Marshal Gaafar Mohammed Nimeiri, president, coup 10. Lt. Gen. Abdel Rahman Swar al Dahab, chairman, coup 11. Ahmed Ali el-Mirghani, president, elected 12. Omar Hassan Ahmad al-Bashir, president, elected	1956-1956 1956-1958 1958-1964 1964-1965 1965-1966 1966-1967 1967-1969 1969-1969 1969-1985 1985-1985 1986-1989 1989-pres
Swaziland Mbabane Great Britain September 6, 1968	1. King Sobhuza II 2. Queen Dzeliwe (Regent) 3. Queen Ntombi (Regent) 4. King Mswati III	1922-1982 1982-1983 1983-1986 1986-pres
Tanzania Dar es Salaam (Dodoma) Great Britain, Germany April, 1964	1. Julius Nyrere, prime minister, elected 2. Rashidi M. Kawawa, prime minister, elected 3. Julius Nyrere, president, elected 4. Ali Hassan Mwinyi, president, elected 5. Benjamin Mkapa, president, elected 6. Jakaya Kikwete, president, elected	1961-1962 1962-1962 1962-1985 1985-1995 1995-2005 2005-pres
Togo Lome Germany, France April 27, 1960	1. Sylvanus Olympio, president, elected 2. Nicolas Grunitzky, president, coup 3. Col. Kleber Dadjo, chairman, coup 4. Gen. Gnassingbe Eyadema, president, coup 5. Faure Gnassingbe, president, elected	1960-1963 1963-1967 1967-1967 1967-2005 2005-pres
Tunisia Tunis France March 20, 1956	1. Habib Bourguiba, president, elected 2. Zine El Abidine Ben Ali, president, coup	1956-1987 1987-pres
Uganda Kampala Great Britain October 9, 1962	1. Milton Obote, prime minister/president, elected 2. Idi Amin, president, coup 3. Yusufu Lule, interim president, coup 4. Godfrey Binaisa, chairman, coup 5. Paulo Mwanga, chairman, elected 6. Milton Obote, president, elected 7. Lt. Gen. Tito Okello, president, coup 8. Yoweri Museveni, president, coup	1962-1971 1971-1979 1979-1979 1979-1980 1980-1980 1980-1985 1985-1986 1986-pres
Zambia Lusaka Great Britain October 24, 1964	1.Kenneth Kaunda, president, elected 2. Frederick Chiluba, president, elected 3. Levy Mwanawasa, president, elected	1964-1991 1991-2002 2002-pres
Zimbabwe Harare Great Britain April 18, 1980	1. Canaan Banana, president, elected 2. Robert Mugabe, prime minister(1980)/ president(1988), elected	1980-1987 1980-pres

BIBLIOGRAPHY

Abernathy, David (1983). *Bureaucratic Growth and Economic Decline in Sub-Saharan Africa.* Annual Meeting of the African Studies Association. Boston, MA.

Adebajo, Adekeye and Chris Landsberg (2000). "Back to the Future: UN Peacekeeping in Africa," *International Peacekeeping*, vol. 7, no. 4 (Winter 2000), pp. 162-188.

Adedeji, Adebayo and Timothy M. Shaw (1985). *Economic Crisis in Africa: African Perspectives on Development Problems and Potentials.* Boulder, CO: Lynne Rienner Publishers.

Adedeji, Adebayo (1993). "Marginalization and Marginality: Contexts, Issues and Viewpoints," in Adedeji (ed.) *Africa Within the World: Beyond Dispossession and Dependence.* London: Zed Books.

____, (1995). "Structural Adjustment, Democratization and Rising Ethnic Tensions in Africa," *Development and Change*, vol. 26, no. 2, pp. 355-374.

____, (1999). "Comprehending African Conflicts," in Adedeji (ed.) *Comprehending African Conflicts: The Search for Sustainable Peace and Good Governance.* London: Zed Books.

African Rights (1995). *Rwanda: Death, Despair and Defiance.* London: African-Rights.

Ake, Claude (1980). *A Political Economy of Africa.* London: Longman.

Alao, Adiodun and Funni Olonisakin (1998). "Post Cold War Africa: Ethnicity, Ethnic Conflict and Security," in Adebayo Oyebade and Abiodun Alao (eds.) *Africa After the Cold War.* Trenton: Africa World Press. Pp. 117-142.

Alao, Charles Abiodun (1999). "The Problem of the Failed State in Africa," in Muthia Alagappa and Takashi Inoguchi (eds.) *International Security Management and the United Nations.* Tokyo: United Nations University Press. Pp. 83-102.

Alesina, Alberto, Reza Baqir and William Easterly (1997). "Public Goods and Ethnic Divisions," *World Banking Paper*, no. 6009.

Ali, Mohamed Nuh (1985). *History in the Horn of Africa, 1000 BC to 1500 AD.* Ph.D. Dissertation. University of California in Los Angeles.

Ali, Taisier and Robert O. Mathews (eds.) (1999). *Civil Wars in Africa: Roots and Resolution.* Montreal: McGill-University Press.

Apter, David (1963). "Political Religion in New States," in Clifford Geertz (ed.) *Old Societies in New States*. Glencoe, IL: Free Press. Pp.57-144.

Aristotle (1958). *Politics*. (Edited and Translated by Ernest Baker). London: Oxford University Press.

Armstrong, Robert P. (1996). Ghana Country Assistance Review: A Study in Development Effectiveness. *World Bank Operations Evaluation Study*, no. 1011-0984.

Auvinen, Juha and E. Wayne Nafziger (1999). "The Sources of Humanitarian Emergencies," *The Journal of Conflict Resolution*, vol. 43, no. 3, pp. 267-290.

Ayittey, George B. N. (1994). "The Somali Crisis: Time For an African Solution," *Policy Analysis*, no. 205 (March 28), p.3.

____, (1998). *Africa in Chaos*. New York, NY: St. Martin Press.

____, (2005). *Africa Unchained*. New York, NY: Palgrave Macmillan.

Ayoob, Mohammed (1995). *The Third World Security Predicament: State Making, Regional Conflict, and the International System*. Boulder, CO: Lynne Rienner Publishers.

Azam, Jean-Paul (2001). "The Redistributive State and Conflicts in Africa," *Journal of Peace Research*, vol. 38, no. 4 (July 2001), pp. 429-444.

Barash, David (1991). *Introduction to Peace Studies*. Belmont, CA: Wadsworth Publishing.

Barnett, Tony (1988). *Social and Economic Development: An Introduction*. New York, NY: The Guilford Press.

Bates, Robert H. (1981). *Markets and States in Tropical Africa: The Political Basis of Agricultural Policies*. Berkeley, CA: University of California Press.

Bayart, Jean-François (1993). *The State in Africa: The Politics of the Belly*. New York, NY: Longman.

Bayart, Jean-François, Stephen Ellis and Béatrice Hibou (1999). *The Criminalization of the State in Africa*. Oxford: James Currey.

Bealy, Frank (1999). *Blackwell Dictionary of Political Science*. Malden, MA: Blackwell Publishers.

Bennett, Valeie P. (1975). "Military Government in Mali," *Journal of Modern African Studies*, vol. 13, no. 2, pp.249–66.

Berdal, Mats R. and David Malone (eds.) (2000). *Greed and Grievance: Economic Agendas in Civil Wars*. Boulder, CO: Lynne Reinner Publishers.

Berg, John C. (1994). *Unequal Struggle: Class, Gender, Race, and Power in the U.S. Congress (Interventions--Theory and Contemporary Politics)*. Boulder, CO: Westview Press.

Brockerhoff Martin and Paul Hewett (2000). *Inequality of Child Mortality among Ethnic Groups in Sub Saharan Africa*. World Health Organization.

Berman, Bruce (1998). "Ethnicity, Patronage, and the African State: The Politics of Uncivil Nationalism," *African Affairs*, vol. 97 (July 1998), pp. 305-341.

Berman, Eric G. and Katie E. Sams. (2000). *Peacekeeping in Africa: Capabilities and Culpabilities*. Geneva: UNIDIR/Pretoria: ISS, 2000.

Berman, Harold J. (1983). *Law and Revolution: The Formation of the Western Legal Tradition*. Cambridge, MA: Harvard University Press.

Bienen, Henry and Jonathan Moore. (1987). "The Sudan: Military Economic Corporations," *Armed Forces & Society*, vol. 13, no. 4, pp. 489–516.

Bienen, Henry (1989). *Armed Forces, Conflict, and Change in Africa*. Boulder, CO: Westview Press.

_____, (1993). "Leaders, Violence and Absence of Change in Africa," *Political Science Quarterly*, vol.108, no. 2, pp. 271-282.

Blanton, Robert G., T. David Mason and Brian Athow (2001). "Colonial Style and Post-Colonial Conflict in Africa," *Journal of Peace Research*, vol. 38, no. 4, pp. 473-491.

Boahen, A. Adu (1986). *Topics in West African History*. New York, NY: Longman.

_____, (1987). *African Perspectives on Colonialism*. The Johns Hopkins Symposia in Comparative History, 15th. Baltimore, MD: Johns Hopkins University Press.

_____, (1990). *Africa under Colonial Domination, 1880-1935*. London: J. Currey.

_____, (1997). "Ghana: Conflict Reoriented," in I. William Zartman (ed.) *Governance as Conflict Management*. Washington DC: Brookings Institution.

_____, (1989). *The Ghanaian Sphinx: Reflections on the Contemporary History of Ghana, 1972-1987*. Accra: Academy of Arts and Sciences Press.

Bogdanor, Vernon (1991). *The Blackwell Encyclopaedia of Political Science.* Cambridge, MA: Blackwell Reference.

Braathen, Einar, Morten Bøås and Gjermund Sæther (2000). "Ethnicity Kills? Social Struggles for Power, Resources, and Identities in the Neo-Patrimonial State," in Braathen, Einar, Morten Bøås and Gjermund Sæther (eds.) *Ethnicity Kills? The Politics of War, Peace and Ethnicity in Sub Sahara Africa.* New York, NY: St. Martin Press.

Bradshaw, York, Paul J. Kaiser and Stephen N. Ndegwa (1995). "Rethinking Theoretical and Methodological Approaches to the Study of African Development," *African Studies Review,* vol. 38, no. 2 (September), pp. 39-65.

Brass, Paul (1985). *Ethnic Groups and the State.* London: Croom Helm.

Bratton, Michael and Nicholas Van de Walle (1997). *Democratic Experiments in Africa: Regime Transitions in Comparative Perspective.* Cambridge: Cambridge University Press.

Brautigam, Deborah (1996). "State Capacity and Effective Governance," in Benno Ndulu and Nicolas van de Walle (eds.) *Agenda for Africa's Economic Renewal.* Washington, DC: Overseas Development Council.

Brown, Michael (1996). *The International Dimension of Internal Conflict.* Cambridge: Center for Science and International Affairs.

Brownsberger, William N. (1983). "Development and Governmental Corruption-Materialism and Political Fragmentation in Nigeria," *The Journal of Modern African Studies,* vol. 21 (February).

Brubaker, Roger (1995). "National Minorities, Nationalizing States, and External National Homelands in the New Europe," *Daedalus* (Spring), pp. 107-132.

Burnside, Craig, and David Dollar (2000). "Aid, Policies, and Growth," *American Economic Review,* vol. 90, no. 4 (September 2000), pp. 847-68.

Buzan, Barry, Charles A. Jones, and Richard Little (1993). *The Logic of Anarchy: Neorealism to Structural Realism.* New York, NY: Columbia University Press.

Callaghy, Thomas M. (1984). *The State-Society Struggle: Zaire in Comparative Perspective.* New York, NY: Columbia University Press.

Callaghy, Thomas M. (1987). *Politics and Culture in Zaire*. Ann Arbor, MI: Center for Political Studies, Institute for Social Research, University of Michigan.

Callagy, Thomas M. (1988). "The State and the Development of Capitalism in Africa: Regime Transitions in Comparative Perspective," in Rothchild and Chazan (eds.) *Precarious Balance: State and Society in Africa*. Berkeley, CA: University of California Press.

Callaghy, Thomas M. and John Ravenhill (1993). "How Hemmed In? Lessons and Prospects of Africa's Responses to Decline," in Callaghy and Ravenhill (eds.) *How Hemmed In? Lessons and Prospects of Africa's Responses to Decline*. New York, NY: Columbia University Press.

Campbell, Donald T. (1975). "Degrees of freedom and the Case Study," *Comparative Political Studies*, vol. 8, pp. 178-185.

Carment, David and Patrick James (eds.) (1997). *Wars in the Midst of Peace: The International Politics of Ethnic Conflict*. Pittsburgh, PA: University of Pittsburgh Press.

Cassanelli, Lee V. and Catherine Besteman (1996). *The Struggle for Land in Southern Somalia: The War Behind the War*. Boulder, CO: Westview Press.

Cassanelli, Lee V. (1982). *The Shaping of the Somali Society*. Philadelphia, PA: University of Pennsylvania Press.

Cerulli, Enrico (1957). *Somalia: Scritti Vari Editi ed Inediti* (Volume one). Rome: Istittuto Poligrafico dello Stato.

Chabal, Patrick and Jean-Pascal Daloz (1999). *Africa Works: Disorder as a Political Instrument*. Oxford: James Currey Publishers.

Chabal, Patrick et. al. (2002). *A History of Postcolonial Lusophone Africa*. London: Hurst & Co.

Chabal, Patrick (1988). "Review Article Revolutionaries in Portuguese Africa," *Journal of African Studies*, vol. 14, no. 3.

____, (2002). "The Quest for Good Government and Development in Africa: Is Nepad the Answer?" *International Affairs*, vol. 78, no. 3, pp. 447-462.

Chazan, Naomi (1983). *An Anatomy of Ghanaian Politics: Managing Political Recession, 1969-1982*. Boulder, CO: Westview Press.

____, (1988). "Patterns of State-Society Incorporation and Disengagement in Africa," in Rothchild and Chazan (eds.) *Precarious Balance: A State and Society in Africa*. Boulder, CO: Westview Publishers

Chazan, Naomi, Robert Mortimer, John Ravenhill and Donald Rothchild (1999). *Politics and Society in Contemporary Africa*. Boulder, CO: Lynne Rienner Publishers.

Cilliers, Jakkie and Peggy Mason (eds.) (1999). *Peace, Profit or Plunder? The Privatisation of Security in War-Torn African Societies*. Halfway House: Institute for Security Studies.

Clapham, Christopher S. (1985). *Third World Politics: An Introduction*. Madison, WI: University of Wisconsin Press.

_____, (1988). " Rwanda: The Perils of Peace Making," *Journal of Peace Research*, vol. 35, no. 2, pp.193-210.

_____, (1997). "International Relations in Africa after the Cold War: Conflict Unleashed," in William Hale and Eberhard Kienle (eds.) *After the Cold War: Security and Democracy in Africa and Asia*. London: I.B. Tauris. Pp. 99-113.

Cohan, Al S. (1957). *Theories of Revolution*. New York, NY: Wiley.

Collier, Paul (2000). "Doing Well out of War: an Economic Perspective," in Mats Berdal and David Malone (eds.) *Greed and Grievance: Economic Agendas in Internal Wars*. Boulder, CO: Lynne Reinner Publishers. Pp.91-112.

Collier, Paul and Anke Hoeffler (1998). "On the Economic Causes of Civil War," Oxford *Economic Papers,* vol. 50, pp. 563-73.

_____, (2000). *Greed and Grievance in Civil War*. Presented at conference on the economics of political violence, Princeton University, March 18-19, 2000. Updated version of "On the Economic Causes of Civil War." (1998).

Communism in Africa. Hearing at the US House of Representatives, Foreign Affairs subcommittee. Presented by David D. Newsome, Under Secretary of Foreign Affairs, US Department of State. October 18, 1979.

Conner, Walker (1972). "Nation-Building or Nation-Destroying?" *World Politics,* vol. 24, no. 3 (April), pp. 319–355.

_____, (1994). *Ethnonationalism: the Quest for Understanding*. Princeton, NJ: Princeton University.

Coser, Lewis (1956). *The Functions of Social Conflict*. Glencoe, IL.: Free Press.

Cramer, Cramer (1999) "The Economics and Political Economy of Conflict in Sub-Saharan Africa," *CDPR Discussion Paper*, no.1099. SOAS, University of London. Pp. 12-16.

Crocker, Chester A., Fen Osler Hampton and Pamela Aall (eds.) (2001). *Turbulent Peace: The Challenges of Managing International Conflict.* Washington, DC: United States Institute of Peace Press.

Darity, William Jr. (1985). "Loan-Pushing: Doctrine and Theory," *International Finance Discussion Paper.* Washington, DC: Board of Governors of the Federal Reserve.

David, Steven R. (1997). "Internal Wars: Causes and Cures," *World Politics*, vol. 49, pp. 552-576.

Davidson, Basil (1992). *The Black Man's Burden: Africa and the Curse of Nation-State.* New York, NY: Times Books.

Davis, Kingsley and Wilbert Moore (1945). "Some Principles of Stratification," *American Sociological Review*, vol. 10, pp. 242-247.

de Waal, Alex (1997). "Contemporary Warfare in Africa," in Mary Kaldor and Basker Vashee (eds.) *Restructuring the Global Military Sector, Vol. I: New Wars.* London: Pinter. Pp.287-332.

Deng, Francis M., Sadikiel Kimaro, Terrence Lyons, Donald Rothchild and I. William Zartman (1996). *Sovereignty as Responsibility: Conflict Management in Africa.* Washington, DC: The Brookings Institution.

Deng, Francis M. (1996). "Anatomy of Conflicts in Africa," in Luc van de Goor, Kumar Rupesinghe and Paul Sciarone (eds.) *Between Development and Destruction: An Enquiry into the Causes of Conflict in Post-Colonial States.* Houndsmills: Macmillan. Pp. 219-236.

____, (2000). "Reconciling Sovereignty with Responsibility: A Basis for International Humanitarian Action," in John W. Harbeson and Donald Rothchild (eds.) *Africa in World Politics: The African State System in Flux.* 3rd edition. Boulder, CO: Westview. pp. 353-378.

De Soysa, Indra (2002). "Paradise is a Bazaar? Greed, Creed, and Governance in Civil War, 1989-99," *Journal of Peace Research*, vol 39, no. 4 (July), pp. 395-416.

Diamond, Larry (1987). "Class Formation in the Swollen African State," *The Journal of Modern African Studies*, vol. 25, no. 4, p. 574.

Dietrich, Chris (2000). "The Commercialisation of Military Deployment in Africa," *African Security Review*, vol. 9, no. 1. Pretoria: Institute for Security Studies. pp. 3-17.

Dorsey, Learthen (1994). *Historical Dictionary of Rwanda.* Metuchen, NJ: Scarecrow Press.

Dorsey, Michael (2000). "Violence and Power-Building in Post-Genocide Rwanda," In Doom, Ruddy, and Jan Gorus (eds.) *Politics of Identity and Economics of Conflict in the Great Lakes Region*. Brussels: VUB University Press. pp. 311-348 327.

Dresang, Dennis L. (1974). "Ethnic Politics, Representative Bureaucracy and Development Administration: The Zambian Case," *American Political Science Review*, vol. 68, no. 4, pp 1605-1617.

Duffield, Mark (1988). "Post-modern Conflict, Warlords, Post-adjustment States and Private Protection," *Journal of Civil Wars* (Spring), pp. 65-102.

Easterly, William and Ross Levine (1997) "Africa's Growth Tragedy: Policies and Ethnic Divisions," *Quarterly Journal of Economics*, vol. 112. no. 4 pp.1203-1250

Easton, David (1965). *Framework for Political Analysis*. Englewood Cliffs, NJ: Prentice Hall.

Eckstein, Harry (1975). "Case Study and Theory in Political Science," in Fred I. Greenstein and N.W. Polsby (eds.) *Handbook of Political Science*. vol. 7. Reading, MA: Addison-Wesley. pp. 79-138.

Economist Intelligence Unit (2000). *EIU Country Profile 2000: Rwanda Burundi*. London: Economist Intelligence Unit.

Economist Intelligence Unit (2001). *EIU Country Profile 2001: Rwanda Burundi*. London: Economist Intelligence Unit.

Economist Intelligence Unit (1992-93). *Somalia: Country Profile*. London: Economist Intelligence Unit.

Edgerton, Robert B. (2002). *Africa's Armies. From Honor to Infamy: A History from 1791 to the Present*. Boulder, CO: Westview.

Ekeh, Peter P. (1975). "Colonialism and the Two Publics in Africa: A Theoretical Statement," *Comparative Studies in Society and History*, vol 17, no 1, pp. 91-112.

_____, (1978). "Colonialism and the Development of Citizenship in Africa: A Study of Ideologies of Legitimation," in Onigu Otite (ed.) *Themes in African Social and Political Thought*. Enugu: Fourth Dimension Publishers. Pp. 302-334.

Englebert, Pierret (2000). *State Legitimacy and Development in Africa*. Boulder, CO: Lynne Rienner Publishers.

Elbadawi, Ibrahim A. and Nicholas Sambanis (2002). "How Much War Will We See? Explaining the Prevalence of Civil War," *Journal of Conflict Resolution*, vol. 46, no. 3, pp. 307-34.

Elbadawi, Ibrahim A. and Nicholas Sambanis (2000). *External Interventions and the Duration of Civil Wars*. World Bank, Development Research Group, Public Economics.

Esman, Milton J. (1966). "The Politics of Development Administration," in John D. Montgomery and William J. Siffin (eds.) *Approaches to Development: Politics, Administration and Change*. New York, NY: McGraw-Hill. Pp. 59–112.

____, (1994). *Ethnic Politics*. Ithaca, NY: Cornell University Press.

Fage, John D. (1995). *A History of Africa*. Third edition. London: Routledge Publications.

Fanon, Frantz (1961). *The Wretched of the Earth*. Translated by Constance Farrington. New York, NY: Grove Press.

Fatton, Robert (1992). *Predatory Rule: State and Civil Society in Africa*. Boulder, CO: Lynne Rienner Publishers.

Ferkiss, Victor C. (1966). *Africa's Search For Identity*. New York, NY: Braziller.

Fleming, Harold C. (1964). "Baiso and Randille: Somali Outliers," *Rassegni di Studi Etopici*, vol. 20, pp. 35-96.

Forsyth, Frederick (1977). *The Making of an African Legend: the Biafra Story*. New York, NY: Penguin Books.

Fosu, K. Yerfi (1992). "The Real Exchange Rate and Ghana's Agricultural Exports," *Aerc Research Paper*, vol. 9. Oxford: Centre for the Study of African Economies.

Freire, Paulo (1972). *Pedagogy of the Oppressed*. Harmondsworth: Penguin Books.

Friedland, Willia and Carl Roseberg, Jr. (1965). *African Socialism*. Stanford, CA: Hoover Institution Press.

Furley, Oliver and Roy May (eds.) (1998). *Peacekeeping in Africa*. Aldershot: Ashgate.

Furley, Oliver (1995). "Africa: The Habit of Conflict," in Oliver Furley (ed.) *Conflict in Africa*. London: Tauris Academic Studies. Pp.1-18.

Gagnon, Valeria P. Jr. (1995), "Ethnic Nationalism and International Conflict: The Case of Serbia," *International Security*, vol.19, no.3, pp.132-163.

Ganguly, Rajat and Raymond C. Taras (1998). *Understanding Ethnic Conflict: the International Dimension.* New York, NY: Longman.

Gassana, Emmanuel et. al. (1999). "Rwanda," in Adebayo Adedeji (ed.) *Comprehending and Mastering African Conflicts: The Search for Sustainable Peace and Good Governance.* London: Zed Books.

Gavshon, Arthur (1981). *Crisis in Africa: Battleground of East and West.* Boulder, CO: Westview Press.

Gavshon, Arthur and Kenneth L. Adelman (1986). "Superpower Arms Sales Have Caused African Instability," in Janelle Rohr (ed.) *Problems of Africa: Opposing Viewpoints.* St Paul, MN: Greenhaven Press. Pp. 84-98.

Geertz, Clifford (1973). *The Interpretation of Cultures.* New York, NY: Free Press.

George, Alexander L. (1979). "Case Studies and Theory Development: the Method of Structured, Focused Comparison," in Paul Gordon Lauren (ed.) *Diplomacy: New Approaches in History, Theory, and Policy.* Pp. 43-68.

George, Susan (1988). *A Fate Worse Than Debt.* Harmonsworth, England: Penguin.

Gershoni, Yekutiel (1997). "War Without an End and an End to a War: The Prolonged War in Liberia and Sierra Leone," *African Studies Review,* vol. 40, no. 3.

Goldstone, Jack A. (1980). "Theories of Revolution: The Third Generation," *World Politics,* vol. 32, no. 3 (April), pp. 425–453.

Gordon, Sandy (1993). "Resources and Instability in South Asia," *Survival,* vol. 35, no. 2 (Summer), pp. 66–87.

Goulding, Marrack (1999): "The United Nations and Conflict in Africa since the Cold War," *African Affairs,* vol. 98, pp.155-166.

Gourevitch, Philip (1998). *We wish to inform you that tomorrow we will be killed with our families: Stories from Rwanda.* New York, NY: Farrar Straus and Giroux.

Gros, Jean-Germain (1996). "Towards a Taxonomy of Failed States in the New World Order: Decaying in Somalia, Liberia, Rwanda and Haiti," *Third World Quarterly,* vol. 17, no. 3.

Grotpeter, John J., Brian V. Siegel and Jim Pletcher (1998). "Historical Dictionary of Zambia," *African Historical Dictionaries,* no. 19. Lanham, MD: Scarecrow Press.

Gupta, Sanjeev, Benedict Clements and Erwin Tiongson (1998). "Public Spending on Human Development," *Finance and Development*, vol 35, no. 3, pp. 10-13.

Gurr, Ted Robert (1970). *Why Men Rebel?* Princeton, NJ: Princeton University Press.

____, (1993). *Minorities At Risk: A Global View of Ethnopolitical Conflicts*. Washington, DC: US Institute of Peace Press.

____, (1994). "Peoples Against States: Ethnopolitical Conflict and the Changing World System," *International Studies Quarterly*, vol. 38, no. 3, pp. 347-377.

Gurr, Ted Robert and Barbara Harff (1994). *Ethnic Conflict and World Politics*. Boulder, CO: Westview Press.

Gurr, Ted Robert, Monty G. Marshall and Deepa Khosla (2000). *Peace and Conflict 2001: A Global Survey of Armed Conflicts, Self-Determination Movement, and Democracy*. University of Maryland, MD: Center for International Development and Conflict Management.

Haas, Michael (1974). *International Conflict*. New York, NY: Bobbs-Merrill.

Hagi, Aves O. and Abdiwahid O. Hagi (1998). *Clan, Sub-clan and Regional Representation in the Somali Government Organization 1960-1990: Statistical Data and Findings*. Washington DC.

Hagopian, Mark (1974). *The Phenomenon of Revolution*. New York, NY: Dodd, Mead.

Hale, William and Eberhard Kienle (eds.) (1997). *After the Cold War: Security and Democracy in Africa and Asia*. London: I.B. Tauris.

Arms Control Disarmament Agency, US Department of State (1987). *Handbook of Arms Transfers and Military Expenditure*.

Harbeson, John W. and Donald Rothchild (eds.) (2000). *Africa in World Politics: The African State System in Flux*. 3rd edition. Boulder, CO: Westview.

Harbeson, John W., Donald Rothchild and Naomi Chazan (eds.) (1994). *Civil Society and the State in Africa*. Boulder, CO: Lynne Rienner Publishers.

Harbeson, John W. (2000). "Externally Assisted Democratization: Theoretical Issues and African Realities," in John W. Harbeson and Donald Rothchild (eds.) *Africa in World Politics: The African State System in Flux*. 3rd edition. Boulder, CO: Westview. Pp. 235-259.

Hardin, Blaine (1991). *Africa: Dispatches from a Fragile Continent.* New York, NY: Norton.

Heady, Ferrel (1991). *Public Administration a Comparative Perspective.* New York, NY: Marcel Dekker Inc.

Helman, Gerald B. and Steven R. Ratner (1992). "Saving Failed States," *Foreign Policy*, no. 89 (Winter 1992–93), pp. 3–20.

Henderson, Errol (1999). *Encyclopedia of Violence, Peace, and Conflict.* San Diego, CA: Academic Press.

Henderson, Errol and David Singer (2000). "Civil War in Post Colonial World, 1946-92," *Journal of Peace Research*, vol. 37, no. 3, pp: 275-299.

Herbst, Jeffrey (1993). "The Politics of Sustained Agricultural Reform," in Thomas M. Callaghy and John Ravenhill (eds.) *Hemmed In: Responses to Africa's Economic Decline.* New York, NY: Columbia University Press. Pp. 280-332.

-------- (1996). "Responding to State Failure in Africa," *International Security*, vol. 21, no. 3 (Winter), pp. 120-144.

------- (1997). "Responding to State Failure in Africa," *International Security*, vol. 21, no. 3 (Winter 1996/97), pp. 120-144.

------ (2000a). *States and Power in Africa: Comparative Lessons in Authority and Control.* Princeton, NJ: Princeton University Press.

------- (2000b). "Western and African Peacekeepers: Motives and Opportunities," in John W. Harbeson and Donald Rothchild (eds.) *Africa in World Politics: The African State System in Flux.* 3rd edition. Boulder, CO: Westview. Pp. 308-323.

Hills, Alice (1997). "Warlords, Militia and Conflict in Contemporary Africa: A Reexamination of Terms," *Small Wars and Insurgencies*, vol. 8, no. 1, pp. 35–51.

Hochschild, Adam (1998). *King Leopold's Ghost: A Story of Greed, Terror, and Heroism in Colonial Africa.* Boston, MA: A Mariner Books.

Holsti, Kalevi J. (1992). "International Theory and War in the Third World," in Brian L. Job (ed.) *The Insecurity Dilemma: National Security of Third World States.* Boulder, CO: Lynne Rienner Publishers. Pp. 37–62

Holsti, Kalevi J. (1996). *The State, War, and the State of War.* New York, NY: Cambridge University Press.

Horowitz, Donald (1985). *Ethnic Groups in Conflict.* Berkley, CA: University of California Press.

Howe, Herbert M. (2001). *Ambiguous Order: Military Forces in African States.* Boulder, CO: Lynne Rienner Publishers.

Hsieh, Ching-Chi and Mark D. Pugh (1993). "Poverty, Income Inequality, and Violent Crime: A Meta-analysis of Recent Aggregate Data Studies," *Criminal Justice Review*, vol. 18, no. 1, pp. 82-202.
http://www.ACDA.gov
http://datacenter2.chass.utotronto.ca/pwt
http://news.bbc.co.uk/1/hi/world/africa/country_profiles/1070329
http://news.bbc.co.uk/1/hi/world/africa/country_profiles/1072611
http://news.bbc.co.uk/hi/english/world/africa/newsid_1308000/1308963.
http://www.cnn.com/WORLD/africa/9804/07/rwanda/
http://www.ethnologue.com/
http://www.guardian.co.uk/fairtrade/story/0,12458,794488,00.html
http://www.hrw.org/reports/1999/rwanda/Geno1-3-11.htm.
http://www.ICRG.org
http://www.imf.org/external/pubs/ft/fandd/1998/09/imfstaf1.htm
http://www.ius.edu/SocialScience/ModelUN/SierraLeone.htm
http://www.keesings.com/
http://www.oecd.org
http://www.SIPRI.org
http://www.usc.edu/dept/LAS/ir/cis/cews/database/Rwanda/rwanda.doc
http://www.worldbank.org
http://www.wto.org/trade_resources/publications/development/ htm

Human Rights Watch (1995). *Human Rights Watch, Playing the "Communal Card": Communal Violence and Human Rights*. New York, NY: Human Rights Watch.

Huntington, Samuel P. (1968). *Political Order in Changing Societies*. New Haven, CT: Yale University Press.

Hutchful, Eboe (2000). "Understanding the African Security Crisis," in Abdel-Fatau Musah and J.'Keyode Fayemi (eds.) *Mercenaries: An African Security Dilemma*. London: Pluto Press. P.211.

Hyden, Goran (1983). *No Shortcuts to Progress: African Development Management in Perspective*. Berkeley, CA: University of California Press.

---- (1990). "Reciprocity and Governance in Africa," in James S. Wunsch and Dele Olowu (eds.) *The Failure of the Centralized State*. Boulder, CO: Westview Press. Pp. 245-269.

------ (1992). "Governance and the Study of Politics," in Goran Hyden and Michael Bratton (eds.) *Governance and Politics in Africa*. Boulder, CO: Lynne Rienner Publishers. Pp. 1-26.

------ (2000). "The Governance Challenge in Africa," in Hyden, et al. (eds) *African Perspectives on Governance*. Trenton, NJ: Africa World Press, Inc.

Hyden, Goran and Bratton Michael (eds.) (1992). *Governance and Politics in Africa*. Boulder, CO: Lynne Rienner Publishers.

Iliffe, John (1995). *Africans: The History of a Continent*. Cambridge: Cambridge University Press.

Jackson, Robert H. and Carl Gustav Rosberg (1982). *Personal Rule in Black Africa: Prince, Autocrat, Prophet, Tyrant*. Berkeley, CA: University of California Press.

Jackson, Tudor (1986). *Law of Kenya*. Nairobi: Kenyan Literature Bureau.

Jackson, Robert H. (1992a). "Juridical Statehood in Sub-Saharan Africa," *Journal of International Affairs*, vol 46, no. 1 (Summer).

------ (1992b). "Pluralism and International Political Theory," *Review of International Studies*, vol 18, no. 3 (July).

Jenkins, J. Craig and Augustine Kposowa (1990). "Explaining Military Coups: Black Africa 1956-1984," *American Sociological Review*, vol. 55, pp. 861-750.

Jenkins, J. Craig and Augustine Kposowa (1992). "The Structural Sources of Military Coups: A LISREL Analysis of Military Interventions in Postcolonial Africa, 1957-1984," *American Journal of Sociology*, vol. 99, pp.126-63.

Jeong, Ho-Won (ed.) (1999). *Conflict Resolution: Dynamics, Process and Structure*. Aldershot: Ashgate.

Jervis, Robert (1978). *Deterrence Theory Revisited*. Los Angeles, LA: University of California.

Job, Brian L (1992). *The Insecurity Dilemma: National Security in the Third World States*. Boulder, CO: Lynne Reinner Publishers.

Johnson, Chalmers (1966). *Revolutionary Change*. Boston, MA: Little, Brown.

Joseph, Richard and Jeffrey Herbst (1997). "Correspondence: Responding to State Failure in Africa," *International Security*, vol. 22, no. 2, pp. 175-184.

Kaiser, Paul J. and Stephen N. Ndegwa (1995). "Rethinking Theoretical and Methodological Approaches to the Study of African Development," *African Studies Review*, vol. 38, no. 2 (September), pp. 39-65.

Kandeh, Jimmy D. (1992). "Politicization of Ethnic Identities in Sierra Leone," *African Studies Review*, vol. 35, no. 1.

Kaplan, Robert D. (1993). *Balkan Ghosts: A Journey Through History*. New York, NY: St. Martin.

Kasfir, Nelson (1983). "Introduction: Relating State to Class in Africa," *Journal in Commonwealth and Comparative Politics*, vol. XXI, p. 5.

Keefer, Philip and Stephen F. Knack (1995). *Polarization, Property Rights, and the Links between Inequality and Growth*. College Park, MD: Center for Institutional Reform and the Informal Sector, University of Maryland at College Park.

Keen, David (1998). "The Economic Functions of Violence in Civil Wars," *Adelphi Paper*, vol. 320. London: IISS.

Keller, Edmond J. and Donald Rothchild (eds.) (1996). *Africa in the New World Order*. Boulder, CO: Lynne Rienner Publishers.

Keller, Edmond J. (1998). "Transnational Ethnic Conflict in Africa," in David A. Lake and Donald Rothchild (eds.) *The International Spread of Ethnic Conflict: Fear, Diffusion and Escalation*. Princeton, NJ: Princeton University Press. Pp. 275-292.

Kilson, Martin (1966). *Political Change in a West African State: A Study of the Modernization Process in Sierra Leone*. Cambridge, MA: Harvard University Press.

Kindleberger, Charles P. (1983). *Historical Perspective on Today's Third World Debt Crisis*. Boston, MA: Department of Economics, MIT.

Kingma, Kees (2000). *Demobilization in Sub-Saharan Africa: The Development and Security Impacts*. Basingstoke: Macmillan.

Kokole, Omari H. (1996). "Ethnic Conflicts Versus Development in Africa," in Luc van de Goor, Kumar Rupesinghe and Paul Sciarone (eds.) *Between Development and Destruction: An Enquiry into the Causes of Conflict in Post-Colonial States*. Houndsmills: Macmillan. Pp. 126-140.

Kposowa, Augustine and J. Craig Jenkins (1992). "The Structural Sources of Military Coups: A LISREL Analysis of Military Intervention in Postcolonial Africa, 1957-1984," *American Journal of Sociology*, vol. 99, pp. 126-163.

Kriesberg, Louis (1998). *Constructive Conflicts: From Escalation to Resolution*. Lanham: Rowman & Littlefield.

Kuran, Timur (1998). "Ethnic Dissimilation and Its National Diffusion," in David A. Lake and Donald Rothschild (eds.) *The*

International Spread of Ethnic Conflict: Fear, Diffusion, and Escalation. Princeton, NJ: Princeton University Press. Pp. 35-60.

Kusow, Abdi (1994). "Peace and Stability in Somalia: Problems and Prospects," *UFAHAMU*, vol. XXII, no. I&II.

____, (1994). "The Genesis of the Somali Civil War: A New Perspective," *Northeast African Studies*, vol. 1, no. 1, pp. 31-47.

____, (1995). "The Somali Origin: Myth or Reality," in Ali Jimale Ahmed (ed.) *The Invention of Somalia.* Pp. 81-106.

La Billion, Philippe (2001). "Fuelling War or Peace Buying: The Role of Corruption in Conflicts," *Discussion Paper*, no. 2001/65. Published by the World Institute for Development Economic

Laggah, John Bobor et. al. (1999). "Sierra Leone," in Adebayo Adedeji (ed.) *Comprehending and Mastering African Conflicts: The Search for Sustainable Peace and Good Governance.* London: Zed Books. Pp. 174-188.

Laitin, David D. and Said Samatar (1987). *Somalia: A Nation in Search of State.* Boulder, CO: Westview Press.

Lapido, Adamolekun (1986). *Politics and Administration in Nigeria.* Ibadan, Nigeria: Spectrum Books Ltd.

Lake, David A. and Donald Rothschild (1998). "Spreading Fear: The Genesis of Transnational Ethnic Conflict," in Lake and Rothschild (eds.) *The International Spread of Ethnic Conflict.* Princeton, NJ: Princeton University Press. Pp. 3-32

Learthen, Dorsey (1994). *Historical Dictionary of Rwanda.* London: Scarecrow Press.

Lefebvre, Jeffrey A. (1991). *Arms for the Horn: U.S. Security Policy in Ethiopia and Somalia, 1953-1991.* Pittsburgh, PA: University of Pittsburgh Press.

Lemarchand, Renè (2000). "The Crisis in the Great Lakes," in John W. Harbeson and Donald Rothchild (eds.) *Africa in World Politics: The African State System in Flux.* 3rd edition. Boulder, CO: Westview. Pp. 324-352.

Leonard, David K. and Scott Strauss (2003). *Africa's Stalled Development: International Causes and Cures.* Boulder, CO: Lynne Reinner.

Lewis, Ioan M. (1961). *A Pastoral Democracy: A Study of Pastoralism and Politics Among the Northern Somali of the Horn of Africa.* London: Oxford University Press.

_____, (1980). *A Modem History of Somalia: Nation and State in the Horn of Africa*. London: Longman

Licklider, Roy (ed.) (1993). *Stopping the Killing: How Civil Wars End*. New York, NY: New York University Press.

Lijphart, Arend (1975). "The Comparable-Cases Strategy in Comparative Research," *Comparative Political Studies*, vol. 8 (July), p. 171.

_____, (1977). *Democracy in Plural Societies*. New Haven, CT: Yale University Press.

Lindgren, Göran Kjell-Åke Nordquist and Peter Wallensteen (eds.) (1993). *Experiences from Conflict Resolution in the Third World*. Uppsala: Department of Peace and Conflict Research, Uppsala University.

Lipsey, Roderick K. von (ed.) (1997). *Breaking the Cycle: A Framework for Conflict Intervention*. New York: St. Martin's Press.

Little, Peter D. and Michael Horowitz (1988). "Agricultural Policy and Practice in Rwanda," *Human Organization*, vol. 46 & 47.

Lofchie, Michael F. (1993). "Economic Policy in Kenya and Tanzania," in Thomas M. Callaghy and John Ravenhill (eds.) *Hemmed In: Response to Africa's Economic Decline*. New York, NY: Columbia University Press.

Lonsdale, J. (1986). "Political Accountability in African History," in Patrick Chabal (ed.) *Political Domination in Africa*. Cambridge: Cambridge University Press. Pp.106-7

Lund, Michael S. (1996). *Preventing Violent Conflicts: A Strategy for Preventive Diplomacy*. Washington, DC: United States Institute of Peace Press.

Macridis, Roy C. and Steven L. Burg (1991). *Introduction to Comparative Politics: Regimes and Change*. 2nd edition. New York, NY: HarperCollins.

Maddox, Gregory (1996). *Custodians of the Land: Ecology & Culture in the History of Tanzania*. Athens, OH: Ohio University Press.

Mahler, Gregory (2003). *Comparative Politics: An Institutional and Cross-National Approach*. Upper Saddle, NJ: Prentice Hall.

Malaquis, Assis (2001). "Diamonds are a Guerrilla's Best Friend: The Impact of Illicit Wealth on Insurgency Strategy," *Third World Quarterly*, vol. 22, no. 3, pp. 311-325.

Mamdani, Mahmood (2001). *When Victims Become Killers: Colonialism Nativism and the Genocide in Rwanda.* Princeton, NJ: Princeton University Press.

_____, (1992). "Democratic Theory and Democratic Struggles in Africa," *Dissent* (Summer), pp. 312-318.

_____, (1996). *Citizen and Subject: 1960 Contemporary Africa and the Legacy of Late Colonialism.* Princeton NJ: Princeton University Press.

Mansfield, Edward D. and Jack Snyder (1995). "Democratization and the Danger of War," *International Security,* vol. 20, no. 1 (Summer), pp. 5–38.

Macridis, Roy C. and Steven L. Burg (1991). *Introduction to Comparative Politics: Regimes and Change.* 2nd edition. London: Harper Collins.

Marchal, Roland (1996). *Final Report on the Post Civil War Somali Business Class.* Paris: European Commission/Somalia Unit.

Marx, Karl and James L. Joynes (1893). *Wages and Capital.* Glasgow: Labour Literature Society.

Mauro, Paolo (1995). "Corruption and Growth," *Quarterly Journal of Economics, vol. 2,* no. 441, pp. 681-712.

Mazrui, Ali A. (1967). *Towards a Pax Africana: A Study of Ideology and Ambition.* London: Weidenfeld and Nicolson.

_____, (1969). *Post Imperial Fragmentation: The Legacy of Ethnic and Racial Conflict.* Denver: University of Denver.

_____, (1969). *Violence and Thought: Essays on Social Tensions in Africa.* Harlow: Longmans.

_____, (1995). "Conflict as a Retreat from Modernity: A Comparative Overview," in Oliver Furley (ed.) *Conflict in Africa.* London: Tauris Academic Studies. Pp.19-27.

_____, (1998). "The Failed State and Political Collapse in Africa," in Olara A. Otunnu and Michael W. Doyle (eds.) *Peacemaking and Peacekeeping for the New Century.* Lanham: Rowman & Littlefield. Pp. 233-244.

Mbaku, John Mukum (ed.) (1999). *Preparing Africa for the Twenty-First Century: Strategies for Peaceful Coexistence and Sustainable Development.* Aldershot: Ashgate.

McGowan, Pat and Thomas H. Johnson (1984). "African Military Coups d'etat and Underdevelopment: A Quantitative Historical Analysis," *Journal of Modern African Studies,* vol. 22, no. 4, pp. 633-666.

McGowan, Pat and Thomas H. Johnson (1986). "Sixty Coups in Thirty Years: Further Evidence Regarding African Military Coup d'etat," *Journal of Modern African Studies*, vol. 24, no. 3, pp. 539–46.

McMillan, James H. and Sally Schumacher (1984). *Research in Education*. Boston, MA: Little, Brown and Company.

Meier, Gerald M. and Dudley Seers (1985). *Pioneers in Development*. Oxford: Oxford University Press.

Melvern, Linda (2000). *A People Betrayed: The Role of West in Rwanda's Genocide*. London: Zed Books.

Médard, Jean-Francois (1982). "The Underdeveloped State in Tropical Africa: Political Clientalism or Neo-Patrimonialism," in C. Clapham (ed.) *Private Patronage and Public Power*. London: Frances Pinter.

_____, (1996). "Patrimonialism, Neopatrimonialism and the Study of the Postcolonial State in Sub-Saharan Africa," in Henrik Secher Marcussen (ed.) *Improved Natural Resource Management: The Role of Formal Organisations and Informal Networks and Institutions*. Roskilde: Roskilde University Press. Pp. 76-97.

Merriam, Sharan B. (1988). *Case Study Research in Education: A Qualitative Approach*. San Francisco, LA: Jossey-Bass.

Migdal, Joel S. (1988). *Strong States and Weak Societies: State-Society Relations and State Capabilities in the Third World*. Princeton, NJ: Princeton University Press.

_____, (2001). *State in Society: Studying How States and Societies Transform and Constitute One Another*. Cambridge: Cambridge University Press.

Mohammed, Nadir A.L. 1999. *Civil Wars and Military Expenditures: A Note*. http://econ.worldbank.org/files/13215_Mohammed.pdf.

Mosca, Gaetano (1896). *Elementi di scienza politica*. Roma: Bocca.

Mubarak, Jamil Abdalla (1996). *From Bad Policy to Chaos in Somalia*. Westport, CT: Praeger Publishers.

Mudimbe, Valentin Y. (1988). *The Invention of Africa: Gnosis, Philosophy, and Order of Knowledge*. Bloomington, IN: Indiana University Press.

Mugabe, Robert. *The Killings Resume*, viewable at
http://www.strategicstudies.org/crisis/rwanda.htm#Uganda-Rwanda.

Mukhtar, Mohamed H. (1989). "The Emergence and Role of Political Parties in the Inter-riverine Region of Somalia from 1947-1960 (independence)," *UFAHAMU*, vol. XVII., no. II (UCLA, Spring).

_____, (1995a). "Islam in Somali History: Fact and Fiction," in Ali Jimale Ahmed (ed.) *The Invention of Somalia*. Lawrenceville: Red Sea Press. Pp.1-28.

_____, (1995b). *Somalia: Searching for The Foundation of Social and Civil Morality*. Unpublished Paper given to me by the author.

Mukhtar, Mohamed H. and Abdi Kusow (1993). *The Bottom-up Approach in Reconciliation in the Inter-river Regions of Somalia*. A Visiting Mission Report (August 18 September 23, 1993).

Musah, Abdel-Fatau and J. 'Kayode Fayemi (eds.) (2000). *Mercenaries: An African Security Dilemma*. London: Pluto Press.

Mwase, George Simeon and Robert I. Rotberg (ed.) (1967). *Strike a Blow and Die: A Narrative of Race Relations in Colonial Africa*. Cambridge, MA: Harvard University Press.

Nafziger, Wayne E. (1993). *The Debt Crisis in Africa*. Baltimore, MD: Johns Hopkins University Press. Pp. 67-71.

Ndulu, Benno and Nicolas van de Walle (eds.) (1996). *Agenda for Africa's Economic Renewal*. Washington, DC: Overseas Development Council.

Newbury, Catherine (1998). "Ethnicity and Politics of History in Rwanda," *Africa Today*, vol. 45, no. 1 (Jan-March), pp. 7-24.

Newbury, David (1997). "Irredentist Rwanda: Ethnic and Territorial Frontiers in Central Africa," *Africa Today*, vol 44, no 2, pp. 211-222.

Newman, Saul (1991). "Does Modernization Breed Ethnic Conflict?" *World Politics*, vol. 43, no. 3 (April), pp. 451–478.

Chasing the Kleptocrats. New York Times (Monday, September 29, 2003). Section A page 22 (column 1).

Nkrumah, Kwame (1964). *Consciencism*. London: Heinemamnn.

_____, (1966). *Neo-Colonialism: The Last State of Imperialism*. New York, NY: St. Marin's Press.

Nugent, Paul (1995). *Big Men, Small Boys, and Politics in Ghana*. Accra: Asempa Press.

Nyerere, Julius (1968). *Freedom and Socialism*. Daar Salaam: Oxford University Press.

Oberdorfer, Don (1992). "Bush Sends Forces To Help Somalia America Must Act,' President Says" *Washington Post* Section A, p.1

Odetola, Olatunde (1982). *Military Regimes and Development*. London: George Allen & Unwin.

———, (1986). *Military Regimes and Development: A Comparative Analysis in African Societies*. London: George Allen & Unwin.

Ofcansky, Thomas P., Rodger Yeager and Laura Kurtz (1997). "Historical Dictionary of Tanzania," *African Historical Dictionaries*, no. 72. Lanham, MD: Scarecrow Press.

Ofiaja, Nicholas D. (1979). *Stability and Instability in Politics: The Case of Nigeria and Cameroon*. New York, NY: Vantage Press.

Okigbo, Pius (1993). "The Future Haunted by the Past," in Adebady Adedeji (ed.) *Africa Within the World*. London: Zed Books. Pp. 28-38.

O'Laughlin, Bridget (2000). "Class and the Customary: The Ambiguous Legacy of the Indigenato in Mozambique," *African Affairs*, vol. 99.

Omitoogun, Wuyi (2003). *Military Expenditure Data in Africa: A Survey of Cameroon, Ethiopia, Ghana, Kenya, Nigeria and Uganda*. New York: Oxford University Press, Inc..

Onimode, Bade (1989). "The IMF, World Bank and the African Debt," in Bade Onimode (ed.) *The IMF, World Bank and the African Debt*. London: Zed Books, Ltd. Vol. I, pp. 1-7.

Oomen, T. (1997). *Citizenship Nationality and Ethnicity: Reconciling Competing Identities*. Cambridge: Polity Press.

Osaghae, Eghosa E. (2000). "Applying Traditional Methods to Modern Conflict: Possibilities and Limits," in I. William Zartman (ed.) *Traditional Cures for Modern Conflicts. African Conflict "Medicine."* Boulder, CO: Lynne Rienner Publishers. Pp. 201-218.

Ottaway, Marina (1999). "Ethnic politics in Africa: Change and Continuity," in Richard Joseph (ed.) *State, conflict, and Democracy in Africa*. Boulder, CO: Lynne Reinner Publishers. Pp. 229-318.

———, (1982). *Soviet and American Influence in the Horn of Africa*. New York, NY: Praeger.

Oyebade, Adebayo and Abiodun Alao (eds.) (1998). *Africa after the Cold War*. Trenton: Africa World Press.

Parenti, Micahel (1989). *The Sword and the Dollar: Imperialism, Revolution, and Arms Race*. New York, NY: St. Martin.

Patton, Adell and NetLibrary Inc. (1996). *Physicians, Colonial Racism, and Diaspora in West Africa*. Gainesville, FL: University Press of Florida.

Peterson, Scott. (2000). *Me against My Brother: At War in Somalia, Sudan, and Rwanda*. New York, NY: Routledge.

Peterson, John (1968). "The Enlightenment and Founding of Freetown," in Christopher Fyfe and Eldred Jones (eds.) *Freetown: A Symposium*. Freetown: Sierra Leone University Press.

Pfaff, William (1993). "Revive Secular Citizenship Above 'Ethnic' Nationality," *International Herald Tribune* (July 20. 1993).

Posen, Barry (1993). "The Security Dilemma and Ethnic Conflict," in Michael E. Brown (ed.) *Ethnic Conflict and International Security*. Princeton, NJ: Princeton University Press. Pp.103-124.

Prunier, Gérard (1997). *The Rwanda Crisis: History of a Genocide*. New York, NY: Columbia University Press.

_____, (1999). *Rwanda in Zaire: From Genocide to Continental War*. London: C. Hurst.

Ragin, Charles C. (1987). *The Comparative Method: Moving Beyond Qualitative and Quantitative Strategies*. Berkley, CA: University of California Press.

Rapoport, Anatol (1989). *The Origins of Violence: Approaches to the Study of Conflict*. New York, NY: Paragon House.

Rasmussen, Jorgen Scott (1969). *The Process of Politics, a Comparative Approach*. New York, NY: Atherton Press.

Ravenhill, John (1986). *Africa in Economic Crisis*. New York, NY: Columbia University Press.

Regan, Patrick M. (2000). *Internal wars and Foreign Powers: Outside Intervention in Interstate Conflicts*. Ann Arbor, MI: University of Michigan Press.

Reno, William (1995). *Corruption and State Politics in Sierra Leone*. Cambridge: Cambridge University Press.

_____, (1996). "The Business of War in Liberia," *Current History*, vol. 93, no 601 (May), pp. 211-215.

_____, (1998). *Warlord Politics and African States*. Boulder, CO: Lynne Rienner Publishers.

_____, (2000) "Africa's Weak States, Nonstate Actors, and the Privatization of Interstate Relations," in John W. Harbeson and Donald Rothchild (eds.) *Africa in World Politics: The African State System in Flux*. 3rd edition. Boulder, CO: Westview. Pp. 286-307.

_____, (2000). "Shadow States and the Political Economy of Internal Wars," in Mats Berdal and David Malone (eds.) *Greed and Grievance: Economic Agendas in Internal Wars*. Boulder, CO: Lynne Reinner Publishers. P. 64.

Reuchler, Luc and Thania Paffenholz (eds.) (2001). *Peacebuilding: A Field Guide*. Boulder, CO: Lynne Rienner Publishers.

Reynolds, Vernon (ed.) (1983). *The Sociobiology of Ethnocentrism*. London: Croom Helm.

Reyntjens, Filip (1999). *Talking or Fighting?: Political Evolution in Rwanda and Burundi, 1998-1999*. Uppsala: Nordiska Afrikainstitutet.

Richard, Joseph (ed.) (1999). *State, Conflict and Democracy in Africa*. Boulder, CO: Lynne Rienner Publishers.

Rodney, Walter (1977). *How Europe Underdeveloped Africa*. Washington, DC: Howard University Press.

Rotberg, Robert I. (1967). *The Rise of Nationalism in Central Africa: The Making of Malawi and Zambia, 1873-1964*. Cambridge, MA: Harvard University Press.

_____, 2003). *Africa's Discontent: Coping with Human and Natural Disasters*. Cambridge, MA: World Peace Foundation.

_____, (2003). *State Failure and State Weakness in a Time of Terror*. Cambridge, MA: World Peace Foundation.

Rothchild, Donald and Naomi Chazan (eds.) 1988. *The Precarious Balance: State and Society in Africa*. Berkeley, CA: University of California Press.

Rothchild, Donald and John W.Harbeson (2000). "The African State and State System in Flux," in John W. Harbeson and Donald Rothchild (eds.) *Africa in World Politics: The African State System in Flux*. 3rd edition Boulder, CO: Westview. Pp. 3-20.

Rothchild, Donald (1996). "Conclusion: Responding to Africa's Post-Cold War Conflicts," in Edmond J. Keller and Donald Rothchild (eds.) *Africa in the New World Order*. Boulder: Lynne Rienner Publishers. Pp. 227-242.

_____, (1997). *Managing Ethnic Conflict in Africa: Pressures and Incentives for Cooperation*. Washington, DC: Brookings Institution Press.

_____, (1999). "Ethnic Insecurity, Peace Agreements, and State Building," in Richard Joseph (ed.) *State, Conflict and Democracy in Africa*. Boulder, CO: Lynne Rienner Publishers. Pp. 319-338.

___, (1981). *Ethnopolitics: A Conceptual Framework*. New York, NY: Columbia University Press.

Rule, James B. (1992). Tribalism and the state. A reply to Michael Walzer", Dissent, Fall 1992, p. 519. .

___, (1988). *Theories of Civil Violence*. Berkeley, CA: University of California Press.

Rummel, Rudolph J. (1997) "Is collective violence correlated with social pluralism?" *Journal of Peace Research*, vol. 34, no. 3. pp. 163-76.

Rupesinghe, Kumar (1998). *Civil Wars, Civil Peace. An Introduction to Conflict Resolution*. London: Pluto Press.

Ryan, Stephen (1995). *Ethnic Conflict and International Relations*. Aldershot: Dartmouth. 2nd edition.

Sachs, Jeffery and Andrew Warner (1997). *Sources of Slow Growth in African Economies*. Oxford: Oxford University Press.

Samarasinghe, Stanley W.R. de A. and Reed Coughlan (eds.) (1991). Economic Dimensions of Ethnic Conflict. London: Pinter Publishers.

Samatar, Ahmed I. (1993). "Undersiege: Blood, Power, and the Somali State," in P. Anyang' Nyong'o (ed.) *Arms and Daggers in the Hearts of Africa*. Nairobi, Kenya: Arrucian Academy of Science.

___, (1988). *Socialist Somalia: Rhetoric and Reality*. New York, NY: Zed Press.

Samatar, Said and David Laitin (1984). *Somalia a Nation in Search of State*. Boulder, CO: Westview Press

Sambanis, Nicholas (2002). "A Review of Recent Advances and Future Directions in the Quantitative Literature on Civil War," *Defence and Peace Economics*, vol. 13, no. 3, pp. 215-43.

Sandbrook, Richard (1993). *The Politics of Africa's Stagnation*. New York, NY: Cambridge University Press

Sandole, Dennis J.D. and Hugo van der Merwe (eds.) (1993). *Conflict Resolution Theory and Practice: Integration and Application*. Manchester: Manchester University Press.

Scherrer, Christian and Hakan Wiberg (eds.) (1999). *Ethnicity and Intra-State Conflict: Types, Causes and Peace Strategies*. Aldershot: Ashgate.

Schroeder, Peter J. (2000). African Politics and Society: A Mosaic in Transformation. Boston, MA: Bedford/St. Martin's.

Sesay, Amadu and Adiodun Alao (1998). "Democracy and Security in Africa: The Changing Nature of a Linkage," in Adebayo Oyebade and Abiodun Alao (eds.) *Africa after the Cold War*. Trenton: Africa World Press. Pp. 53-62.

Shaw, R. Paul and Yuwa Wong (1989). *Genetic Seeds of Warfare: Evolution, Nationalism, and Patriotism*. London: Unwin Hyman.

Shaw, Timothy (1976). "The Foreign Policy System of Zambia," *African Studies Review*, vol. 19 (April), pp. 31-66.

Shaw, Martin (1997). "The State of Globalization," *Review of International Political Economy*, vol. 4, no. 3, pp. 497-513.

Shills, Edward (1957). "Primordial, Personal, Sacred and Civil Ties," *British Journal of Sociology*, vol. 7, pp.13-45.

Shoumatoff, Alex (1992). "Rwanda's Aristocratic Guerrillas," *New York Times Magazine*, (December 13), p. 44.

Sislin John and Frederic Pearson (2001). *Arms and Ethnic Conflict*. Lanham, MD: Rowman & Littlefield.

Sklar, Richard L. (1963). *Nigerian Political Parties: Power in an Emergent African Nation*. Princeton: Princeton University Press.

Slater, Robert O. (1986). "Controversy: Explaining African Coups d'etat," *American Political Science Review*, vol. 80, pp. 225-49

Smillie, Ian, Lansana Gberie and Ralph Hazelton (2000). *The Heart of the Matter: Sierra Leone, Diamonds, and Humans Security*. Ontario: Partnership Africa Canada Publication.

Snow, Donald M. (1996). *UnCivil Wars: International Security and the New Pattern of Internal War*. Boulder, CO: Lynne Rienner Publishers.

Somalia: "Country Profile." *The Economist Intelligence Unit*. 1992-93.

Stedman, Stephen John (1996). "Conflict and Conciliation in Sub-Saharan Africa," in Michael E. Brown (ed.) (1996). *The International Dimensions of Internal Conflict*. Cambridge, MA: MIT Press. Pp. 235-266.

Steinberg, Stephen (1981). *The Ethnic Myth: Race, Ethnicity and Class in America*. New York, NY: Atheneum.

Strauss, Anselm L. and Juliet M. Corbin (1990). *Basics of Qualitative Research: Grounded Theory Procedures and Techniques*. Newbury Park, CA: Sage Publications.

Tandon, Yash (ed.) (1996). African Conceptions of Democracy and Good Governance. *Basic Document Series*. Harare: International South Group Network.

Tangri, Roger K. (1985). *Politics in Sub-Saharan Africa*. London; Portsmouth, N.H.: J. Currey:

The Washington Times, 13 December 1998, A10.

Thomas, Caroline and Peter Wilkin (eds.) (1999). "Introduction," in Ida (eds.) *Globalization, Insecurity, and the African Experience*. Boulder, CO: Lynne Rienner Publishers. Pp. 1-19.

Tilly, Charles (1973). "Does Modernization Breed Revolution?" *Comparative Politics*, vol. 5, no. 3 (April), pp. 425–447.

_____, (1985). *From Mobilization to Revolution*. Reading, MA: Addison-Wesley.

_____, (1992). *Coercion, Capital, and European States, AD 990-1992*. Cambridge: Blackwell.

Toure, Amadou Toumani (1999). "Mastering African Conflicts," in Adebayo Adedeji (ed.) *Comprehending and Mastering African Conflicts: The Search for Sustainable Peace and Good Governance*. London: Zed Books. Pp. 22-30.

Touval, Saadia (1963). *Somali Nationalism*. Boston, MA: Harvard University Press.

Turton, E.R. (1975). "Bantu, Galla and Somali Migrations in the Horn of Africa: A Reassessment of the Jubba/Tana Area," *Journal of African History*, vol. 16, pp.519-537.

Udogu, E. Ike (1999). "Ethnicity and Democracy in Sub-Saharan Africa," in John M. Mbaku (ed.) *Preparing Africa for the Twenty-First Century: Strategies for Peaceful Coexistence and Sustainable Development*. Aldershot: Ashgate Publishers. Pp. 151-176.

United Nations Conference on Trade and Development (UNCTAD) (1995). Foreign Direct Investment in Africa. *United Nations Publication*, Sales No. E. 95.II.A.6. Geneva: United Nations.

UNDP (1999). *Sierra Leone Human Development Report*. New York, NY: United Nations.

United Nations Development Program (UNDP) (2001). *Human Development Report* (Annually). New York, NY: United Nations.

United States Committee for Refugees at www.refugees.org

US Department of State (1986). *World Military Expenditures and Arms Transfers*. Arms Control and Disarmament Agency.

Vail, Leroy (1989). "The Creation of Tribalism in Southern Africa," in Vail (ed.) *The Creation of Tribalism in Southern Africa*. London: Currey Books.

van den Berghe, Pierre (1981). *The Ethnic Phenomenon*. New York, NY: Elsevier

van de Walle, Nicolas (2001). *African Economies and the Politics of Permanent Crisis, 1979-1999*. Cambridge: Cambridge University Press.

Vasquez, John, James Turner Johnson, Sanford Jaffe and Linda Stamato (eds.) (1995). *Beyond Confrontation: Learning Conflict Resolution in the Post-Cold War Era*. Ann Arbor, MI: University of Michigan Press.

Vidal, John (1992). *Black Need, but only Whites Receive: Race appears to be Skewing the West's Approach to Aid. Look at Kosovo. Then look at Africa.* http://www.guardian.co.uk/comment/story/0,3604,280594,00.html

Wallensteen, Peter (2002). *Understanding Conflict Resolution: War, Peace and the Global System*. London: Sage.

Wallenstein, Peter and Margareta Sollenberg (1999). "Armed Conflict, 1989-98," *Journal of Peace Research*, vol. 36, no. 5, pp. 539-606.

Wells, Alan (1974). "The Coups d'etat in Theory and Practice: Independent Black Africa in the 1960s," *American Journal of Sociology*, vol. 79, no. 4, pp. 871-888.

Welsh, David (1996). "Ethnicity in Sub Saharan Africa," *International Affairs*, vol. 72, no. 3, pp. 477-491.

Wiarda, Howard (1999). *Introduction to Comparative Politics: Concepts and Processes*. 2d edition. Belmont, CA: Wadsworth.

Wiking, Staffan (1983). *Military Coups in Sub-Saharan Africa: How to Justify Illegal Assumptions of Power*. Uppsala Offcenter, AB.

Woods, Dwayne (1992). "Civil Society in Europe and Africa: Limiting State Power Through a Public Sphere," *African Studies Review*, vol. 35, no. 2, pp. 77-100.

Woodward, Susan L. (1995). *Balkan Tragedy: Chaos and Dissolution After the Cold War*. Washington, DC: The Brookings Institution.

World Bank (1981). *Accelerated Development in Sub-Saharan Africa*. Washington, DC: World Bank.

_____, (1989). *Sub-Saharan Africa: From Crisis to Sustainable Growth*. Washington, DC: World Bank.

_____, (1992). *World Development Report*. Washington, DC: World Bank.

_____, (1995). "Ghana: Is Growth Sustainable? Operations Evaluations Department," *Report No. 99*. Washington, DC: World Bank Publications.

_____, (1995). *A Continent in Transition: Sub-Saharan Africa in the Mid-1990s*. Washington, DC: World Bank.

_____, Africa Database 1998/99.

_____, Report 2000/2001. *World Development Report*. Washington, DC: World Bank.

_____, (1989). Sub-*Saharan Africa: From Crisis to Sustainable Growth*. Washington, DC: World Bank.

_____, (1991). "Intra-regional Trade in Sub-Saharan Africa," World Development Reports, 1993. Washington, DC: World Bank.

Wuyi, Omitoogu (2001). "Military Expenditure and Conflict in Africa," *DPMN Bulletin*, vol. VIII, no. 1 (July).

Wylie, Kenneth C. (1977). *The Political Kingdoms of the Temne: Temne Government in Sierra Leone, 1825-1910*. New York, NY: Africana Pub. Co.

Wyse, Akintola J. G., (1989). *The Krio of Sierra Leone: An Interpretive History*. London: Hurst in association with the International African Institute.

Yin, Robert K. (1989). Case Study Research: Design and Methods. Beverly Hills, CA: Sage Publishing.

_____, (1994). Case Study Research: Design and Methods. *Applied Social Research Methods Series*. 2nd edition. Thousand Oaks, CA: Sage Publications.

Young, Crawford and Thomas Turner (1985). *The Rise and Decline of the Zairian State*. Madison, WI: University of Wisconsin Press.

_____, (1985). *African Relations with the Major Powers. African Independence: The First Twenty-Five Years*. Bloomington, IN: Indiana University Press.

_____, (1982). *Ideology and Development in Africa*. New Haven, CT: Yale University Press.

_____, (1988). "The African Colonial State and Its Political Legacy," in Donald Rothschild and Naomi Chazan (eds.) T*he Precarious Balance: State and Society in Africa*. Boulder, CO: Westview. Pp.25-66.

_____, (1994). *The African Colonial State in Comparative Perspective*. New Haven, CT: Yale University Press.

_____, (1998). *Ethnic Diversity and Public Policy: A Comparative Inquiry*. New York, NY: St. Martin's Press in association with UNRISD.

_____, (1999). "The Third Wave of Democratization in Africa," in Richard Joseph (ed.) *State, Conflict and Democracy in Africa*. Boulder, CO: Lynne Rienner Publishers. Pp. 15-38.

_____, (2000). "The Heritage of Colonialism," in John W. Harbeson and Donald Rothchild (eds.) *Africa in World Politics: The African State System in Flux*. 3rd edition. Boulder, CO: Westview. Pp. 23-42.

Zakaria, Fareed (2003). *The Future of Freedom: Illiberal Democracy at Home and Abroad*. New York, NY: W. W. Norton & Company.

Zartman I. William (1997), "Introduction," in Zartman (ed) *Governance as Conflict Management: Politics and Violence in West Africa*. Washington, DC: The Brookings Institution Press.

_____, (ed.) (2000). *Traditional Cures for Modern Conflicts: African Conflict "Medicine."* Boulder, CO: Lynne Rienner Publishers.

_____, (2000). "Inter-African Negotiations and State Renewal," in John W. Harbeson and Donald Rothchild (eds.) *Africa in World Politics: The African State System in Flux*. 3rd edition. Boulder, CO: Westview. Pp. 139-159.

_____, (2000). "Introduction: African Traditional Conflict "Medicine"," in ida *Traditional Cures for Modern Conflicts: African Conflict "Medicine"*. Boulder, CO: Lynne Rienner Publishers. Pp. 1-11.

_____, (1995). "Introduction: Posing the Problem of State Collapse," in Zartman (ed.) *Collapsed States: The Disintegration and Restoration of Legitimate Authority*. Boulder, CO: Lynne Rienner Publishers. Pp. 1–11;

_____, (ed.) (1995). *Collapsed States. The Disintegration and Restoration of Legitimate Authority*. Boulder, CO: Lynne Rienner Publishers.

Zimmerman, Robert F. (1993). *Dollars, Diplomacy, and Dependency : Dilemmas of U.S. Economic Aid*. Boulder, CO: Lynne Rienner Publishers.

Zimmermann, Warren (1995). "The Last Ambassador: A Memoir of the Collapse of Yugoslavia," *Foreign Affairs*, vol. 74, no. 2 (March–April), pp. 2–20.

INDEX

A

Acheampong, I.K., 113, 117
adjustment programs, 40, 41, 74, 76, 99, 134
AFRC. *See* Armed Forces Revolutionary Council
Afrifa, A.A., 117
Afro-Marxism. *See* Marxism
Afro-Shirazi Party, 121
Ahidjo, Ahmadou, 32
Ahmed, Abdulahi Yusuf, 90, 168
Aidid, Mohammed Farah, 89
Akazu, 72
Akuffo, Frederick, 117, 166
All People's Congress, 78, 82, 83, 84
Amin, Idi, 46, 121, 169
Angola, 16, 41, 47, 55, 60, 124, 126, 127, 128, 132, 159, 164
Ankrah, Joseph, 113, 117, 166
anti-colonial. *See* anti-colonialism
anti-colonialism, 112, 114
APC. *See* All People's Congress
Armed Forces Revolutionary Council, 79, 117
Arusha Declaration, 121
Ashanti, 52, 111, 112, 115
ASP. *See* Afro-Shirazi Party
autocratic. *See* autocratism
autocratism, 27, 45, 51, 100, 101, 152

B

Balewa, Abubakar Tafawa, 46, 168
Banda, Hastings, 46
Barre, Mohamed Siad, 46, 56, 62, 168
Barre, Siad, 87, 89, 91, 92, 93, 94, 95, 96, 97, 101, 108, 109, 119, 152, 156
Belgium, 23, 36, 66, 68, 70, 71, 76, 98, 104, 105, 121, 164, 165, 168
Bemba, 128, 129, 130, 131
Benin, 16, 164
Bio, Julius Maada, 79, 168
Bizimungu, Pasteur, 67, 73, 168
Bokassa, Jean-Bedel, 46
Botswana, 16, 22, 23, 29, 30, 35, 54, 142, 156, 159, 164
British South Africa Company, 127, 129, 133
Burkina Faso, 16, 76, 111, 154, 164
Burundi, 36, 64, 65, 66, 70, 104, 105, 106, 119, 164
Busia, Kofi, 113, 117, 166

C

Cameroon, 32, 61, 164
Cardew, Frederic, 80
CCM. *See* Chama cha Mapinduzi
Central African Republic, 46, 165
Chama cha Mapinduzi, 121, 122, 123
Chiluba, Frederick, 128, 131, 136, 169
China, 47, 74, 96, 118, 154
Christianity, 75, 77, 80
citizenship, 17, 37, 44
civic public, 37, 38
civil war, 26, 86, 97, 119, 123
civilian regime, 44, 45

Cold War, 15, 17, 30, 35, 49, 51, 55, 57, 63, 87, 90, 93, 96, 97, 99, 110, 118, 136, 146, 151, 152, 153
colonial. See colonialism
colonial rule. See colonialism
colonial state, 17, 32, 36, 44, 48, 49, 68, 71, 91, 113, 122, 152
colonialism, 17, 20, 23, 30, 31, 35, 36, 37, 38, 42, 43, 45, 46, 48, 52, 53, 55, 61, 63, 68, 69, 71, 75, 78, 79, 80, 81, 86, 88, 89, 90, 91, 93, 98, 104, 107, 108, 110, 113, 122, 129, 130, 132, 133, 134, 140, 143, 153, 162, 164
context, 22, 33, 35, 59, 63, 97, 110, 111, 142, 143, 152, 157
contextual factor, 21, 22, 39, 42, 43, 54, 64, 97, 100, 111, 133, 142, 143, 150, 162
contextual perspective, 20, 27, 33, 75, 104, 140
contextual variable. See contextual factor
Convention People's Party, 112, 114, 116
Côte d'Ivoire, 46, 61, 111
coup, 18, 26, 32, 47, 48, 51, 62, 67, 70, 73, 78, 79, 83, 84, 86, 95, 97, 100, 102, 113, 114, 117, 128, 132, 133, 136, 137, 146, 147, 148, 151, 158, 161, 164, 165, 166, 167, 168, 169
coup d'Etat de Gitarama, 70
CPP. See Convention People's Party
Creole, 77, 81

D

Darood, 56, 91, 92, 94, 107
democracy, 15, 16, 24, 27, 29, 43, 67, 94, 101, 110, 116, 117, 119, 125, 154, 156, 159

democratic. See democracy
Democratic Republic of Congo, 16, 29, 35, 36, 41, 46, 47, 49, 60, 61, 64, 65, 105, 119, 126, 127, 152, 165
democratization. See democracy
Dhulbahante, 56, 92
dictatorial state, 33, 46
Direct Development Assistance, 40
Direct Foreign Investment, 39, 40
Djibouti, 87, 89, 108, 154, 165

E

Economic Community of West African States, 79
economic development, 17, 19, 33, 39, 59, 73, 95, 96
Economic Recovery Programs, 136
Egypt, 46, 74, 75, 88, 154, 165, 169
Eritrea, 26, 165
Ethiopia, 26, 47, 87, 88, 89, 91, 93, 95, 96, 108, 165, 166
ethnic. See ethnicity
ethnic groups, 21, 23, 36, 37, 38, 81, 114, 119, 122, 126, 127, 129, 131, 140, 143, 158, 161
ethnicity, 17, 20, 23, 34, 35, 37, 38, 52, 60, 66, 68, 72, 75, 81, 91, 113, 114, 120, 122, 126, 129, 143, 146, 152, 161, 162
ethnic-primordialism, 17
European Union, 23, 69
exploitation, 23, 30
Eyadema, Gnassingbe, 46, 169

F

favoritism, 31, 38, 51, 69, 80, 95
foreign aid, 17, 23, 39, 43, 69, 83, 93, 100, 116, 128, 134, 144
France, 23, 36, 46, 68, 74, 75, 77, 88, 89, 90, 164, 165, 166, 167, 168, 169

Freetown, 77, 80, 81, 168

G

Gadhafi, Moammar, 76
Gendarmerie National Rwandaise, 70
genocide, 26, 64, 65, 67, 73, 74, 75, 76, 104, 106
Germany, 66, 68, 96, 98, 112, 121, 122, 133, 140, 141, 164, 167, 168, 169
Ghana, 16, 46, 49, 52, 62, 77, 104, 110, 111, 112, 113, 114, 115, 116, 118, 119, 122, 123, 126, 133, 134, 135, 136, 137, 138, 139, 140, 143, 144, 145, 147, 148, 149, 150, 159, 166
Gini Coefficient, 53, 54, 62, 107
Gini score. *See* Gini Coefficient
governability, 28
governance, 15, 17, 19, 20, 22, 24, 27, 28, 29, 30, 31, 32, 33, 34, 35, 36, 37, 38, 41, 43, 44, 45, 48, 50, 51, 54, 55, 59, 60, 63, 64, 85, 86, 93, 103, 104, 110, 139, 140, 142, 150, 151, 152, 153, 154, 155, 157, 159, 162
Great Britain, 23, 36, 63, 77, 78, 79, 80, 81, 83, 86, 88, 90, 98, 107, 108, 110, 111, 112, 113, 114, 118, 119, 121, 122, 127, 130, 133, 164, 165, 166, 167, 168, 169
Guinea, 46, 76, 77, 81, 84, 117, 165, 166

H

Habyarimana, Juvenal, 65, 67, 69, 70, 71, 72, 73, 74, 75, 100, 106, 156, 168
Houphouet-Boigny, Félix, 46
Human Development Index, 86
Hut Tax, 80

Hutu, 64, 65, 66, 67, 68, 69, 70, 71, 72, 73, 74, 75, 98, 104, 105, 106
Hutu Emancipation Movement. *See* Parmehutu

I

ICA. *See* International Coffee Agreement
IFI. *See* International Financial Institutions
Igaal, Mohamed Ibrahim, 94
IMF. *See* International Monetary Fund
imperialism, 17, 30, 47, 88
Impuzamugambi, 74, 106
independent state, 32, 49
infrastructure, 23, 29, 33, 73, 114, 118, 163
institutionalism, 30, 33
institutionalist. *See* institutionalism
Interahamwe, 74, 106
Inter-Country Risk Guide, 34, 35, 36, 45, 59, 60, 104, 139, 150, 159, 162
internal war, 15, 16, 17, 19, 20, 21, 22, 23, 24, 25, 26, 27, 29, 31, 33, 34, 35, 36, 42, 50, 51, 53, 57, 59, 60, 63, 64, 69, 73, 79, 83, 85, 86, 89, 95, 96, 97, 98, 99, 100, 104, 106, 110, 111, 113, 119, 120, 126, 132, 133, 135, 140, 142, 143, 144, 145, 146, 147, 148, 149, 150, 151, 152, 155, 157, 158, 159, 160
internally displaced persons, 15, 26, 87
International Coffee Agreement, 69, 72
International Financial Institutions, 24, 63
International Monetary Fund, 33, 40, 53, 113, 116, 153, 155
Isaaq, 91, 92, 95, 96
Islam, 77, 88, 120

Italy, 36, 53, 88, 90, 91, 93, 96, 98, 107, 118, 165, 166, 167, 168

J

Juxon-Smith, Andrew, 78

K

Kabbah, Ahmad Tejan, 79, 101
Kagame, Paul, 67, 168
Kambona, Oscar, 121
Kapwepwe, Simon, 130
Karume, Abeid Amani, 121
Kaunda, Kenneth, 46, 126, 127, 128, 130, 131, 132, 136, 156, 169
Kayibanda, Grégoire, 65, 67, 70, 72, 100, 168
Keita, Modibo, 46, 167
Kenya, 49, 50, 52, 56, 61, 87, 88, 89, 90, 108, 119, 166
Kigeri V, 70
Kikwete, Jakaya, 122, 125, 169
Kinyarwanda, 68, 72
kleptocracy, 31, 43, 50, 51, 59, 61, 76, 79, 83, 85, 93, 136, 152
Konkomba, 119, 140
Koroma, Johnny Paul, 79, 168
Koroma, Sorie, 85
Krio, 77, 80, 81, 98
Kufuor, John, 113, 118, 166

L

Lansana, David, 78, 166
Lebanon, 80, 82, 98
Lenshina, Alice, 128, 132
Lesotho, 23, 26, 166
Liberia, 16, 22, 29, 36, 41, 57, 76, 77, 79, 81, 86, 106, 119, 154, 156, 159, 166
Libya, 76, 79, 86, 118, 167
Limann, Hilla, 113, 117
Limba, 78, 81, 82, 85

Lumpa, 128, 132

M

Mahdi, Mohammed Ali, 89
Majertinia, 90, 92, 109
Malawi, 46, 50, 119, 126, 127, 129, 167
Mali, 16, 46, 167
Marehaan, 56, 62, 92, 95
Margai, Albert, 78, 83
Margai, Milton, 78, 81, 82, 83, 168
Marx, Karl, 51, 53
Marxism, 52, 94
Mauritius, 16, 156, 167
mechanistic theory of government, 28
Mende, 78, 80, 81, 82, 83, 85, 98, 107
militarization, 25, 74, 75, 95, 96, 149, 152, 156
military regime, 44, 45, 54
militia, 57, 75, 87, 89, 106
Minah, Francis, 85
Mkapa, Benjamin, 122, 125, 169
MNRD. *See* Mouvement Révolutionnaire National pour le Développement
Mobutu, 61, 64, 152, 165
Moi, Daniel Arap, 61, 166
Momoh, Joseph, 79, 84, 85, 86, 156, 168
Momoh, Joseph Saidu, 78
Mosca, Gaetano, 53
Mouvement Révolutionnaire National pour le Développement, 67, 71
Movement for Multiparty Democracy party, 128
Mozambique, 16, 47, 119, 123, 124, 126, 128, 132, 167
Mudug, 90, 91, 92, 109
Mwami, 65, 66, 68, 164
Mwanawasa, Levy, 129, 131, 169

Mwinyi, Ali Hassan, 122, 124, 125, 136, 169

N

Namibia, 126, 167
Nanumba, 119, 140
Nasser, Gamal Abdel, 46
National Liberation Council, 113, 117
National Redemption Council, 117
National Reformation Council, 78, 83, 84
Ndahindurwa, Kigeri, 67
neo-colonialism, 17, 30, 35, 47, 63, 110, 153
neo-patrimonial state. *See* neo-patrimonialism
neo-patrimonialism, 31, 32, 59, 152
nepotism, 31, 38, 51, 93, 94, 95, 123, 128, 131, 144
Newly Industrializing Countries, 39
Nigeria, 16, 26, 32, 46, 49, 50, 56, 62, 77, 81, 86, 108, 168
Nkrumah, Kwame, 17, 46, 52, 62, 112, 113, 114, 115, 116, 117, 136, 166
NLC. *See* National Liberation Council
normative perspective, 24, 54
no-war country, 22, 24, 25, 34, 35, 42, 43, 48, 54, 57, 58, 59, 98, 103, 104, 110, 111, 129, 132, 135, 136, 137, 138, 139, 144, 145, 146, 147, 148, 149, 150, 151, 153
NRC. *See* National Reformation Council
Ntaryamira, Cyprien, 65, 164
Nyerere, Julius, 32, 46, 52, 62, 120, 121, 122, 123, 124, 125, 131, 132, 134, 136, 156

O

Obasanjo, General Olusegun, 32
ODA. *See* Official Development Assistance
Official Development Assistance, 39, 40, 99, 100, 124, 134, 135, 140, 144, 145, 150, 151, 158, 160, 163
Ogaden, 56, 89, 92, 93, 96, 108
Ogaden People's Liberation Front, 89
organic theory of government, 28
Organization for Economic Co-operation and Development, 33, 50
Organization of Africa Unity, 136
Osman, Adan Abdulle, 32, 101

P

Parmehutu, 66, 67, 70
Party of the Revolution. *See* Chama cha Mapinduzi
peace-to-peace country. *See* no-war country
peace-to-war country. *See* war country
People's National Party, 117
personalism, 31, 32
Physical Quality of Life Index, 41, 146, 158, 160
policy, 24, 33, 34, 54, 57, 73, 85, 95, 102, 103, 118, 125, 132, 138, 139, 148, 149, 158, 161, 163, 179
policy factor, 21, 22, 34, 64, 111, 142, 148, 162
policy perspective, 20, 27, 33, 59, 75, 104, 140
policy variable. *See* policy factor
political system, 15, 17, 20, 28, 43, 46, 54, 73, 90, 128, 136, 162
Portugal, 23, 76, 91, 98, 112, 120, 126, 164, 165, 166, 167, 168
Postcolonial. *See* postcolonialism

postcolonial state, 17, 18, 19, 21, 23, 31, 35, 37, 43, 44, 45, 47, 50, 51, 55, 81, 85, 91, 98, 107, 112, 142, 143, 157

postcolonialism, 32, 33, 36, 37, 64, 70, 73, 75, 98, 114, 121, 136, 150

poverty, 16, 24, 35, 40, 41, 48, 61, 73, 78, 79, 82, 85, 97, 101, 102, 119, 142, 148, 154

pre-colonial. *See* pre-colonialism

pre-colonialism, 64, 75, 98, 133

primordial public, 37, 38

privatization, 24, 41, 72, 152

Progress Party, 117

Provisional National Defence Council, 118, 136

R

Rawlings, Jerry, 113, 116, 117, 118, 119, 136, 156, 166

regime, 18, 24, 29, 30, 31, 41, 43, 44, 45, 51, 54, 56, 57, 65, 70, 71, 72, 73, 74, 75, 78, 79, 83, 86, 87, 89, 91, 92, 93, 94, 95, 96, 97, 99, 100, 101, 108, 111, 118, 119, 126, 131, 132, 133, 156, 158, 161, 163

Revolutionary United Front, 76, 79, 86

Rhodes, Cecil, 127, 129, 133

Rhodesia, 127, 128, 130, 131

RPF. *See* Rwandan Patriotic Front

Rudahigwa, Mutara, 66, 70

RUF. *See* Revolutionary United Front

rule of law, 15, 18, 29, 33, 43, 154

Rwanda, 16, 26, 36, 63, 64, 65, 66, 67, 68, 69, 70, 71, 72, 73, 74, 75, 78, 85, 86, 88, 97, 98, 99, 100, 101, 102, 103, 104, 105, 106, 119, 126, 133, 143, 144, 145, 148, 149, 150, 159, 168

Rwandan Patriotic Front, 65, 67, 73, 74, 75, 76, 156

S

Sankoh, Foday, 76, 79, 86

SAP. *See* Structural Adjustment Programs

security, 18, 28, 29, 32, 33, 37, 45, 54, 55, 56, 57, 87, 92, 95, 118, 149, 162, 163

Seko, Mobutu Sese, 46, 61

Senegal, 16, 22, 32, 168

Senghor, Leopold, 32

Shermarke, Abdirashid Ali, 89, 101

Sierra Leone, 16, 22, 29, 32, 41, 53, 57, 63, 76, 77, 78, 79, 80, 81, 82, 83, 84, 85, 86, 97, 98, 99, 100, 101, 102, 103, 104, 106, 107, 119, 143, 145, 148, 149, 154, 156, 159, 168

Sierra Leone People's Party, 78, 79, 82, 84

Sierra Leone Produce Marketing Board, 83

SLPP. *See* Sierra Leone People's Party

SMC. *See* Supreme Military Council

Somali National Movement, 95, 96

Somalia, 16, 22, 23, 26, 29, 32, 36, 46, 56, 57, 60, 62, 63, 86, 87, 88, 89, 90, 91, 92, 93, 94, 95, 96, 97, 98, 99, 100, 101, 102, 103, 104, 107, 108, 109, 119, 143, 144, 145, 148, 149, 150, 152, 154, 159, 168

South Africa, 16, 26, 55, 96, 124, 126, 127, 128, 131, 132, 156, 167, 169

Soviet Union, 15, 51, 89, 90, 93, 95, 99, 118

SRC. *See* Supreme Revolutionary Council

statism, 47, 131

Stevens, Siaka, 32, 78, 82, 84, 85, 156, 168
Strasser, Valentine, 79
Structural Adjustment Programs, 18, 24, 40, 43, 60, 72, 99, 116, 145, 158, 163
structural factor, 21, 22, 24, 54, 64, 70, 83, 94, 97, 100, 102, 111, 116, 124, 130, 133, 135, 137, 142, 146, 148, 161, 162, 163
structural perspective, 20, 27, 33, 75, 104, 140
structural variable. *See* structural factor
structuralism, 30, 33
structuralist. *See* structuralism
structure, 24, 33, 34, 146
Sudan, 16, 26, 32, 88, 108, 159, 169
Supreme Military Council, 117
Supreme Revolutionary Council, 89, 94
Swareddahab, Abdul Rahman, 32
Swaziland, 23, 169
Syria, 80

T

Tanganyika, 119, 121, 126, 133, 141
Tanganyika African National Union, 121
TANU. *See* Tanganyika African National Union
Tanzania, 16, 22, 23, 29, 32, 46, 49, 54, 64, 104, 110, 111, 119, 120, 121, 122, 123, 124, 125, 126, 128, 130, 131, 132, 133, 134, 135, 136, 137, 138, 139, 140, 141, 143, 144, 145, 147, 148, 149, 150, 159, 169
Taylor, Charles, 41, 76, 166
Temne, 76, 77, 78, 80, 81, 82, 83, 84, 85, 98, 107
Togo, 46, 111, 113, 140, 169
totalitarian. *See* totalitarianism
totalitarianism, 44, 70, 94

Touré, Ahmed Sékou, 46, 117, 166
tribalism, 37, 38, 60, 63, 94, 110, 132
Tutsi, 64, 65, 66, 67, 68, 69, 70, 71, 73, 74, 75, 98, 104, 105, 156
Twa, 68, 71

U

ubuhake, 65, 66, 69
UDP. *See* United Democratic Party
Uganda, 46, 50, 64, 70, 73, 75, 76, 105, 119, 121, 123, 125, 154, 169
ujamaa, 121, 122, 124, 125, 131, 134, 137
Union Nationale Rwandaise, 66
UNIP. *See* United National Independence Party
United Democratic Party, 84
United National Independence Party, 127, 130, 131
United Nations, 55, 61, 66, 70, 76, 79, 90, 95, 106, 119, 160
United States, 26, 36, 46, 50, 51, 55, 60, 69, 72, 76, 89, 90, 93, 99, 118, 156, 160

W

war country, 22, 24, 25, 34, 35, 42, 43, 48, 54, 57, 58, 59, 63, 100, 102, 103, 104, 110, 111, 119, 135, 137, 138, 139, 140, 144, 145, 146, 147, 148, 149, 150, 151, 153, 159, 162
World Bank, 22, 24, 26, 30, 33, 40, 53, 60, 61, 62, 92, 113, 116, 120, 123, 124, 142, 153, 155, 160, 162

Y

Yemen, 88

Z

Zaire. *See* Democratic Republic of Congo

Zambia, 46, 49, 104, 110, 111, 119, 126, 127, 128, 129, 130, 131, 132, 133, 134, 135, 136, 137, 138, 139, 140, 143, 144, 145, 148, 149, 150, 159, 169

Zanzibar, 88, 119, 121, 122, 123, 125, 133, 141

Zimbabwe, 124, 126, 127, 130, 132, 169

www.ingramcontent.com/pod-product-compliance
Lightning Source LLC
Chambersburg PA
CBHW071229170426
43191CB00032B/1219